Moritz Hennemann | Gordian Konstantin Ebner
Benedikt Karsten | Gregor Lienemann | Marie Wienroeder

Data Act

An Introduction

Nomos

Suggested citation: Author in Hennemann et al., Data Act, p. ...

The open access publication of this title was made possible by the umbrella initiative „Hochschule.digital Niedersachsen" of the German state of Lower Saxony.

The Deutsche Nationalbibliothek lists this publication in the Deutsche Nationalbibliografie; detailed bibliographic data are available on the Internet at http://dnb.d-nb.de

ISBN 978-3-7560-1342-5 (Print)
978-3-7489-1869-1 (ePDF)

British Library Cataloguing-in-Publication Data
A catalogue record for this book is available from the British Library.

ISBN 978-3-7560-1342-5 (Print)
978-3-7489-1869-1 (ePDF)

Library of Congress Cataloging-in-Publication Data
Hennemann, Moritz | Ebner, Gordian Konstantin | Karsten, Benedikt
Lienemann, Gregor | Wienroeder, Marie
Data Act
An Introduction
Moritz Hennemann | Gordian Konstantin Ebner | Benedikt Karsten
Gregor Lienemann | Marie Wienroeder
254 pp.
Includes bibliographic references.

ISBN 978-3-7560-1342-5 (Print)
978-3-7489-1869-1 (ePDF)

1st Edition 2024

Published by
Nomos Verlagsgesellschaft mbH & Co. KG
Waldseestraße 3–5 | 76530 Baden-Baden
www.nomos.de

Production of the printed version:
Nomos Verlagsgesellschaft mbH & Co. KG
Waldseestraße 3–5 | 76530 Baden-Baden

ISBN 978-3-7560-1342-5 (Print)
ISBN 978-3-7489-1869-1 (ePDF)
DOI https://doi.org/10.5771/9783748918691

Online Version
Nomos eLibrary

Authors

Moritz Hennemann is a Full University Professor, holding the Chair of Civil Law, Information Law, Media Law, and Internet Law, University of Freiburg Law Faculty since 2023. His research focuses on private law, business law, data law, media law, and information law, including from a comparative perspective. He holds degrees in Law from the Universities of Heidelberg (2009), Oxford (M.Jur., 2011), and Freiburg (Dr. jur., 2011). He was a postdoctoral researcher at the University of Freiburg (Habilitation, 2019), a visiting researcher at University of Oxford Law Faculty's Institute of European and Comparative Law (2023) and at Harvard Law School (2018) as well as an affiliate to the Berkman Klein Center for Internet & Society, Harvard Law School (2018-2020). Between 2020 and 2023 he was holding the Chair of European and International Information Law, University of Passau Law Faculty and was Director of the University of Passau Research Centre for Law and Digitalisation (FREDI).

Gordian Ebner is pursuing his legal clerkship (*Referendariat*) at the Higher Regional Court of Munich since October 2022 and has been an academic research assistant at the Chair of European and International Information Law, University of Passau Law Faculty from 2020 to 2023. His research focuses on data protection law, especially data-related information duties, including from a comparative perspective. He holds degrees in Law from the University of Passau (2020; Dr. jur., 2022 and LL.M., 2024).

Benedikt Karsten is an academic research assistant and doctoral candidate in Law at the University of Passau Research Centre for Law and Digitalisation (FREDI) since 2022. His research focuses on data (economy) law. He holds a degree in Law from the University of Passau (2020) and is a fully qualified lawyer (Ass. jur., 2022 and LL.M., 2024).

Gregor Lienemann is an academic research assistant and doctoral candidate in Law at the Chair of European and International Information Law, University of Passau Law Faculty since 2021. His research focuses on data portability and on the intersection of data protection and competition law, including from a comparative perspective. He holds degrees in Law from the Universities of Munich (2020) and Reading (LL.M., 2021).

Marie Wienroeder is an academic research assistant and doctoral candidate in Law at the Chair of European and International Information Law, University of Passau Law Faculty since 2022. Her research focuses on data law. She holds a degree in Law from the University of Passau (2022).

Foreword

Dear Fellow Reader,

In February 2022, the EU Commission released the Proposal for a Data Act. From then on, manifold discussions within the political realm as well as in academia have taken place. In December 2023, a final version was agreed on by the respective EU actors – and the Data Act finally entered into force in January 2024.

Against this background, this volume aims to provide those interested in the Act (but maybe not engaged with this piece of regulation so far) with a concise, but detailed introduction to the new regulation, its articles, and its recitals. The Data Act, its concept, and its instruments are presented, explained, evaluated, and put into context. References to the actual wording of articles and recitals were oftentimes included. Reference is given throughout to the significant share of literature on the Data Act and, if needed to, the proposal(s). Inevitably, being an Introduction, we could not deep dive into every detail of the Data Act.

We like to highlight, however, that this introduction also puts an emphasis on aspects of the Act that have been less discussed so far, for example a deep-dive has been made in Chapter IX with regard to the highly important provisions on switching and interoperability between data processing services (Art. 23-31, 33-35). Furthermore, the bibliography at the end of this volume provides you – as comprehensively as possible – with further literature on the final version of the Act as well as on the draft version(s).

This Introduction to the Data Act is based on and has partly been prepublished in an earlier version (mirroring the legislative process and the proposals of the Data Act) as Hennemann, M. / Karsten, B. / Wienroeder, M. / Lienemann, G. / Ebner, G. (Eds.), The Data Act Proposal – Literature Review and Critical Analysis, Part I – III (2023) *University of Passau IRDG Research Paper Series No. 23-01, 23-02, 23-03.* We have, however, made substantial changes to this earlier version and have updated all parts to the final version of the Act.

This Introduction to the Data Act also builds upon further publications by the authors to the final version of the Data Act (Hennemann, M. / Steinrötter, B., Der Data Act – Neue Instrumente, alte Friktionen, strukturelle Weichenstellungen, *Neue Juristische Wochenschrift (NJW)* 2024 (1), 1-8; Wienroeder, M., Sind der Data Act und die DSGVO miteinander kompatibel?, Privacy in Germany (PinG) 2024 (3), 103-108) as well as to the draft version of the Data Act (Hennemann, M. / Steinrötter, B., Data Act – Fundament des neuen EU-Datenwirtschaftsrecht?, *Neue Juristische Wochenschrift (NJW)* 2022 (21), 1481-1486; Ebner, G., Information Overload 2.0? – Die Informationspflichten gemäß Art. 3 Abs. 2 Data Act-Entwurf, *Zeitschrift für Datenschutz (ZD)* 2022 (7), 364-369; Karsten, B. / Wienroeder, M., Der Entwurf des Data Act – Auswirkungen auf die Automobilindustrie, *Recht Automobil Wirtschaft (RAW)* 2022, 99-105; Hennemann, M., Datenrealpolitik – Datenökosysteme, Datenrecht, Datendiplomatie (2022) *University of Passau IRDG Research Paper Series No. 22-18*; Hennemann, M. / Lienemann, G., The Data Act – Article-by-Article Synopsis of the Commission Proposal (2022) *University of Passau IRDG Research Paper Series No. 22-07*).

We are more than happy to hear your thoughts on this introduction, about what we have missed and – maybe also – what you liked. Please drop us an e-mail to moritz.hennemann@jura.uni-freiburg.de.

We like to thank the entire team at the chair of European and International Information and Data Law and at the Research Centre for Law and Digitalisation (FREDI) at University of Passau Law Faculty for their extremely valuable support in the drafting process and for taking the burden of formatting the document. FREDI and this publication is supported by the Bavarian State Ministry of Science and Culture. We are very grateful for this support.

Finally, we very much thank Marco Ganzhorn for the – in every way – splendid and invaluable coordination from the publisher's side. We are also more than thankful for Nomos supporting and the umbrella initiative "Hochschule.digital Niedersachsen" for ensuring an Open Access publication format.

Sincerely yours,

Moritz Hennemann, Gordian Ebner, Benedikt Karsten,
Gregor Lienemann & Marie Wienroeder

Freiburg and Passau, February 2024

Contributions by Authors

Hennemann	Chapters I.-III.
Ebner	Chapters I., IV.
Karsten	Chapters I., VI.-VII.
Lienemann	Chapters I., V.-VI., IX.
Wienroeder	Chapters I., IV.-V., VIII., X.-XII.

Contributions by Chapters

Chapter I.	*Hennemann/Ebner/Karsten/Lienemann/Wienroeder*
Chapter II.	*Hennemann*
Chapter III.	*Hennemann*
Chapter IV.	*Ebner/Wienroeder*
Chapter V.	*Lienemann/Wienroeder*
Chapter VI.	*Karsten/Lienemann*
Chapter VII.	*Karsten*
Chapter VIII.	*Wienroeder*
Chapter IX.	*Lienemann*
Chapter X.	*Wienroeder*
Chapter XI.	*Wienroeder*
Chapter XII.	*Wienroeder*

Table of Contents

I. Executive Summary

1. The Data Act is a push into the right direction. Its focus on non-personal and personal data use and data usability deserves applause. Its actual design is, however, not in every way convincing.
2. The Data Act is first and foremost seeking to enhance compulsory data sharing with regard to different actors and in commercial and non-commercial data ecosystems.
3. The Act is introducing statutory data access rights in the favour of users of IoT-products (Art. 4 et seq.) as well as public authorities in specific cases (Art. 14 et seq.). In the context of IoT-products, the access rights are linked to the data 'generated by the use' and are dependent on a user's request to grant direct access to himself and / or to a third-party recipient. There are no access rights to the benefit of the public and / or the market participants / the economy in general.
4. The data access is combined with underlying contracts / agreements enabling data use. The Data Act is fostering contractual agreements between (nearly) all relevant parties (data use agreement, data access contract (on FRAND terms), non-disclosure-agreements (NDAs)). The Data Act is supporting a process of "contractualisation" of data law. It is against this background rightly criticized that the Data Act does not stipulate any conflicts of law-rules.
5. Despite this process of "contractualisation", the Data Act does not provide (beside Art. 13) any specific rules in detail for the central data use agreement according to Art. 4(13). Generally, the rules on standard terms control are rather limited in substance. The Data Act does not contain rules for data contracts vis-à-vis consumers (and leaves this to the member states). On the basis of Art. 41, however, model contract clauses will be developed.
6. The data access is restricted by various rules – especially with respect to a data use with regard to competing products / competing markets (Art. 4(10), 5(6), 6(2)(e)) as well as with regard to gatekeepers according to the DMA (which are considered to be illegitimate as third-party recipients, Art. 5(3), 6(2)(d)).
7. It is highly debated whether and to what extent the data access regime sets – from a Law & Economics perspective – functionally calib-

rated, sensible, and thought-through parameters and incentives. It is discussed whether the user activation (the Data Act relies on) will work in practice. It is considered whether sectoral approaches should be favoured in opposition of the one size fits all-framework of the Data Act. Furthermore, it is questioned whether the exclusion of gatekeepers as third-party recipients is serving innovation and the common wealth. Finally, the (setting of) FRAND conditions (Art. 8(1)) is confronted with doubts with regard to practicability.

8. From a mostly, but not only, doctrinal point of view it is heavily debated whether and to what extend the data access regime introduces and / or paves the way for some type of 'IP-like' right regarding non-personal data. This debate has to be seen against the background that – on the basis of the current law – non-personal data (if one has access and notwithstanding any trade secret law regime) can be used freely and without some form of consent and / or agreement by the 'producer'. The final version of the Data Act heavily underlines the central role of the user. The need for a data use agreement with the user according to Art. 4(13) points to some form of 'attribution' (without constituting an absolute right) of the respective data to the user. It is another question whether and in which settings users will actually negotiate and / or value this agreement in practice. It is therefore an open question whether the Act will manifest the current factual setting in favour of the data holder.
9. The Act also introduces new access rights for public sector bodies. In contrast to Chapter II, these access rights are independent from a user – meaning that the public sector body can request data directly from the data holder. The public sector body has to demonstrate an exceptional need to access data. Furthermore, the access rights do differentiate between non-personal and personal data. However, the scope of the access rights is limited.
10. The Data Act seeks to regulate providers of data processing services (i.e. cloud and edge computing businesses). Commentators have called into question the technical feasibility of, in particular, the withdrawal of switching charges (Art. 29) and the mandate for functional equivalence of service at the destination (Art. 23(1)(d), read jointly with Art. 30(1)). Likewise, the fact that differently sized (IaaS) cloud providers have to meet these requirements has drawn criticism.

11. With smart contracts being regarded as a viable avenue for data sharing, Art. 36 aims for standardisation of these self-executing protocols through key requirements.
12. The rule on international transfer of non-personal data (Art. 32) comes along with similar uncertainties as the parallel norm in Art. 31 Data Governance Act.
13. From a legal point of view, it is highly unsatisfying that the Data Act for all parts does not really "solve" and / or complicates the relationship to and its interplay with data protection law / the General Data Protection Regulation (GDPR).
14. Additionally, and even more surprising, it is hard to comprehend that the Data Act does not substantially tackle the relationship to and its interplay with the Data Governance Act. Specific rules are limited and no incentives are set (for example to the benefit of data intermediaries). As data intermediaries do potentially fulfil a central function in order to enable data exchanges / data contracts (*inter alia* between users and third-party recipients), the gap opposes the general aim of the Data Act to enhance and foster data sharing and data use.
15. The Data Act increases the regulatory complexity for the data economy significantly. With regard to the aim of boosting data access and fairness in data markets, it is to be welcomed that the Data Act does introduce specific rules to the benefit of and some exceptions regarding micro, small, or medium-sized enterprises.
16. The Data Act – and especially its access rights – will be complemented by sector-specific EU legislation (in particular by European Data Spaces legislation). It is, however, not entirely clear whether and to what extent the Data Act leaves room for member state legislation in specific sectors.
17. Finally, the Data Act is rather vague on the central question whether and to what extent a monetarisation of personal and – especially – non-personal data shall be possible. Different follow-on rules of the access right (e.g., Art. 4(10), 5(6), 6(2)(c) and (e)) limit – next to data protection law – a full monetarisation. At least slightly, Art. 4(13) and (14) as well as Art. 6(2)(h) might be interpreted to point to the user as being the prime actor to monetarise.
18. With the Data Act and the Data Governance Act, the EU has again been a first mover in the 'market of regulatory ideas.' With regard to the criticism from an Economics angle as well as with regard to the missing interplay between the two Acts and between the Acts and

the GDPR, it is at least doubtful that the Data Act (and the Data Governance Act) will be able to unleash its full potential. It is, for example, rather foreseeable that unchanged data protection restrictions will serve as a barrier for data holders to grant access.

II. Introduction

On February 23 2022, the Commission unveiled its long-awaited Proposal for a Data Act[1]. From there on, the debate gained significant momentum – including intense and fierce political and academic discussions about the conceptual clarity, the aims pursued, the instruments chosen, and the structural roads taken of and by the Act.[2] Finally, on January 11 2024, the regulation[3] came into force.[4] The Data Act[5] is part (and fundamental cornerstone) of a greater legislative agenda of the EU Commission which was laid down in the European Strategy on Data[6] in 2020.[7]

The Data Act combines provisions in substance (e.g., access rights), provisions targeted at tech regulation (e.g., with regard to interoperability) as well as provisions on enforcement structures (e.g., *public enforcement* and alternative dispute settlement mechanisms). The new Act includes access rights to datasets to the benefit of both private and public entities, and accentuates a contractual angle into regulating the exchange and use of data in the digital economy. It strives for general accessibility, interoperability, and portability of data with technical safeguards (e.g., smart contracts) and

---

1 Commission, 'Proposal for a Regulation of the European Parliament and of the Council on harmonised rules on fair access and use of data (Data Act)' COM(2022) 68 final.

2 Cf. e.g., – and with further references to the debate – Hennemann, M. / Steinrötter, B., *NJW* 2024, 1 (6 et seqq.) as well as the critique from an economics point of view by Krämer, J., Improving The Economic Effectiveness of the B2B and B2C Data Sharing Obligations in the Proposed Data Act, CERRE, 2022; Kerber, W., *GRUR-Int* 2023, 120; Eckardt, M. / Kerber, W., Property rights theory, bundles of rights on IoT data, and the EU Data Act (December 2023).

3 Supporting this approach (and not the instrument of a directive) Leistner, M. / Antoine, L., IPR and the use of open data and data sharing initiatives by public and private actors, 2022, p. 72.

4 Commission, 'European Data Act enters into force, putting in place new rules for a fair and innovative data economy', https://digital-strategy.ec.europa.eu/en/news/european-data-act-enters-force-putting-place-new-rules-fair-and-innovative-data-economy.

5 Regulation (EU) 2023/2854 of the European Parliament and of the Council of 13 December 2023 on harmonised rules on fair access to and use of data and amending Regulation (EU) 2017/2394 and Directive (EU) 2020/1828 (Data Act).

6 Commission, 'A European strategy for data' COM(2020) 66 final. Cf. in detail Veil, W. / Weindauer, F., in: Hennemann, M. (ed.), Global Data Strategies, 2023, pp. 51 et seqq.

7 For an overview on different data strategies worldwide see Hennemann, M. (ed.), Global Data Strategies, 2023.

sets limitations for re-use in and along the data lifecycle (e.g., by starting with the product design, Art. 3(1)).[8] Generally, the Data Act thereby mirrors the non-rival nature of data / codified information. Rec. 1 rightly highlights: "The same data may be used and reused for a variety of purposes and to an unlimited degree, without any loss of quality or quantity."

The Act aims to unleash the enormous potential of data. Especially, the Data Act fosters data trade with respect to non-personal data, but is targeted – in conjunction with the Data Governance Act (DGA)[9] – at all societal dimensions of non-personal and personal data usability, data use, data sharing, and data innovation.[10] The key instruments and elements of the new data access, data use, and data sharing regime established by the Chapters II. – V. of the Data Act and by the Data Governance Act are illustrated by figure 1:

8 See Hennemann, M. / Steinrötter, B., *NJW* 2024, 1 (3).

9 Regulation (EU) 2022/868 of the European Parliament and of the Council on European data governance.

10 Cf. also rec. 1.

Figure 1: © Hennemann, M. / Steinrötter, B., NJW 2024, 1 (2) (translated version).

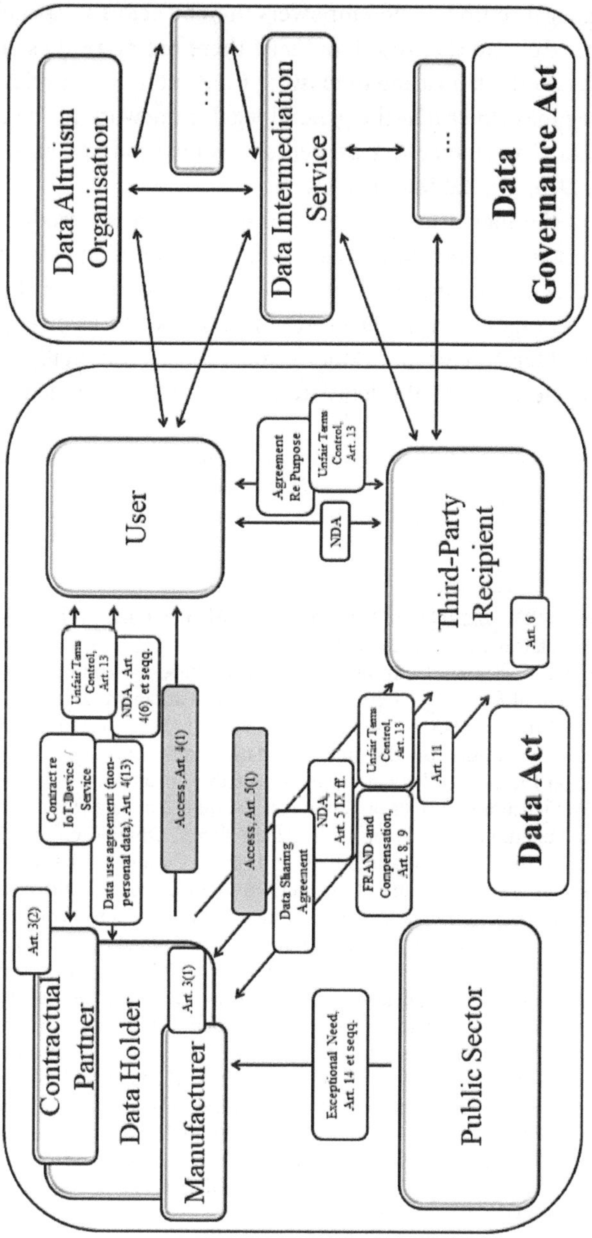

Despite its name, however, the Data Act does not regulate all legal aspects with respect to data (as the Data Governance Act does not regulate all aspects of data governance). Rather, the Data adds specific instruments to the existing legal setting – and empowers thereby actors in specific scenarios. The Data Act and its provisions must therefore be read as (important) puzzle pieces to the landscape of existing (and future) data-relevant norms and legal regimes (*inter alia* the general legal framework for data contracts and the Data Governance Act as well as competition law and Regulation (EU) 2022/1925 (Digital Markets Act)[11]).

In light of the increasing legislative complexity, this introduction to the Data Act hopefully contributes to a better understanding how this legislative piece fits with the broader legislative setting. Against this background, this volume engages with the Data Act in detail as well as engages with the cumbersome literature on the Data Act proposal. Additionally, this volume also makes references to the legislative debate which has led to the final version.[12]

11 Regulation (EU) 2022/1925 of the European Parliament and of the Council on contestable and fair markets in the digital sector.

12 Cf. *inter alia* Parliament Committee on Industry, Research and Energy, 'Draft report on the proposal for a regulation of the European Parliament and of the Council on harmonised rules on fair access to and use of data (Data Act)', 14 September 2022; Parliament Committee on the Internal Market and Consumer Protection, 'Draft Opinion on the proposal for a regulation of the European Parliament and of the Council on harmonised rules on fair access to and use of data (Data Act)', 4 October 2022; Parliament Committee on Legal Affairs, 'Draft Opinion on the proposal for a regulation of the European Parliament and of the Council on harmonised rules on fair access to and use of data (Data Act)', 6 October 2022; Parliament Committee on Civil Liberties, Justice and Home Affairs, 'Draft Opinion on the proposal for a regulation of the European Parliament and of the Council on Harmonised rules on fair access to and use of data (Data Act)', 19 October 2022. Council Presidency, 'Note on the Proposal for a Regulation of the European Parliament and of the Council on harmonised rules on fair access to and use of data (Data Act) - Second Presidency compromise text (Chapters I-V)', 21 October 2022; Council Presidency, 'Note on the Proposal for a Regulation of the European Parliament and of the Council on harmonised rules on fair access to and use of data (Data Act) - Second Presidency compromise text (Chapters VI-XI)', 3 November 2022; Council Presidency, 'Note on the Proposal for a Regulation of the European Parliament and of the Council on harmonised rules on fair access to and use of data (Data Act) – Third Presidency compromise text', 8 December 2022.

1. General Setting and Goals

The challenges to be tackled by and the goals pursued with the Data Act are diverse.[13] The Act is mainly pointing to the unwillingness to share data by those who have access and is targeted at fostering data sharing, especially to boost innovation in aftermarkets.[14] Although the most prominent part of the Act is directed at *internet of things*-products and related services (Art. 4 et seq.), the Act is not primarily concerned with competition on these primary markets.[15]

Rec. 1 highlights:

> "In recent years, data-driven technologies have had transformative effects on all sectors of the economy. The proliferation of products connected to the internet in particular has increased the volume and potential value of data for consumers, businesses and society. High-quality and interoperable data from different domains increase competitiveness and innovation and ensure sustainable economic growth. The same data may be used and reused for a variety of purposes and to an unlimited degree, without any loss of quality or quantity."

On this basis, rec. 6 sets the general regulatory setting of the Act:

> "Data generation is the result of the actions of at least two actors, in particular the designer or manufacturer of a connected product, who may in many cases also be a provider of related services, and the user of the connected product or related service. It gives rise to questions of fairness in the digital economy as the data recorded by connected products or related services are an important input for aftermarket, ancillary and other services. In order to realise the important economic benefits of data, including by way of data sharing on the basis of voluntary agreements and the development of data-driven value creation by Union enterprises, a general approach to assigning rights regarding access to and the use of data is preferable to awarding exclusive rights of access and use. This Regulation provides for horizontal rules which could be

13 Cf. also rec. 31 and 119.

14 See Krämer, J., Improving The Economic Effectiveness of the B2B and B2C Data Sharing Obligations in the Proposed Data Act, CERRE, 2022, p. 5, who has strong doubts whether the Act's design will fulfil this goal (cf. p. 19).

15 Krämer, J., Improving The Economic Effectiveness of the B2B and B2C Data Sharing Obligations in the Proposed Data Act, CERRE, 2022, p. 6.

> followed by Union or national law that addresses the specific situations of the relevant sectors."

Rec. 2 outlines the main "[b]arriers to data sharing" the Act is willing to tackle and which "prevent an optimal allocation of data for the benefit of society":

> "a lack of incentives for data holders to enter voluntarily into data sharing agreements, uncertainty about rights and obligations in relation to data, the costs of contracting and implementing technical interfaces, the high level of fragmentation of information in data silos, poor metadata management, the absence of standards for semantic and technical interoperability, bottlenecks impeding data access, a lack of common data sharing practices and the abuse of contractual imbalances with regard to data access and use."

Rec. 4 underlines that the Act "respond[s] to the needs of the digital economy and (...) remove[s] barriers to a well-functioning internal market for data" (the latter is inter alia underlined by the rules on switching between data processing services according to Art. 23-31). The Data Act seeks to promote innovation by access and to incentivise data production. Rec. 32 elaborates in this regard:

> "The aim of this Regulation is not only to foster the development of new, innovative connected products or related services, stimulate innovation on aftermarkets, but also to stimulate the development of entirely novel services making use of the data concerned, including based on data from a variety of connected products or related services. At the same time, this Regulations aims to avoid undermining the investment incentives for the type of connected product from which the data are obtained, for instance, by the use of data to develop a competing connected product which is considered to be interchangeable or substitutable by users, in particular on the basis of the connected product's characteristics, its price and intended use. (...)"

Rec. 30 additionally points to – also with regard to the protection of trade secrets – that "[i]t is important to preserve incentives to invest in products with functionalities based on the use of data from sensors built into those products."

2. *From a Reaction to Market Failures to a new Market Design*

The various aforementioned drivers in favour of the Data Act underline a general tendency in European Data Law. First, the different instruments do not – and do not want to – fit neatly into specific fields of law. Central questions, e.g., the nature of specific rights, remain open. They often combine different, not always directly connected, fields aspects of data governance. This is especially true for the Data Governance Act which tackles only selected fields like public sector information, data intermediation services, and data altruism – and does not strive to set coherent rules.

Second and most importantly, it has already become clear from the Data Governance Act that the legislator does not only strive to counter perceived or actual market failures – as a traditional Economics perspective would advise to do.[16] Rather, the Acts must be described as a form of *market design law* or *market infrastructure law*.[17] The different Acts are not only meant as setting boundaries for specific activities – neatly underlined by the fact that the Acts pursue a horizontal approach and are not only e.g., applicable to a specific sector[18] or only to dominant undertakings[19]. The Data Act is consequently described as a "horizontal fundamental piece of regulation for all sectors"[20]. Therefore, the Acts are rather directed at establishing and boosting distinct market actors (e.g., users, data intermediation services)

---

16 See Leistner, M. / Antoine, L., IPR and the use of open data and data sharing initiatives by public and private actors, 2022, p. 77. Cf. in detail on the economic justification of the Act, Max Planck Institute for Innovation and Competition, Position Statement, 2022, pp. 15 et seq. n. 32 et seq.

17 Hennemann, M. / Steinrötter, B., *NJW* 2024, 1 (6); Leistner, M. / Antoine, L., IPR and the use of open data and data sharing initiatives by public and private actors, 2022, p. 78; Schweitzer, H. / Metzger, A. / Blind, K. / Richter, H. / Niebel, C. / Gutmann, F., The legal framework for access to data in Germany and in the EU, BMWK, 2022, p. 117; Schweitzer, H. / Metzger, A., *ZEuP* 2023, 42 (50). Cf. also Max Planck Institute for Innovation and Competition, Position Statement, 2022, pp. 17 et seq. n. 39.

18 Demanding respective complementary sectoral rules, Krämer, J., Improving The Economic Effectiveness of the B2B and B2C Data Sharing Obligations in the Proposed Data Act, CERRE, 2022, p. 6; Max Planck Institute for Innovation and Competition, Position Statement, 2022, p. 3 n. 3.

19 Schweitzer, H. / Metzger, A. / Blind, K. / Richter, H. / Niebel, C. / Gutmann, F., The legal framework for access to data in Germany and in the EU, BMWK, 2022, pp. 211, 213; Max Planck Institute for Innovation and Competition, Position Statement, 2022, pp. 15 et seq. n. 33.

20 Podszun, R. / Pfeifer, C., *GRUR* 2022, 953 (955).

as well as shaping existing and in part creating new markets.[21] Contrary to traditional doctrine, but in line with modern Economics approaches of market shaping (*Mazzucato*)[22], the legislative instruments are to be understood – and might be regarded as justified – as being targeted at a distinct *transformation* of underlying market structures[23].[24]

Finally, however and in contrary, this is not to say that the Data Act – next to its *market design* approach – does not actually address market failures in question.[25] The opposite is true. The Act for example tackles the fact that "access [to data] is frequently restricted where one actor holds them in the system or due to a lack of interoperability between data, between data services or across borders." (rec. 3).

3. *"Contractualisation" of Data (Economy) Law*

The Acts strives "to realise the important economic benefits of data, including by way of data sharing on the basis of voluntary agreements and the development of data-driven value creation by Union enterprises" and supports "a general approach to assigning rights regarding access to and the use of data" (rec. 6). Such an approach is regarded as superior to the award of "exclusive rights of access and use" (rec. 6). Accordingly – and referring to the broad debate on "data property" or absolute rights to data – rec. 5 states that the Act "should not be interpreted as recognising or conferring any new right on data holders to use data generated by the use of a connected product or related service."[26] (cf., however, the discussion

---

21 Schweitzer, H. / Metzger, A. / Blind, K. / Richter, H. / Niebel, C. / Gutmann, F., The legal framework for access to data in Germany and in the EU, BMWK, 2022, p. 116; Hennemann, M. / Steinrötter, B., *NJW* 2024, 1 (6).

22 Mazzucato, M., A collective response to our global challenges: a common good and market-shaping approach, UCL Institute for Innovation and Public Purpose Working Paper 2023-01, pp. 9 et seq.

23 Cf. also rec. 6 and 32.

24 Schweitzer, H. / Metzger, A. / Blind, K. / Richter, H. / Niebel, C. / Gutmann, F., The legal framework for access to data in Germany and in the EU, BMWK, 2022, p. 116.

25 See in detail Kerber, W., *GRUR Int.* 2023, 120 (121).

26 Similar rec. 25: "This Regulation should not be understood to confer any new right on data holders to use product data or related service data."

on Art. 4(13) below).[27] Voluntary agreements are also not barred by the new access regime (Art. 1(10)).

On that basis, the Data Act is driven by a *contractualisation* of the relevant relationships between data holder, data user, and data recipient.[28] The Act underlines that data (economy) law is driven by contract law. Rec. 5 stipulates respectively that "[p]rivate law rules are key in the overall framework for data sharing" and that "[t]herefore, this Regulation adapts rules of contract law and prevents the exploitation of contractual imbalances". Accordingly, the Data Act does not introduce a (direct) right to access of a competitor / third party that is fully independent of a user or its contractual relationship(s) (cf. also Art. 4(13) and (14)).[29]

As a default, the Act refers to a scenario where a product or service is used on a contractual basis and data is generated in the context of this very contract.[30] However, it has to be borne in mind that the data holder (being obliged to grant access) and the contractual partner of the user might be two different persons (cf. also Art. 3 (3)(d)). Furthermore, data access is generally combined with underlying (bilateral) contracts / agreements enabling data use.[31] The Act is consequently fostering contractual agreements between (nearly) all relevant parties (data use agreement, data access contract (on FRAND terms), non-disclosure-agreements (NDAs; cf. rec. 31) (cf. figure 1 above).[32] *Leistner* and *Antoine* correctly point to a "contractual design and enforcement in larger, multipolar networks" (and the missing rules of the Data Act in this regard).[33] Furthermore, the definition of a user as well as the operationalisation via user accounts (cf. rec. 21) mirrors the contractual setting. In addition, the contract law approach is strongly underlined by the fact that – on the basis of Art. 41 – model contractual

27 Cf. also Max Planck Institute for Innovation and Competition, Position Statement, 2022, p. 16 n. 34.

28 Cf. Hennemann, M. / Steinrötter, B., *NJW* 2024, 1 (4 et seq., 6 et seq.). For a detailed account Staudenmeyer, D., *EuZW* 2022, 596 (596 et seq.). Cf. also Max Planck Institute for Innovation and Competition, Position Statement, 2022, p. 27 n. 68; Leistner, M. / Antoine, L., IPR and the use of open data and data sharing initiatives by public and private actors, 2022, p. 74.

29 Hennemann, M. / Steinrötter, B., *NJW* 2022, 1481 (1483).

30 Hennemann, M. / Steinrötter, B., *NJW* 2022, 1481 (1483).

31 Staudenmeyer, D., *EuZW* 2022, 596 (596); Hennemann, M. / Steinrötter, B., *NJW* 2024, 1 (6 et seq.).

32 Staudenmeyer, D., *EuZW* 2022, 596 (596 et seq.); Hennemann, M. / Steinrötter, B., *NJW* 2024, 1 (6 et seq.).

33 Leistner, M. / Antoine, L., IPR and the use of open data and data sharing initiatives by public and private actors, 2022, p. 75.

terms and standard contractual terms shall be developed. The provisions on *smart contracts* (Art. 11(1), 36(1)) complement this contractual strive.

Despite this process of *contractualisation*, the Data Act does provide data contract law rules only to a limited extent.[34] Substantial aspects are missing.[35] This gap does not only refer to substantial rules, but it is also rightly criticised that the Data Act does not stipulate any conflicts of law-provisions.[36]

However, the rules on the unfair terms control (Art. 13) stipulate first parameters in substance, but do not contain rules for data contracts vis-à-vis consumers (leaving this dimension to the member states). Furthermore, the Act does not regulate substantially the central data use agreement according to Art. 4(13).[37]

Finally, and also with the new Art. 14 et seqq. in mind, Art. 1(6) Sentence 1 clarifies that the Data Act "does not apply to or pre-empt voluntary arrangements for the exchange of data between private and public entities, in particular voluntary arrangements for data sharing."[38]

4. User Activation

The Data Act heavily relies on an activation of the user.[39] Thereby, the access regime of the Data Act adopts a similar approach as the right to data portability according to Art. 20 Regulation (EU) 2016/679 (General Data Protection Regulation (GDPR))[40] does (which is faced with many obstacles and is said to be ineffective and / or under-used in practice).

---

34 Hennemann, M. / Steinrötter, B., *NJW* 2024, 1 (4).

35 Hennemann, M. / Steinrötter, B., *NJW* 2024, 1 (7).

36 See in this regard Hennemann, M. / Steinrötter, B., *NJW* 2024, 1 (7 et seq.).

37 Bomhard, D. / Merkle, M., *RDi* 2022, 168 (174); Leistner, M. / Antoine, L., IPR and the use of open data and data sharing initiatives by public and private actors, 2022, p. 74.

38 Council Presidency 2022/0047(COD) – 13342/22, p. 36.

39 Hennemann, M. / Steinrötter, B., *NJW* 2024, 1 (6).

40 Regulation (EU) 2016/679 of the European Parliament and of the Council on the protection of natural persons with regard to the processing of personal data and on the free movement of such data.

The user has – not only formally[41] – a central role in the Data Act framework.[42] A processing of non-personal data by the data holder is only possible on the basis of a contractual agreement with the user (Art. 4(13)). Only the user may request access to the data generated by the user's use of an IoT-product – in favour of himself / herself (Art. 4(1)) or to the benefit of a third party (Art. 5(1)). The user is also free to use both rights cumulatively.[43] Any access of a third party is dependent on the user (Art. 5(1)) – and consequently oftentimes on a respective contractual agreement with the user. The third party will practically have to set (financial) incentives in order to 'activate' the user respectively.[44] Furthermore, the third party may not hinder the user to grant access to further third parties (Art. 6(2)(h)).

In addition and finally, Art. 4 (14) underlines the strong position of the user by stipulating that "[d]ata holders shall not make available non-personal product data to third parties for commercial or non-commercial purposes other than the fulfilment of their contract with the user."

It was and will be heavily discussed whether this activation will actually on will work in practice.[45]

5. Monetarisation of Data?

Furthermore, the final version of the Data Act provides us with some clarity on the central question whether and to what extent a monetarisation of personal and – especially – non-personal data shall be possible.[46]

The general purpose of the Act, the different access rights stipulated by the Act as well as a well-understood interplay with data intermediation services generally – and rightly – foster an understanding towards a monet-

41 Cf. also Podszun, R. / Pfeifer, C., *GRUR* 2022, 953 (956). Cf. also Kerber, W., *GRUR-Int.* 2023, 120 (121).

42 Cf. for the respective discussion Leistner, M. / Antoine, L., IPR and the use of open data and data sharing initiatives by public and private actors, 2022, pp. 80, 98.

43 Specht-Riemenschneider, L., *MMR-Beil.* 2022, 809 (816).

44 Krämer, J., Improving The Economic Effectiveness of the B2B and B2C Data Sharing Obligations in the Proposed Data Act, CERRE, 2022, p. 15.

45 Cf. e.g., Leistner, M. / Antoine, L., IPR and the use of open data and data sharing initiatives by public and private actors, 2022, pp. 81, 97; Podszun, R. / Pfeifer, C., *GRUR* 2022, 953 (956).

46 Cf. Hennemann, M. / Steinrötter, B., *NJW* 2024, 1 (7). In detail with regard to the proposal Max Planck Institute for Innovation and Competition, Position Statement, 2022, pp. 7 et seq. n. 14 et seq.

arisation.[47] Especially, Art. 4(13) and Art. 6(2)(h) might be interpreted in such way that these provisions point to the user as being the prime actor to monetarise.[48] Also, Art. 4 (14) and also Art. 6(2)(c) give ground in this regard (cf. also rec. 5, 7, 25, 26, 33).[49]

Different follow-on rules of the access right (e.g., Art. 4(10), 5(6), 6(2)(c) and (e)), however, limit – next to data protection law – a full monetarisation.

6. *Enforcement*

The Data Act is generally rather silent on mechanisms of *private enforcement* and / or contractual consequences of violations of the Act's obligations.[50] Whereas rec. 9 highlights that national contract law shall not be affected, it is often not clear whether and to which extent obligations following from the Act are of a contractual nature.[51] Provisions like, *inter alia*, Art. 13(1), (7) and (9), however, underline the private law effects of the Act.

Furthermore, Art. 47 and 48 transports the Data Act to the (collective) enforcement mechanism of Regulation (EU) 2017/2394[52] and Directive (EU) 2020/1828 (Directive on Representative Actions)[53] which annexes are amended respectively.

---

47 In detail Hennemann, M. / Steinrötter, B., *NJW* 2024, 1 (7).

48 See also Max Planck Institute for Innovation and Competition, Position Statement, 2022, p. 18 n. 42. Cf. for doubts from an Economics perspective in this regard Krämer, J., Improving The Economic Effectiveness of the B2B and B2C Data Sharing Obligations in the Proposed Data Act, CERRE, 2022, p. 21.

49 Cf. Hennemann, M. / Steinrötter, B., *NJW* 2024, 1 (7).

50 Hennemann, M. / Steinrötter, B., *NJW* 2024, 1 (8); Bomhard, D. / Merkle, M., *RDi* 2022, 168 (174); Leistner, M. / Antoine, L., IPR and the use of open data and data sharing initiatives by public and private actors, 2022, pp. 13, 74; Max Planck Institute for Innovation and Competition, Position Statement, 2022, pp. 4 et seq. n. 6 and 8. This is also criticized from an Economics perspective, cf. Krämer, J., Improving The Economic Effectiveness of the B2B and B2C Data Sharing Obligations in the Proposed Data Act, CERRE, 2022, p. 10.

51 Cf. also rec. 5, 42, 104.

52 Regulation (EU) 2017/2394 of the European Parliament and of the Council on cooperation between national authorities responsible for the enforcement of consumer protection laws.

53 Directive (EU) 2020/1828 of the European Parliament and of the Council on representative actions for the protection of the collective interests of consumers.

In addition, in the context of a third-party recipient access specific provisions on alternative dispute settlement and on further protection measures are stipulated by Art. 10 and 11 (cf. also rec. 52 et seqq.).

To the opposite, the Act provides detailed provisions on *public enforcement.* Art. 37 points to the respective (mandatory) authorities and data coordinators.[54] Art. 40 stipulates rules on sanctions to be provided with the national implementing laws.[55]

7. Trade Agreements / Other Union Legal Acts Governing Rights and Obligations on Data and Use (Art. 44) / Options for Member States

Trade Agreements

Rec. 4 underlines that the Data Act and Union law "should be without prejudice to obligations and commitments in the international trade agreements concluded by the Union."

Union Law

Furthermore, the Data Act should not affect specific provisions of acts of the Union adopted in the field of data sharing between businesses, between businesses and consumers and between businesses and public sector bodies that were adopted prior to the date of the entering into force of the Data Act, Art. 44(1).

Most prominently, the Data Act is without prejudice to future Union law that specifies further requirements with regard to sector specific legislation, to the common European data space regulation, and to areas of public interest, Art. 44(2). Art. 44(2) points explicitly to "technical aspects of data access" (lit. a), "limits on the rights of data holders to access or use certain data provided by users" (lit. b), and "aspects going beyond data access and use" (lit. c) (see also rec. 115).

---

54 Cf. also rec. 107 et seqq.
55 Cf. rec. 109.

Member States

In addition, the EU as well as the member states may further regulate ("with the exception of Chapter V") access to and use of data for scientific research purposes, Art. 44(3) (cf. also rec. 115 as well as 49, 63, and 76 in this regard).

Furthermore, however, rec. 4 states that member states "should not adopt or maintain additional national requirements regarding matters falling within the scope of this Regulation" in order to guarantee the "direct and uniform application" of the Act. Exceptions must be explicitly named within the Act. Next to Art. 44(3) this is *inter alia* the case in Art. 18(2) pointing to sectoral legislation. In addition, rec. 4, 6, 20, 25, 27, 52, and 115 point to further options. For example, only within the recitals (rec. 25), it becomes apparent that the Act allows – in the context of the compulsory data licence agreement according to Art. 4(13) – for rather broad sector-specific deviations[56]:

> "Moreover, this Regulation does not prevent sector-specific regulatory requirements under Union law, or national law compatible with Union law, which would exclude or limit the use of certain such data by the data holder on well-defined public policy grounds."

Rec. 27 elaborates in this regard the sector-specific demands and challenges:

> "In sectors characterised by the concentration of a small number of manufacturers supplying connected products to end users, there may only be limited options available to users for the access to and the use and sharing of data. In such circumstances, contracts may be insufficient to achieve the objective of user empowerment, making it difficult for users to obtain value from the data generated by the connected product they purchase, rent or lease. Consequently, there is limited potential for innovative smaller businesses to offer data-based solutions in a competitive manner and for a diverse data economy in the Union. This Regulation should therefore build on recent developments in specific sectors, such

56 Cf. Podszun, R. / Pfeifer, C., *GRUR* 2022, 953 (955); Specht-Riemenschneider, L., *MMR-Beil.* 2022, 809 (811). Demanding respective rules from an Economics perspective, Kerber, W., *GRUR-Int.* 2023, 120 (135); Krämer, J., Improving The Economic Effectiveness of the B2B and B2C Data Sharing Obligations in the Proposed Data Act, CERRE, 2022, p. 6. Cf. also Leistner, M. / Antoine, L., IPR and the use of open data and data sharing initiatives by public and private actors, 2022, p. 78.

as the Code of Conduct on agricultural data sharing by contract. Union or national law may be adopted to address sector-specific needs and objectives."

Outside the Scope of Union Law

Art. 1(6) Sentences 4 and 5 add that the Act shall not apply to fields of law that do not fall into the scope of Union law (e. g., defence, national security, tax matters).

8. Evaluation and Review (Art. 49)

By September 12 2028, the Commission has to carry out an evaluation of the Data Act, Art. 49. Art. 49(1)(a)-(m) list the content of the respective report.[57] The evaluation shall serve as the basis to revise the Act.[58]

9. Entry into Force and Application (Art. 50)

Art. 50 regulates – differently for different chapters – the application of the Act. The Data Act generally applies from September 12 2025 "[i]n order to allow actors (…) to adapt to the new rules", Art. 50(1) and rec. 117. Obligations according to Art. 3(1) should apply to connected products and related services placed on the market from September 12 2026 onwards, Art. 50(2). The provisions of Chapter IV should apply to contracts concluded after September 12 2025; an exception is, however, made for contracts concluded on or before September 2025. If they are of indefinite duration or have an expiry date of at least January 11 2034, Chapter IV applies from September 12 2027, Art. 50.

57 Cf. Leistner, M. / Antoine, L., IPR and the use of open data and data sharing initiatives by public and private actors, 2022, p. 122; Specht-Riemenschneider, L., *MMR-Beil.* 2022, 809 (826).

58 Leistner, M. / Antoine, L., IPR and the use of open data and data sharing initiatives by public and private actors, 2022, p. 122.

10. Competence

With regard to the competence of the EU, the Data Act is based on Art. 114 TFEU. Rec. 119 adds in this regard that "the objectives of this Regulation, namely ensuring fairness in the allocation of value from data among actors in the data economy and fostering fair access to and use of data in order to contribute to establishing a genuine internal market for data, cannot be sufficiently achieved by the Member States". It is underlined that these goals "can rather, by reason of the scale or effects of the action and cross-border use of data, be better achieved at Union level". Rec. 119 further points to the legislator's assessment that the principle of subsidiarity has been met and that the Data Act "does not go beyond what is necessary in order to achieve [the aforementioned] objectives".

III. Regulatory Scope (Art. 1-2, Art. 43)

Chapter I ('General Provisions'; Art. 1-2) frames the Act in terms of scope and terminology, defining key concepts, and the complementary relationships with applicable legislation on e.g., data protection, electronic communications, and criminal matters. It is complemented by Chapter X ('*Sui Generis* Right under Directive 1996/9/EC'; Art. 43), which explicitly denies protection granted to databases (by way of the *sui generis* right) "when data is obtained from or generated by a connected product or related service falling within the scope of [the Data Act] (...)."

1. Scope (Art. 1 paras. 1-3)

Material Scope

Art. 1(1) lays down the material scope of the Data Act. In substance, the Data Act provides for different, but intertwined instruments.[59] Rec. 5 summarises:

> "This Regulation ensures that users of a connected product or related service in the Union can access, in a timely manner, the data generated by the use of that connected product or related service and that those users can use the data, including by sharing them with third parties of their choice. It imposes the obligation on data holders to make data available to users and third parties of the user's choice in certain circumstances. It also ensures that data holders make data available to data recipients in the Union under fair, reasonable and non-discriminatory terms and conditions and in a transparent manner. (...) This Regulation also ensures that data holders make available to public sector bodies, the Commission, the European Central Bank or Union bodies, where there is an exceptional need, the data that are necessary for the performance of a specific task carried out in the public interest. In addition, this Regulation seeks to facilitate switching between data processing services and

59 Hennemann, M. / Steinrötter, B., *NJW* 2022, 1481 (1482).

to enhance the interoperability of data and of data sharing mechanisms and services in the Union."

Art. 1(2) provides chapter-by-chapter details on the respective scope of application. Chapters VIII-XI are not explicitly mentioned as they are of a supporting nature to the other chapters. Art. 1(2) first and foremost highlights that the Data Act, in general, regulates personal and non-personal data.[60] In the following, however, precise differentiations are made with regard to the scope of application:

- Chapter II: data concerning the performance, use and environment of connected products and related services (but without content) (lit. a)
- Chapter III: private sector data relevant for the statutory data sharing obligations (lit. b)
- Chapter IV: private sector data accessed and used on the basis of b2b-contract (lit. c)
- Chapter V: private sector data, but "with a focus on non-personal data" – this (probably) refers to the fact that Art. 15 is mainly targeted at non-personal data (lit. d)
- Chapter VI: data and services processed for data processing services (lit. e)
- Chapter VII: non-personal data held in the Union by data processing service providers (lit. f)

Personal and Territorial Scope

Following this setting, Art. 1(3) defines the personal and territorial scope of the Act. Art. 1(3) lists the different (major) actors regulated by the Data Act:

- *manufacturers* of connected products placed on the market in the Union (irrespective of the place of establishment) (lit. a)
- *providers* of related services (irrespective of the place of establishment) (lit. a)
- *users* in the Union of connected products or related services (lit. b)
- *data holders* (irrespective of their place of establishment) that make data available to data recipients in the Union (lit. c)

60 This approach is mostly welcomed, cf. e.g., Krämer, J., Improving The Economic Effectiveness of the B2B and B2C Data Sharing Obligations in the Proposed Data Act, CERRE, 2022, p. 9.

- *data recipients* in the Union to whom data are made available (lit. d)
- *public sector bodies*, the Commission, the European Central Bank and Union bodies that request data holders to make data available where there is an exceptional need for those data for the performance of a specific task carried out in the public interest and to the data holders that provide those data in response to such request (lit. e)
- *data processing service providers* (irrespective of their place of establishment) providing such services to customers in the Union (lit. f)[61]
- *participants* in data spaces[62] and *vendors* of applications using smart contracts and *persons* whose trade, business or profession involves the deployment of smart contracts for others in the context of executing an agreement (lit. g)

It is important to note that Art. 1(3) combines the personal and territorial scope of the Data Act.[63] With references to products and services "placed on the market in the Union" (lit. a) as well as to "providing such services to customers in the Union" (lit. f) the Data Act mirrors the well-known market principle. At first sight, the Data Act should be interpreted in line with existing data regulation – inter alia Art. 3(2)(a) and rec. 23 GDPR as well as Art. 11(3) and rec. 42 DGA (with its reference to "envisage offering services" (rec. 23 GDPR)).[64]

Virtual Assistants

Art. 1(4) clarifies that "[w]here this Regulation refers to connected products or related services, such references are also understood to include virtual assistants insofar as they interact with a connected product or related service." According to Art. 2(31) virtual assistant refers to "software that can process demands, tasks or questions including those based on audio, written input, gestures or motions, and that, based on those demands, tasks or questions, provides access to other services or controls the functions of connected products".

Rec. 23 underlines and elaborates on the central role virtual assistants play in today's connected society. The recital further clarifies the data

61 Cf. the (different) terminology and the concept sub Ch. VI. below. Cf. also Hennemann, M. / Steinrötter, B., *NJW* 2022, 1481 (1482).

62 Cf. also rec. 27 and 103 as well as Art. 30 lit. h DGA.

63 Hennemann, M. / Steinrötter, B., *NJW* 2022, 1481 (1482).

64 Hennemann, M. / Steinrötter, B., *NJW* 2022, 1481 (1482).

covered ("only the data arising from the interaction between the user and a connected product or related service through the virtual assistant should be covered by this Regulation.").

2. Interplay with Existing Rules (Art. 1 paras. 5 and 6, Art. 43)

Manifold questions arise regarding the interplay of the Data Act with existing rules in other fields of laws.[65]

Contract Law

Rec. 9 underlines that the Data Act "does not affect national contract law, including rules on the formation, validity or effect of contracts, or the consequences of the termination of a contract."[66] In addition, Art. 1(10) stresses that the Data Act "does not preclude the conclusion of voluntary lawful data sharing contracts, including contracts concluded on a reciprocal basis, which comply with the requirements laid down in this Regulation." Furthermore, Art. 1(6) Sentence 1 clarifies that "[t]his Regulation does not apply to or pre-empt voluntary arrangements for the exchange of data between private and public entities, in particular voluntary arrangements for data sharing."[67]

Unfair Terms Law and Consumer Law

Art. 1(9) underlines that the Data Act only complements and is without prejudice to EU consumer law – in particular the Directive 2005/29/EC

65 Cf. Hennemann, M. / Steinrötter, B., *NJW* 2024, 1 (5 et seq.) as well as Max Planck Institute for Innovation and Competition, Position Statement, 2022, p. 96 n. 267 et seq. See also Leistner, M. / Antoine, L., IPR and the use of open data and data sharing initiatives by public and private actors, 2022, pp. 73 et seq. Questions of Trade Secrets Law are discussed below in the context of the relevant norms. Cf. in detail in this regard Max Planck Institute for Innovation and Competition, Position Statement, 2022, p. 100 n. 277 et seq., for questions with regard to private international law cf. pp. 120 et seq. n. 333 et seq.

66 Council Presidency 2022/0047(COD) – 15035/22, p. 9.

67 Council Presidency 2022/0047(COD) – 13342/22, p. 36.

(Unfair Commercial Practices Directive)[68], the Directive 2011/83/EU[69], and the Directive 93/13/EEC[70].[71] Rec. 28 underlines especially that Art. 13 does not apply to b2c-contracts, but that respective contracts are subject to Directives 93/13/EEC and 2005/29/EC.

Intellectual Property Law

Fundamentally, Art. 43 curbs protection granted to databases by way of a *sui generis* right within the ambit of the Act.[72] Art. 7 of Directive 96/9/EC (Database Directive)[73] shall not apply to databases containing data obtained from or generated by the use of a product or a related service. The goal of this provision is in particular that the exercise of the access (and use) right of users according to Art. 4 and the right to share such data with third parties according to Art. 5 is not hindered.[74] However, the scope of Art. 43 remains unclear.[75] Rec. 112 underlines that the Data Act is seeking to "eliminate the risk that holders of data (...) claim" the *sui generis* right and rec. 71 refers – in the context of the Art. 14 et seqq. – to the fact that "[w]here the sui generis database rights under [Database Directive] (...) apply in relation to the requested datasets, data holders should exercise their rights in such a way that does not prevent the public sector body, the Commission, the European Central Bank or Union body from obtaining the data, or from sharing it, in accordance with this Regulation."

68 Directive 2005/29/EC of the European Parliament and of the Council concerning unfair business-to-consumer commercial practices in the internal market.

69 Directive 2011/83/EU of the European Parliament and of the Council on consumer rights.

70 Directive 93/13/EEC on unfair terms in consumer contracts. Directive (EU) 2019/2161 of the European Parliament and of the Council amending Council Directive 93/13/EEC and Directives 98/6/EC, 2005/29/EC and 2011/83/EU of the European Parliament and of the Council as regards the better enforcement and modernisation of Union consumer protection rules.

71 Cf. also rec. 9.

72 Cf. in detail for intellectual property rights beyond Art. 43 Max Planck Institute for Innovation and Competition, Position Statement, 2022, p. 96 n. 268 et seq. as well as Leistner, M. / Antoine, L., IPR and the use of open data and data sharing initiatives by public and private actors, 2022, p. 76.

73 Directive 96/9/EC of the European Parliament and of the Council on the legal protection of databases.

74 Cf. also rec. 112.

75 Cf. for a discussion in detail Max Planck Institute for Innovation and Competition, Position Statement, 2022, p. 90 n. 254 et seq.

Data Protection Law

The omnipresent question of the interplay between the Data Act – as applying to personal and non-personal data alike – and data protection law[76] sought to be answered by Art. 1(5). According to Art. 1(5) Sentence 1, the Data Act shall not affect the applicability of Union law on the protection of personal data, in particular the GDPR and Directive 2002/58/EC (ePrivacy Directive)[77] (including the powers and competences of supervisory authorities). Rec. 7 confirms that these acts (as well as the Regulation (EU) 2018/1725[78] mentioned there) "provide the basis for sustainable and responsible data processing, including where datasets include a mix of personal and non-personal data".

The Data Act obligations are – as far as the processing of personal data is concerned – added to the existing data protection law duties of processors[79]: "In the event of a conflict between this Regulation and Union law on the protection of personal data or privacy, or national legislation adopted in accordance with such Union law, the relevant Union or national law on the protection of personal data or privacy shall prevail." (Art. 1(5) Sentence 4)[80]

Rec. 7 explicitly underlines that "[n]o provision of this Regulation should be applied or interpreted in such a way as to diminish or limit the right to the protection of personal data or the right to privacy and confidentiality of communications."[81] In many cases, it needs to be evaluated carefully

76 Cf. for a discussion in detail Max Planck Institute for Innovation and Competition, Position Statement, 2022, pp. 105 et seq. n. 291 et seq.

77 Directive 2002/58/EC of the European Parliament and of the Council concerning the processing of personal data and the protection of privacy in the electronic communications sector.

78 Regulation (EU) 2018/1725 of the European Parliament and of the Council on the protection of natural persons with regard to the processing of personal data by the Union institutions, bodies, offices and agencies and on the free movement of such data.

79 Hennemann, M. / Steinrötter, B., *NJW* 2022, 1481 (1482); Leistner, M. / Antoine, L., IPR and the use of open data and data sharing initiatives by public and private actors, 2022, p. 91.

80 Cf. also Art. 6(2)(b).

81 But cf. Art. 18(5) and 21 (sub VIII. 6. and 9.).

whether and to what extent a joint controllership (Art. 26 GDPR) exists (cf. also rec. 34).[82]

Rec. 8 additionally highlights the data protection law principles of data minimisation[83] and data protection by design and by default as well as the technical and organisational measures going along with these principles (cf. inter alia Art. 24 and 32 GDPR).[84] With respect to respective measures rec. 8 insists that "[s]uch measures include not only pseudonymisation and encryption, but also the use of increasingly available technology that permits algorithms to be brought to the data and allow valuable insights to be derived without the transmission between parties or unnecessary copying of the raw or structured data themselves."

In Particular: Legal Basis According to Art. 6(1)(c) and (3) GDPR

One of the main disputes around the Data Act is whether and to what extent the obligations set by the Act, especially to grant access, are to be read a constituting a legal obligation according to Art. 6(1)(c) (as well as Art. 6(1)(e) and (3)) GDPR – justifying the respective data processing (transfer to user and / or third party).[85] It is obvious that the route taken in this regard is fundamentally shaping the effectiveness of the Data Act.[86] The matter was clarified (to some extent) during the legislative process.[87] It is fair to say that many uncertainties remain. Rec. 7 stipulates[88]:

> "Any processing of personal data pursuant to this Regulation should comply with Union data protection law, including the requirement of a valid legal basis for processing under [Art. 6 GDPR] and, where relevant, the conditions of [Art. 9 GDPR] and of [Art.] 5(3) of Directive 2002/58/EC."

82 Cf. in this regard Leistner, M. / Antoine, L., IPR and the use of open data and data sharing initiatives by public and private actors, 2022, pp. 90 et seq., 99.

83 Cf. also rec. 20.

84 Cf. also rec. 24 with regard to the duration of data storing.

85 Strongly in favour Leistner, M. / Antoine, L., IPR and the use of open data and data sharing initiatives by public and private actors, 2022, pp. 90 et seq.; Specht-Riemenschneider, L., *MMR-Beil.* 2022, 809 (810 et seq.).

86 Cf. also Leistner, M. / Antoine, L., IPR and the use of open data and data sharing initiatives by public and private actors, 2022, p. 75.

87 Cf. also the proposal by LIBE, PE737.389, pp. 23 et seq.

88 Cf. also rec. 20 and 24.

With regard to the access regime in Art. 4 et seq. rec. 7 further highlights:[89]

> "This Regulation does not constitute a legal basis for the collection or generation of personal data by the data holder. This Regulation imposes an obligation on data holders to make personal data available to users or third parties of a user's choice upon that user's request. Such access should be provided to personal data that are processed by the data holder on the basis of any of the legal bases referred to in [Art. 6 GDPR]. Where the user is not the data subject, this Regulation does not create a legal basis for providing access to personal data or for making personal data available to a third party and should not be understood as conferring any new right on the data holder to use personal data generated by the use of a connected product or related service."

Rec. 7, however, also slightly opens the door for a legal basis according to Art. 6(1)(f) GDPR: "it could be in the interest of the user to facilitate meeting the requirements of [Art. 6 GDPR]."

With regard to the access regime in Art. 14 et seq. rec. 69 underlines:

> "In accordance with [Art. 6(1) and (3) GDPR], a proportionate, limited and predictable framework at Union level is necessary when providing for the legal basis for the making available of data by data holders, in cases of exceptional needs, to public sector bodies, the Commission, the European Central Bank or Union bodies, both to ensure legal certainty and to minimise the administrative burdens placed on businesses."[90]

In Particular: Art. 20 GDPR

Art. 1(5) Sentence 2 confirms that the right to access (Art. 15 GDPR) and especially the right to data portability (Art. 20 GPDR) remain untouched ("complement") by what is prescribed in Chapter II of the Act – despite the similar nature of the right to access according to Art. 4(1) and 5(1). No such complementary relationship with Art. 20 GDPR is stated for the rights in relation to switching between data processing services under Chapter VI of the Act.[91]

---

89 Cf. also rec. 69 and 72 as well as Art. 17(1)(h).

90 Cf. in detail below sub VIII. 11.

91 Cf. in detail below sub IX. 9.

Data Governance Act

Whilst the Commission proposal was rather silent on the interplay with the Data Governance Act, the final version of the Data Act now rightly – in rec. 26 and 33 – highlights the prospects and needs in this regard:

> "[d]ata intermediation services[92], as regulated by [the Data Governance Act] could facilitate [the] data economy by establishing commercial relationships between users, data recipients and third parties and may support users in exercising their right to use data, such as ensuring the anonymisation of personal data or aggregation of access to data from multiple individual users."

as well as

> "[b]usiness-to-business data intermediaries and personal information management systems (PIMS), referred to as data intermediation services in [the Data Governance Act], may support users or third parties in establishing commercial relations with an undetermined number of potential counterparties for any lawful purpose (...). They could play an instrumental role in aggregating access to data so that big data analyses or machine learning can be facilitated, provided that users remain in full control of whether to provide their data to such aggregation and the commercial terms under which their data are to be used."

This is not to say that these recitals seem sufficient. Although the Data Act clarifies that data intermediation services may be a third-party recipient according to Art. 5 (cf. rec. 39), the Data Act does not substantially tackle the relationship to and its interplay with the Data Governance Act[93] (rec. 70 being an exception clarifying the relationship between the Art. 14 et seq. and the Data Governance Act). A minor (positive) fragment in this regard is rec. 30 where it is highlighted that the user may use data intermediation services to act on the user's behalf in the context of exercising the Data Act rights and any (subsequent) data sharing.

In general, specific rules are missing and no incentives are set. As data intermediaries do fulfil a central function in order to enable data

92 Cf. also Art. 2(10).

93 Cf. e.g., Schweitzer, H. / Metzger, A. / Blind, K. / Richter, H. / Niebel, C. / Gutmann, F., The legal framework for access to data in Germany and in the EU, BMWK, 2022, p. 236.

exchanges / data contracts, this gap opposes the general aim of the Data Act to enhance and foster data sharing and data use.

Some further aspects with regard to public sector information, the European Data Innovation Board (EDIB), the committee procedure, and the evaluation process are, however, regulated by Art. 17(3), 33(11), 42, 46, 49(1)(a) (see also rec. 103).

Free Flow of Data-Regulation

The Data Act complements the Regulation (EU) 2018/1807 (Free Flow of Data Regulation) (Art. 1(7)) – especially by the additional requirements for cloud switching (cf. also rec. 79).

Competition Law

According to rec. 116, the Data Act does not touch Competition Law (Art. 101 et seq. TFEU).[94] The instruments spelled out in the Act shall not be used in way that does not comply with Art. 101 et seq. TFEU.[95]

Criminal Law / Criminal Procedural Law / Digital Services Act

Art. 1(6) Sentence 2 states in addition that the Act shall not affect criminal law and related fields (cf. also rec. 10).

This shall include Regulations (EU) 2021/784[96], (EU) 2022/2065 (Digital Services Act)[97] and (EU) 2023/1543 and Directive (EU) 2023/1544[98] as well

---

94 Cf. also on the question whether competition law instruments are granting adequate solutions for the situations tackled by the Data Act Proposal Max Planck Institute for Innovation and Competition, Position Statement, 2022, pp. 17 et seq. n. 36 et seq.

95 Cf. also Bomhard, D. / Merkle, M., *RDi* 2022, 168 (172).

96 Regulation (EU) 2021/784 of the European Parliament and of the Council on addressing the dissemination of terrorist content online.

97 Regulation (EU) 2022/2065 of the European Parliament and of the Council on a Single Market For Digital Services.

98 Directive (EU) 2023/1544 of the European Parliament and of the Council of 12 July 2023 laying down harmonised rules on the designation of designated establishments and the appointment of legal representatives for the purpose of gathering electronic evidence in criminal proceedings.

as international cooperation in this regard. Rec. 10 refers to the Budapest Convention[99] in particular.

Furthermore, the Data Act does not apply to collection, sharing, access or use of data with regard to Regulation (EU) 2015/847[100] and Directive (EU) 2015/849[101].

Product Safety / Accessibility Requirements for Products and Services

Rec. 11 and 12 confirm respectively that product-specific regulations regarding physical design and data requirements as well as accessibility requirements on certain products and services (in particular Directive 2019/882[102]) shall remain unaffected.

3. Definitions (Art. 2)

Art. 2 defines a vast number of terms to which will be referred within the following chapters. The central ones shall be highlighted in the following.[103]

Data

According to Art. 2(1) data means "any digital representation of acts, facts or information and any compilation[104] of such acts, facts or information, including in the form of sound, visual or audio-visual recording".[105] Data therefore encompasses personal as well non-personal data. This definition

---

99 Council of Europe 2001 Convention on Cybercrime.

100 Regulation (EU) 2015/847 of the European Parliament and of the Council on information accompanying the transfer of funds.

101 Directive (EU) 2015/849 of the European Parliament and of the Council on the prevention of the use of the financial system for the purposes of money laundering and terrorist financing.

102 Directive (EU) 2019/882 of the European Parliament and of the Council on the accessibility requirements for products and services.

103 Details are also discussed, where relevant, in the following chapters.

104 Cf. in regard this rather vague term Max Planck Institute for Innovation and Competition, Position Statement, 2022, p. 23 n. 57.

105 Similar to ISO-Norm ISO/IEC 2382:2015, IT Vocabulary, 2121272. Cf. also in general Zech, H., Information als Schutzgegenstand, 2012, pp. 32 et seq.; Zech, H., *CR* 2015, 137 (138 et seq.).

is a sensible one – as it does not just equal data to information (as Art. 4(1) GDPR does).[106] It is underlined that data is a "transport layer" for information.[107] Art. 2(3), however, defines personal data in line with the Art. 4(1), whereas Art. 2(4) stipulates more broadly that non personal data is data other than personal data.

The Act further provides definitions for metadata (Art. 2(2)), for product data (Art. 2(15)) and related service data (Art. 2(16))[108] as well as for readily available data (Art. 2(17) and rec. 20), and exportable data (Art. 2(38) and rec. 82). Rec. 15 stipulates further details in this regard, also with respect to "data in raw form", "pre-processed data", and "information inferred or derived from such data".

The term data must be separated from the term "digital assets" which is defined in Art. 2(32) as "elements in digital form, including applications, for which the customer has the right of use, independently from the contractual relationship with the data processing service it intends to switch from" – relevant in the context of Art. 23(c), 25, 29(5) (cf. also rec. 83).

Connected Product

According to Art. 2(5) a connected product is referring to "an item that obtains, generates or collects data concerning its use or environment and that is able to communicate product data via an electronic communications service[109], physical connection or on-device access, and whose primary function is not the storing, processing or transmission of data on behalf of any party other than the user". This definition mainly refers to Internet of Things-products.[110] Rec. 14 confirms and clarifies in this regard:

> "Connected products that obtain, generate or collect, by means of their components or operating systems, data concerning their performance, use or environment and that are able to communicate those data via an electronic communications service, a physical connection, or on-device

106 Hennemann, M. / Steinrötter, B., *NJW* 2022, 1481 (1482).
107 Hennemann, M. / Steinrötter, B., *NJW* 2022, 1481 (1482).
108 But cf. also rec. 20 and potential definitions of relevant data by further Union law and national law.
109 Rec. 14 explains that „electronic communications services include, in particular, land-based telephone networks, television cable networks, satellite-based networks and near-field communication networks."
110 Hennemann, M. / Steinrötter, B., *NJW* 2022, 1481 (1482).

access, often referred to as the Internet of Things, should fall within the scope of this Regulation, with the exception of prototypes. (...) Connected products are found in all aspects of the economy and society, including in private, civil or commercial infrastructure, vehicles, health and lifestyle equipment, ships, aircraft, home equipment and consumer goods, medical and health devices or agricultural and industrial machinery."

Different to the original proposal of the Act, the definition of connected products is not further specified. Rec. 16, however, underlines that the Act does not cover settings of specific products (by narrowing the definition of – *inter alia* – relevant 'product data' – also mirroring the scope set by Art. 1(2)(a)):

> "It is important to delineate between, on the one hand, markets for the provision of such sensor-equipped connected products and related services and, on the other, markets for unrelated software and content such as textual, audio or audiovisual content often covered by intellectual property rights. As a result, data that such sensor-equipped connected products generate when the user records, transmits, displays or plays content, as well as the content itself, which is often covered by intellectual property rights, inter alia for use by an online service, should not be covered by this Regulation. This Regulation should also not cover data which was obtained, generated or accessed from the connected product, or which was transmitted to it, for the purpose of storage or other processing operations on behalf of other parties, who are not the user, such as may be the case with regard to servers or cloud infrastructure operated by their owners entirely on behalf of third parties, inter alia for use by an online service."

Related Service

According to Art. 2(3) related service is referring to "digital service, other than an electronic communications service, including software, which is connected with the product at the time of the purchase, rent or lease in such a way that its absence would prevent the connected product from performing one or more of its functions, or which is subsequently connected to the product by the manufacturer or a third party to add to, update or adapt the functions of the connected product".[111]

Definitional References to Other Legal Acts

The Act frequently references other pieces of EU (digital) legislation. For example, Art. 2(3), (11) and (20) point to the GDPR definitions for personal data, data subject, and profiling. Art. 2(10) transplants the notion of data intermediation services from Art. 2(11) DGA[112], as do Art. 2(18) and (19) for the concept of trade secrets and trade secret holder introduced in Art. 2(1) and (2) of Directive (EU) 2016/943. These definitions and references do support a coherent interpretation of the relevant terms under European data law.

111 Cf. also rec. 15, 17 and 18.

112 Cf., in detail, Specht-Riemenschneider, L., in id. / Hennemann, M. (ed.), *Data Governance Act: DGA*, Nomos 2023, Art. 2 para. 64 et seq.

IV. SME-Exemption (Art. 7), Product Design, Service Design, and Informational Duties (Art. 3)

Chapter II ('Business to Consumer and Business to Business Data Sharing', Art. 3-7) increases the options for consumers and businesses to access data generated by the products or related services they own, rent or lease.[113]

1. Exemption of Micro and Small Enterprises; Mandatory Nature (Art. 7)

Art. 7(2) stipulates the mandatory nature of the user's rights under Chapter II while also providing exemptions for micro-, small- and medium-sized enterprises (SMEs) (Art. 7(1)).

Definition of Enterprise

According to Art. 2(8) the notion of an enterprise refers to a natural or legal person which in relation to contracts and practices covered by the Data Act is acting for purposes which are related to that person's trade, business, craft or profession. The definition for 'enterprise' is both relevant in the context of privileges and exemptions afforded to micro, small, or medium-sized enterprises (Art. 7-9 and 13-14; cf. the respective definition under Art. 2 of the Annex to Recommendation 2003/361/EC) as well as in other respects. Art. 8(3) refers to enterprises as a category of data recipients, Art. 13 as the contractual counterpart, and Art. 49(1)(d) as beneficiaries under Art. 5 whose exclusion should be evaluated (likely beyond gatekeepers within the meaning of the DMA, which are already barred from receiving data pursuant to Art. 5(2)(c)).

113 Commission, COM(2022) 68 final Explanatory Memorandum, p. 14.

Exemption of Micro and Small Enterprises

Art. 7(1) stipulates that "the obligations of [Chapter II] shall not apply to data generated by the use of products manufactured or related services provided by (...) micro or small enterprises".[114] Respective enterprises shall "not have partner enterprises or linked enterprises[115] which do not qualify as a micro or small enterprise" and should not be "subcontracted to manufacture or design a connected product or to provide a related service".

The exemption stipulated by Art. 7(1) is rather unclear.[116] The norm may be read in that way that micro and small enterprises shall not have the burden to fulfil the Art. 3-6. However, the norm does only point to the products and services itself (and not to the enterprises). Furthermore, the exemption also seems to cover scenarios where bigger enterprises – as data holders – use the products / services of micro and small enterprises. Rec. 37 sheds some light on this question. It becomes clear that respective enterprises do not have duties according to Art. 3(1):

> "Given the current state of technology, it is overly burdensome to impose further design obligations in relation to products manufactured or designed and related services provided by micro and small enterprises. That is not the case, however, where a micro or small enterprise is sub-contracted to manufacture or design a product. In such situations, the enterprise, which has sub-contracted to the micro or small enterprise, is able to compensate the sub-contractor appropriately."

Furthermore, respective enterprises do not fall under the personal scope of Art. 4 and 5 if they are manufacturer of a product or provider of a service. However, respective enterprises may be covered in other scenarios as rec. 37 spells out

> "A micro or small enterprise may nevertheless be subject to the requirements laid down by this Regulation as data holder, where it is not the manufacturer of the product or a provider of related services."

114 Cf. the respective definition in Art. 2 Annex to Recommendation 2003/361/EC.

115 Cf. the respective definition in Art. 3 Annex to Recommendation 2003/361/EC.

116 A proposal to delete or at least to modify Art. 7 was made by Max Planck Institute for Innovation and Competition, Position Statement, 2022, pp. 35 et seq. n. 96.

Exemption of medium-sized enterprises

Art. 7(1) Sentence 2 offers the same exemption for "medium-sized enterprises" (Art. 2 Annex to Recommendation 2003/361/EC) "that meet the threshold of that category for less than one year or that where it concerns products that a medium-sized enterprise has been placed on the market for less than one year".

Mandatory Nature

According to Art. 7(2) "[a]ny contractual term which, to the detriment of the user, excludes the application of, derogates from or varies the effect of the user's rights under this Chapter shall not be binding on the user." A respective general rule is far from doubt; especially with regard to an Economics perspective.[117] The rule applies to any contractual term – deviating to the detriment of the user – including the contract to buy or lease the product. Thus, it could be understood that even the seller or lessor is obliged to ensure the protection of the user's rights by the data holder.[118]

2. Product Design, Service Design (Art. 3(1))

According to Art. 3(1) connected products (cf. Art. 2(5)) shall be designed and manufactured, and related services (cf. Art. 2(6)) shall be designed and provided, in such a manner that product data and related service data, including the relevant metadata necessary to interpret and use the data, are, by default, easily, securely, free of charge, in a comprehensive, structured, commonly used and machine-readable format, and, where relevant and technically feasible, directly accessible to the user. Art. 1(4) highlights that connected products and related services might also encompass virtual assistants (as defined in Art. 2(31)) "insofar as they interact with a connected product or related service". The provision shall facilitate the user's access to the data generated by the product.[119]

117 Cf. also below VI. 2.
118 Schmidt-Kessel, M., *MMR-Beil.* 2024, 75 (77).
119 Cf. Metzger, A. / Schweitzer, H., *ZEuP* 2023, 42 (52); Schmidt-Kessel, M., *MMR-Beil.* 2024, 75 (78).

Rec. 20 states correctly that "not all data generated by products or related services are easily accessible to their users" and that "there are often limited possibilities for the portability of data generated by products connected to the internet".[120] Due to that fact Art. 3(1) ensures in technical terms "that users of a product or related service in the Union can access, in a timely manner, the data generated by the use of that product or related service and that those users can use the data, including by sharing them with third parties of their choice".[121] By enabling "data access by default", Art. 3(1) creates the technical basis for an effective exercise of the rights under Art. 4 et seq. vis-à-vis data holders.[122] Art. 2(13) defines the data holder as a legal or natural person who has the right or obligation, in accordance with this Regulation, applicable Union law or national legislation implementing Union law, to use and make available data, including, where contractually agreed, product data or related service data which it has retrieved or generated during the provision of a related service.

The access option shall simplify, for example, "switching between data processing services and to enhance the interoperability of data and data sharing mechanisms and services in the Union".[123] To allow developers to respond to the "far-reaching"[124] requirements of Art. 3(1), the obligation shall only apply to connected products and the services related to them placed on the market after 12 September 2026 (Art. 50).[125]

Personal Scope

The wording of Art. 3(1) does not make entirely clear what the relationship between Art. 3(1) and the underlying contract is as well as who is to be obliged by the provision.[126] In particular, rec. 24 explicitly refers only to the information obligations pursuant to Art. 3(3). With regard to the obligation under Art. 3(1), a distinction should correctly be made between connected

120 Rec. 19.

121 Rec. 5.

122 Cf. rec. 24; Metzger, A. / Schweitzer, H., *ZEuP* 2023, 42 (52); Schmidt-Kessel, M., *MMR-Beil.* 2024, 75 (78); Hennemann, M. / Steinrötter, B., *NJW* 2022, 1481 (1483).

123 Rec. 5.

124 Kerber, W., *GRUR-Int.* 2023, 120 (125).

125 The regulation in Art. 50 was a reaction to the criticism, among others, in the BDI Stellungnahme zum Legislativvorschlag des EU-Data Act, 2022, p. 12.

126 Max Planck Institute for Innovation and Competition, Position Statement, 2022, p. 30 n. 74.

products and related services. For connected products, only the manufacturer can guarantee compliance with Art. 3(1) regarding the production and design of products.[127] Sellers or lessors are not able to technically design the products if they are merely distributors and not manufacturers themselves. In contrast, providers of related services can regularly monitor compliance with Art. 3(1) themselves.

Material Scope

The Data Act addresses "product data and related service data, including the relevant metadata necessary to interpret and use the data". Correspondingly, rec. 15 states that the Data Act applies to product data and related service data.[128] According to Art. 2(15) 'product data' means data generated by the use of a connected product, that the manufacturer designed to be retrievable, via an electronic communications service, physical connection or on-device access, by a user, data holder or a third party, including, where relevant, the manufacturer. Art. 2(16) defines 'related service data' as data representing the digitisation of user actions or of events related to the connected product, recorded intentionally by the user or generated as a by-product of the user's action during the provision of a related service by the provider. Pursuant to Art. 2(2) 'metadata' means a structured description of the contents or the use of data facilitating the discovery or use of that data. Supplementary rec. 15 describes different scenarios all of which are covered:

(1) "data recorded intentionally or data which result indirectly from the uscr's action"
(2) "data about the connected product's environment or interactions"
(3) "data on the use of a connected product generated by a user interface or via a related service", which covers "all data that the product generates as a result of such use, such as data generated automatically by sensors and data recorded by embedded applications, including applications indicating hardware status and malfunctions"

---

127 Max Planck Institute for Innovation and Competition, Position Statement, 2022, p. 30 n. 74 and Wiebe A., *GRUR* 2023, 1569 (1571) generally regard the manufacturer as the one obligated; Assion, S. / Willecke, L., *MMR* 2023, 805 (807) as well as Schmidt-Kessel, M., *MMR-Beil.* 2024, 75 (79) focus without distinction on the actual seller, lessor and service provider.

128 Cf. also above III. 2.

(4) "data generated by the connected product or related service during times of inaction by the user", e.g. when the product is in stand-by or switched off
(5) "data which are not substantially modified, meaning data in raw form"
(6) "data which have been pre-processed for the purpose of making them understandable and useable prior to subsequent processing and analysis"
(7) pre-processed data also covers the relevant metadata, "including its basic context and timestamp, to make the data usable, combined with other data"

In particular: Derived Data

It was furthermore highly disputed whether and to what extent "derived and inferred data" has to be made accessible.[129] The Draft Opinion of the Committee on Civil Liberties, Justice and Home Affairs (LIBE) advocated in this regard.[130] The Council Presidency explicitly denied such a broad access[131] and was able to prevail. Rec. 15 now states:

> "By contrast, information inferred or derived from such data, which is the outcome of additional investments into assigning values or insights from the data, in particular by means of proprietary, complex algorithms, including those that are a part of proprietary software, should not be considered to fall within the scope of this Regulation and consequently should not be subject to the obligation of a data holder to make it available to a user or a data recipient, unless otherwise agreed between the user and the data holder."

Rec. 15 adds that this could also cover intellectual property rights, which is why the derived data should rightly not be included in the scope of the regulation.

129 Cf. Krämer, J., Improving The Economic Effectiveness of the B2B and B2C Data Sharing Obligations in the Proposed Data Act, CERRE, 2022, p. 23: Max Planck Institute for Innovation and Competition, Position Statement, 2022, pp. 10 et seq. n. 20 et seq.
130 LIBE PE737.389, p. 31. Cf. also Max Planck Institute for Innovation and Competition, Position Statement, 2022, p. 11 n. 25.
131 Council Presidency 2022/0047(COD) – 15035/22, p. 11.

Mechanisms of Access

The numerous requirements for data accessibility of Art. 3(1) are rather vague in terms of content.[132] It has been partly argued that Art. 3(1) is to be understood more as a general principle and less as an enforceable claim.[133] In fact, Art. 3(1) itself does not provide a right of access.[134]

First and foremost, it is discussed whether and to what extent the Data Act allows a mere *in-situ* access of the user.[135] Partly, it was strongly argued with reference to rec. 22 the Act does not oblige the data holder to actually transmit the data in question, but under all circumstances may restrict its obligation to offering practically an interface only.[136] Others point to the difference between the *access by design*-obligation of Art. 3 and the access right of Art. 4(1). Whilst Art. 3(1) shall be regarded as the general rule, Art. 4(1) – a rule that would otherwise not be necessary – shall offer a right to access that goes beyond *in-situ*.[137]

Rec. 21 states that when designing a product or connected service, it is important to ensure that, in the case of multiple contracting parties on the user side, each user[138] should be able to benefit equally from the measures of facilitated data access.[139] Regarding a product that is typically used by several persons, this includes, for example, the possibility of creating separate user accounts for individual users (which can be used by all users, if necessary).[140] This also ensures individual data management. Thereby, Art. 3(1) seeks to lay the foundation for Art. 4(1) and (5) Sentence 2.

Rec. 21 also refers to the fact that data shall be "granted to the user on the basis of a simple request mechanism granting automatic execution and not

132 Gerpott, T., *CR* 2022, 271 (275).

133 Leistner, M. / Antoine, L., IPR and the use of open data and data sharing initiatives by public and private actors, 2022, p. 85; for enforcement issues, see below.

134 Grapentin, S., *RDi* 2023, 173 (177).

135 Cf. Max Planck Institute for Innovation and Competition, Position Statement, 2022, pp. 26 et seq. n. 65 et seq.

136 See especially Specht-Riemenschneider, L., *MMR-Beil.* 2022, 809 (815 et seq.).

137 Pointing to the open formulation of Art. 4(1) Podszun, R. / Pfeifer, C., *GRUR* 2022, 953 (957); cf. also Max Planck Institute for Innovation and Competition, Position Statement, 2022, pp. 26 et seq. n. 66 and p. 32 n. 79. See – in contrary – Specht-Riemenschneider, L., *MMR-Beil.* 2022, 809 (815).

138 Council Presidency 2022/0047(COD) – 15035/22, p. 13.

139 Cf. rec. 21.

140 Rec. 21; this is also the direction of the proposal by Specht-Riemenschneider, L., *MMR-Beil.* 2022, 809 (815).

requiring examination or clearance by the manufacturer or data holder".[141] Furthermore, the data is to be made available free of charge.

The restriction "relevant and technically feasible" is irritating.[142] Rec. 22 only mentions therefore that "direct" availability refers to availability from an on-device data storage as well as from a remote server.[143] In line with the MPIIC, it is not clear why the reservation ("where relevant and technically feasible") refers only to "direct" accessibility and not to easy, safe, free of charge and comprehensive accessibility in a structured, commonly used and machine-readable format.[144]

The Council Presidency's proposal to include the words "in a structured, commonly used and machine-readable format"[145] made it into the final version. This is to be welcomed, as it ensures that users can make use of the information provided.[146] With this in mind, it is of particular relevance that the user can (technically) 'read' and 'understand' the data provided.

Enforcement

It remains unclear to what extent and against whom private enforcement measures in the event of non-compliance are possible. *Metzger* and *Schweitzer* rightly point to the fact that private enforcement on the basis of unfair competition law could be possible.[147]

3. *Information Duties*

Art. 3(2) and Art. 3(3) stipulates numerous information duties that must be considered before concluding a contract for a connected product or the

141 Rec. 21.

142 See also Max Planck Institute for Innovation and Competition, Position Statement, 2022, p. 30 n. 73.

143 Rec. 22.

144 Max Planck Institute for Innovation and Competition, Position Statement, 2022, p. 30 n. 73.

145 Council Presidency 2022/0047(COD) – 13342/22, p. 40; LIBE PE737.389, p. 31; ITRE PE732.704, p. 33.

146 Unfortunately, the proposal of the LIBE Draft Opinion (LIBE PE737.389, p. 31) to design products in such a way that data subjects can directly exercise their rights under Art. 15 et seq. GDPR did not make it into the final version of the Data Act.

147 Metzger, A. / Schweitzer, H., *ZEuP* 2023 42 (52).

provision of a related service. Respective duties shall effectuate the access rights of Art. 4 and 5.[148] Art. 3(2) is targeted at a contract to purchase, rent or lease a connected product. A contract for the provision of a related service is regulated by Art. 3(3). This separation is not convincing. The two paragraphs do not substantially differ. Both paragraphs are therefore discussed together, before differing details are highlighted.

Personal Scope

Art. 3(2) explicitly addresses the "the seller, the rentor or the lessor, which can be the manufacturer" of a connected product.[149] This is reasonable and consistent, as the information duty must (only) be fulfilled vis-à-vis the user before concluding a contract, so that only the user's contractual partner can be obliged to provide information.[150]

Art. 3(3) does not specify who exactly is obliged to provide the information.[151] Rec. 24 merely concretises this to the effect that, the information obligation "before concluding a contract for the provision of a related service should lie with the prospective data holder, independently of whether the data holder concludes a contract for the purchase, rent or lease of a connected product." This concept is suboptimal, as the data holder will not always be identical to the contractual partner.[152] For reasons of practicability, only the contractual partner should be obliged to provide the information.[153]

The contractual partner is in both cases responsible for the actual provision. The content of the information given will typically been provided by the manufacturer beforehand – to the user's contractual partner and – in practical terms – also to all intermediate instances.[154] According to the wording, the information duties also apply in c2c-relationships, for example in a non-commercial resale of a smart product. Whether this was

148 Cf. Metzger, A. / Schweitzer, H., *ZEuP* 2023 42 (53).

149 Cf. rec. 23; in the original proposed version (COM(2022) 68 final) Art.3(2) did not specify who exactly is obliged to provide the information; cf. also Max Planck Institute for Innovation and Competition, Position Statement, 2022, p. 31 n. 77.

150 Cf. also Specht-Riemenschneider, L., *MMR-Beil.* 2022, 809 (817); Schmidt-Kessel, M., *MMR-Beil.* 2024, 75 (79).

151 Cf. Schmidt-Kessel, M., *MMR-Beil.* 2024, 75 (79).

152 Cf. already Metzger, A. / Schweitzer, H., *ZEuP* 2023, 42 (53).

153 Also Schmidt-Kessel, M., *MMR-Beil.* 2024, 75 (79).

154 Cf. also Max Planck Institute for Innovation and Competition, Position Statement, 2022, p. 31 n. 77.

the legislator's intention is highly questionable. In such situations, neither the data holder nor the primary contractual partner of the non-commercial re-seller can be held liable for the provision of the information.[155]

According to Art. 7(1), the information duties do not apply for data generated by the use of products manufactured or related services provided by enterprises that qualify as micro or small enterprises, as defined in Art. 2 of the Annex to Recommendation 2003/361/EC, provided those enterprises do not have partner enterprises or linked enterprises as defined in Art. 3 of the Annex to Recommendation 2003/361/EC which do not qualify as a micro or small enterprise and where the micro and small enterprise is not subcontracted to manufacture or design a product or provide a related service.[156] This exception is particularly useful for small(er) companies.[157]

General Requirements for Providing Information

Art. 3(2) and Art. 3(3) are only referring to a *provision* of information. The contractual partner of the user is not obliged to ensure that the information is actually acknowledged, read or understood by the user.

Rec. 24 sheds light on the purpose of the information duties by referring to the fact that these duties are intended to "provide transparency over the data generated and to enhance the easy access for the user". First, the information duties shall counter the fear of losing 'control' over the one's "own" data[158].[159] At the same time, the user should be given the opportunity to consider the underlying contractual agreement.[160]

Art. 3(2) and Art. 3(3) merely state that the information must be provided before the contract is concluded. Neither in Art. 3(2) and Art. 3(3) nor in the recitals any further references are given with regard to a specific timing. In any case, it would at least be useful to provide the information not just before the conclusion of the contract, but at a time before the

155 Cf. Max Planck Institute for Innovation and Competition, Position Statement, 2022, pp. 31 et seq. n. 77.

156 A different view, which is not compatible with the wording of Art. 7(1), is held by Hartmann, B. / McGuire, M. / Schulte-Nölke, H., *RDi* 2023 49 (58).

157 Ebner, G., *ZD* 2022, 364 (367).

158 Commission, Special Eurobarometer 487a "The General Data Protection Regulation", 2019, p. 39.

159 Ebner, G., *ZD* 2022, 364 (367).

160 Cf. Ebner, G., *ZD* 2022, 364 (367); Hennemann, M. / Steinrötter, B., *NJW* 2022, 1481 (1483).

contract is finalised[161] that guarantees a substantial reflection of the conclusion of the contract. Due to the various settings covered by the Act, it is, however, not possible to specify a general time period.

According to rec. 24, the user should also be informed if the "information changes during the lifetime of the connected product or the contract period for the related service, including" cases in which "the purpose for which those data are to be used changes from the originally specified purpose".[162] However, it is questionable how the lifetime of certain products is to be determined. In any case, it should only be based on an average lifetime to be determined objectively and not on the individual lifetime of the individual product. In this respect, the determination of a general period of approximately five years could be appropriate. With regard to the duration of the contract period for the related service, there are no obstacles in this respect. Changes in the corresponding information are subject to notification throughout the entire duration of the contract.

According to the wording of Art. 3(2) ("purchase, rent or lease"), one might argue that the information duty only applies in cases of a contract with a *monetary consideration*.[163] Cases in which products are handed over entirely without monetary consideration should be rare, but nevertheless cannot be excluded. It was therefore already rightly mentioned that this wording of Art. 3(2) leaves room for avoiding the information duty when products are provided at no cost[164], for example in the case of a free trial use of a product. Needless to say, that the information in Art. 3(2) is, however, relevant, after all, when using the product, regardless of whether a contract with a monetary consideration has been concluded. At least, if instead of a monetary payment the generated data is actually constituting the counter-performance (according to the prevailing understanding[165] data can constitute consideration[166]), the threshold "purchase, rent or lease" is met – and Art. 3(2) applies. The same applies to the information obligation under Art. 3(3) for a contract for the provision of a related service.

161 Ebner, G., *ZD* 2022, 364 (367).
162 This amendment was proposed by the Council Presidency 2022/0047(COD) – 15035/22, p. 14.
163 Cf. Bomhard, D. / Merkle, M., *RDi* 2022, 168 (173).
164 Bomhard, D. / Merkle, M., *RDi* 2022, 168 (173).
165 Cf. Art. 3(2) Digital Content Directive and Sec. 327 German Civil Code.
166 Alternatively, the conclusion of a data use agreement according to Art. 4(13).

Rec. 24 adds further that "it is, in any case, necessary that the user is able to store the information in a way that is accessible for future reference and that allows the unchanged reproduction of the information stored."

According to Art. 3(2) and Art. 3(3) the information must be provided in a clear and comprehensible manner. These formal requirements lag far behind what is required by Art. 12(1) and (7) GDPR.[167] This is unfortunate. Insights from a behavioural economic analysis of Art. 12-14 GDPR and of privacy notices based thereon in particular point to the fact that relevant information must be communicated in a short and concise manner and in a way that is easy to comprehend.[168] Otherwise, there is a high probability that the information will either not be read by their addressees or might be misunderstood in terms of content.[169] Therefore, a wording similar to Art. 12(1) GDPR as well as a provision of information in a short and meaningful way, for example by using icons, keywords or certificates[170] (comparable to Art. 42 et seq. GDPR) would have been appropriate for Art. 3(2) and Art. 3(3).[171]

Rec. 24 nevertheless points out that "the information obligation could be fulfilled, for example by maintaining a stable [...] URL on the web, which can be distributed as a web link or QR code, pointing to the relevant information, which could be provided by the seller, the rentor or the lessor [...] to the user before concluding the contract for the purchase, rent or lease of a connected product". This reference is a step in the right direction. However, when using these methods, it must be considered that users might not reach out to the information 'behind' the link. In conclusion, it can therefore be stated that the provision of information via "media break" is generally permissible, but should be viewed critically from the user's perspective.

At best, Art. 3(2) and (3) would have been designed in a way that encourages (in digital environments) the use of electronic information systems,

167 Ebner, G., *ZD* 2022, 364 (367); also Steinrötter, B., *GRUR* 2023, 216 (224 et seq.).
168 Ebner, G., Weniger ist Mehr?, 2022, pp. 104 et seq.
169 Cf. Gerpott, T., *CR* 2022, 271 (275); Ebner, G., Weniger ist Mehr?, 2022, pp. 111 et seq.
170 Gerpott, T., *CR* 2022, 271 (275).
171 Cf. for further options (e.g., implementing an obligation to explain the non-use of icons) Ebner, G., Weniger ist Mehr?, 2022, p. 321 pointing to § 161 German Stock Corporation Act (AktG).

such as PIMS[172] or privacy bots[173].[174] They offer the most effective way of tackling one's *information overload*.[175] For the development, establishment and implementation of PIMS or privacy bots, incentives must be created in general, not just in the provisions of the Data Act. However, the establishment of PIMS would be particularly useful in the context of the Data Act.[176]

The current design of Art. 3(2) and Art. 3(3), however, will not lead to a significantly different presentation of information compared to Art. 13 GDPR. The contractual partners will also use the methods known from the GDPR, such as multi-layered-notices[177] or one-pagers, to provide the notices in accordance with Art. 3(2) and Art. 3(3).

Rec. 24 underlines the "obligation to provide information does not affect the obligation for the controller to provide information to the data subject pursuant to Art. 12, 13 and 14 [GDPR]". Consequently, this means that the information of Art. 3(2) and Art. 3(3) must be communicated in addition to that of Art. 13 GDPR.[178] Even if the relation to Regulation (EU) 2019/1150 (P2B-Regulation)[179] is not explicitly mentioned, it can be assumed that Art. 3(2) applies in addition to Art. 9(2) Regulation (EU) 2019/1150.[180]

In order to avoid any confusion among data subjects, it is important to provide the information under Art. 3(2) and Art. 3(3) explicitly separated from that under Art. 13 GDPR.[181] Nevertheless, it is to be expected that the 'new' data (protection) notices will be equated by laypersons with those

172 For further information to PIMS see Efroni, Z. / Metzger, J. / Mischau, L. / Schirmbeck, M., *EDPL* 2019, 352 (357 et seq.); Specht-Riemenschneider, L. / Blankertz, A. / Sierek, P. / Schneider, R. / Knapp, J. / Henne, T., *MMR-Beil.* 2021, 25 (27); Kollmar, F. / El-Auwad, M., *K&R* 2021, 73 (77 et seq.); Richter, F., *PinG* 2017, 122 (123); Kettner, S. / Thorun, C. / Vetter, M., Wege zur besseren Informiertheit, 2018, p. 83.

173 For further information to privacy bots see Nüske, N. / Olenberger, C. / Rau, D. / Schmied, F., *DuD* 2019, 28 (29); Geminn, C. / Francis, L. / Herder, K., *ZD-Aktuell* 2021, 05335.

174 Cf. Gerpott, T., *CR* 2022, 271 (275).

175 Cf. Ebner, G., Weniger ist Mehr?, 2022, pp. 137 et seq.

176 See in detail Ebner, G., *ZD* 2022, 364 (367).

177 After all, the German courts now explicitly allow the use of these "multi-layered-notices", cf. Ebner, G., *ZD* 2023, 282 (285 et seq.).

178 Hennemann, M. / Steinrötter, B., *NJW* 2022, 1481 (1483); Bomhard, D. / Merkle, M., *RDi* 2022, 168 (174); Ebner, G., *ZD* 2022, 364 (367); Specht-Riemenschneider, L., *ZEuP* 2023, 638 (663).

179 Regulation (EU) 2019/1150 of the European Parliament and of the Council on promoting fairness and transparency for business users of online intermediation services.

180 Gerpott, T., *CR* 2022, 271 (275).

181 Ebner, G., *ZD* 2022, 364 (367); following this Steinrötter, B., *GRUR* 2023, 216 (224).

of Art. 13 and 14 GDPR and, at worst, perceived as equally annoying[182].[183] As it is the case with existing privacy notices, there is a high risk of an *information overload* and a *click and forget*-behaviour.[184]

The Different Informational Elements in Detail

Art. 3(2) specifies in four, Art. 3(3) in nine letters several notices which must "at least" be communicated to the user before the conclusion of a corresponding contract. Using the words "at least" is not ideal as it leaves room for further 'unnamed' information duties.[185] Since the words "at least" were unfortunately not deleted in the legislative process for the Data Act (unlike that of the GDPR[186]) unnamed information obligations may potentially come into play. In this respect, there are numerous possibilities for further informational elements which are likely to depend primarily on the respective product or service. Despite the legal uncertainty caused by this, contractual partners should be very reluctant to provide unnamed information. For "usual cases", the canon of mandatory information duties is to be regarded as sufficient. In general, when assessing what information (still) needs to be communicated, the risk of one's *information overload* must always be taken into account.

The Different Informational Elements of Art. 3(2)

According to Art. 3(2) at least the following information shall be provided to the user before concluding a contract for the purchase, rent or lease of a *connected product.*

According to Art. 3(2)(a) the user shall receive information regarding the type, format and estimated volume of product data which the connected product is capable of generating. The notice is generally useful because not all users will know exactly what data a product collects.[187] The user can

182 Cf. Roßnagel, A., *DuD* 2016, 561 (563).

183 Ebner, G., *ZD* 2022, 364 (367).

184 Hennemann, M. / Steinrötter, B., *NJW* 2022, 1481 (1483); Bomhard, D. / Merkle, M., *RDi* 2022, 168 (173); Ebner, G., *ZD* 2022, 364 (367).

185 See in detail Ebner, G., *ZD* 2022, 364 (368).

186 Cf. Art. 14 GDPR in Commission, COM(2012) 11 final.

187 Metzger, A. / Schweitzer, H., *ZEuP* 2023 42 (53); for further details to information asymmetries see Ebner, G., Weniger ist Mehr?, 2022, pp. 45 et seq., 168.

also assess the intensity of data generation by the product or related service. Rec. 24 states that "this could include information on data structures, data formats, vocabularies, classification schemes, taxonomies and code lists, where available [...]".

However, this list could tempt to communicate too much information (which is not necessarily useful for the users). It should not be interpreted in such a way that all information mentioned in it must always be provided. Instead, the contracting parties should primarily use Art. 3(2)(a) as a guide.

The type of the data can be easily presented (e.g., via icons) and divided into categories. When creating categories, it is important not to create categories that are too detailed or too broad. The depth of detail of the categorisation is up to each contractual partner and depends on the type of data processing.

The information regarding the format of the data can ultimately be described in one or two words (e.g.: "*format: pdf*").

The "estimated volume" refers to the amount of data that the connected product is capable of generating. However, the determination will depend above all on the user's behaviour and might therefore be difficult to communicate (in advance). Conceivable are abstract references to values within the scope of average use, which could be briefly described.[188] Nevertheless, the added value of this information for users is questionable.

According to Art. 3(2)(b) the user shall be provided with the information whether the connected product is capable of generating data continuously and in real-time. This information can be easily visualised with icons and allows conclusions about the volume of data generation. One might indeed interpret the wording in such a way that information can be omitted if the data is generated neither continuously nor in real time. However, this would be contrary to the purpose and a correct understanding of the wording ("whether"). Therefore, it must also be stated that these practices do not occur.

According to Art. 3(2)(c) the user must be informed whether the connected product is capable of storing data on-device or on a remote server, including the intended duration of retention. With regard to the exact content of the information on the duration of retention, the principles developed for Art. 13(2)(a) GDPR can be used as a guideline. In any case, the beginning and the duration of the storage should be specified as precisely as

188 Ebner, G., *ZD* 2022, 364 (368).

possible (i.e. in hours, days, weeks and years, depending on the processing situation).[189] The information regarding the retention period does not make sense at least for cases within the scope of the GDPR, because this information is already provided via Art. 13(2)(a) GDPR.[190] In these cases, one note should be sufficient as long as it indicates that it refers to both Art. 13(2)(a) GDPR and Art. 3(2)(c) Data Act.

According to Art. 3(2)(d) the user needs to know how she or he may access, retrieve, or where relevant, erase the data, including the technical means to do so, as well as their terms of use and quality of service. Rec. 24 adds that this includes information on the "terms of use and quality of service of application programming interfaces or, where applicable the provision of software development kits". The extensive mentioning in rec. 24 already indicates the high relevance of the right of access to data (Art. 4(1))[191] and the corresponding information. The information enables users to "access the access" of the generated data. It thereby provides and increases transparency for the users about what data is collected[192] and in which way it is accessible.[193] In this respect, it is necessary to provide an abstract reference to the existence of the right of access, retrieval and deletion on the one hand and to their concrete execution on the other hand ("including the technical means to do so"). For example, it would make sense to provide a brief reference and a link or QR-Code that leads to a corresponding portal of the contractual partner of the user.[194] Especially with regard to the terms of use and the quality of service, it is important to ensure that users are not overloaded with too much information to avoid an *information overload.*

The Different Informational Elements of Art. 3(3)

According to Art. 3(3) at least the following information shall be provided to the user before concluding a contract for the provision of a *related service.*

---

189 Ebner, G., Weniger ist Mehr?, 2022, pp. 193 et seq.

190 Incidentally, a reference to the storage period and the deletion concept should have been avoided as well, since the relevance in this respect is less high for non-personal data and unnecessarily threatens the risk of *information overload.*

191 Hennemann, M. / Steinrötter, B., *NJW* 2022, 1481 (1485).

192 Rec. 23.

193 Rec. 5.

194 Ebner, G., *ZD* 2022, 364 (368); see also Ebner, G., *ZfDR* 2023, 299 (304).

Pursuant to Art. 3(3)(a) the user shall receive information regarding the nature, estimated volume and collection frequency of product data that the prospective data holder is expected to obtain and, where relevant, the arrangements for the user to access or retrieve such data, including the prospective data holder's data storage arrangements and the duration of retention. The regulation combines elements of Art. 3(2)(a) and Art. 3(2)(c). The use of the word "nature" is inconsistent in view of Art. 3(2)(a). In this respect, a drafting mistake is likely. "Nature" is to be interpreted as "type".[195] In this respect and with regard to the "estimated volume", reference can be made to the above. The collection frequency should be communicated as accurately as possible at the time the information is provided. With regard to the modalities to access or retrieve data, as well as the data holder's data storage and retention policy, reference can be made to the above (Art. 3(2)(c)).

According to Art. 3(3)(b) the user must be informed about the nature and estimated volume of *related service data* to be generated, as well as the arrangements for the user to access or retrieve such data, including the prospective data holder's data storage arrangements and the duration of retention. In contrast to Art. 3(3)(a), Art. 3(3)(b) explicitly addresses related service data. The informing actor is therefore advised to make a clear distinction between product data and related service data when providing the information.

According to Art. 3(3)(c) the user needs to know whether the prospective data holder expects to use readily available data itself and the purposes for which those data are to be used, and whether it intends to allow one or more third parties to use the data for purposes agreed upon with the user. It is very surprising that the regulation only explicitly addresses "readily available data" as defined in Art. 2(17). The data holder will already know at the time of providing the information whether he wants to use data that will be available later. The value of the reference to the intention to use by the manufacturer supplying the product or by the service provider remains unclear. In the event of an intended use of non-personal data (for example) by the seller, a separate data licence agreement with the user is required pursuant to Art. 4(13) Sentence 1. In this respect, the user might be aware of the provider's own use.[196] However, this is not the case if the agreement

195 This was already argued for Art. 3(2)(a) of the commission draft (COM(2022) 68 final), see Ebner, G., *ZD* 2022, 364 (368).

196 See already Ebner, G., *ZD* 2022, 364 (368).

pursuant to Art. 4(13) Sentence 1 is concluded after the information has been provided.

In contrast, the fact that the data is passed on to third parties, just like the purposes of use, can have a decisive influence on the user's decision to conclude a contract. Therefore, they should be communicated in any case.[197] Insofar as the data generated is personal data, there may be duplications with Art. 13(1)(c) and (e) GDPR at the time of collection. However, since the data subject already received the relevant information due to Art. 3(2)(d), there could be no need to inform them again in accordance with Art. 13(4) GDPR. It should be noted, however, that unlike Art. 13(1)(e) GDPR, Art. 3(2)(d) does not require the naming of specific recipients or categories. In this respect, the information in Art. 13(1)(e) GDPR can have an independent value in addition to Art. 3(2)(d).[198] If the provider is also the controller in terms of the GDPR, it is advisable for the controller to already provide information about specific recipients or at least categories of recipients in the information pursuant to Art. 3(2)(d). The purposes of use could be clearly displayed with icons, which would make it much easier for users to receive information.[199]

According to Art. 3(3)(d) the user shall be provided with information on the identity of the prospective data holder, such as its trading name and the geographical address at which it is established and, where applicable, other data processing parties. Notices regarding the identity of the data holder contains information "such as its trading name and the geographical address at which it is established". At least in the context of Art. 13 GDPR, it is the established opinion that the summonable address, consisting of (trade) name and geographical address, is the most important identity feature.[200] The words "such as" are actually redundant in this respect.[201] The identity must in fact be described as precisely as possible.[202] Therefore, legal persons should be named with the legal form suffix and natural persons

197 With a corresponding proposal to amend the wording Council Presidency 2022/0047(COD) – 13342/22, p. 40; ITRE PE732.704, p. 34.

198 Ebner, G., *ZD* 2022, 364 (368).

199 See in detail Ebner, G., *ZfDR* 2023, 299 (307 et seq.).

200 Cf. Ehmann, E. / Selmayr, M. / Knyrim, R., DS-GVO, 3rd ed. 2024, Art. 13 n. 44 „postalische Anschrift muss als Minimum wohl in jedem Fall genannt werden".

201 In order to prevent inconsistencies and attempts at circumvention, the "such as" should have been deleted, cf. Ebner, G., *ZD* 2022, 364 (368).

202 At least for Art. 13 GDPR Article 29 Data Protection Working Party, WP 260 – Guidelines on transparency under Regulation 2016/679, 31.

with their first name, surname and address.[203] In case there are also other processing parties, their trading name and geographical address must also be mentioned.

According to Art. 3(3)(e) the user must be aware of the means of communication which make it possible to contact the prospective data holder quickly and to communicate with the data holder efficiently. Due to the close connection of the notices in Art. 3(3)(d) and (e), they could also have been combined in one paragraph. In the context of Art. 13(1)(a) GDPR, accessibility by telephone and electronic means have emerged as the most relevant contact options.[204] In this respect, telephone hotlines, online contact forms and e-mail addresses are ideal as "quick" and "effective" communication tools.[205]

According to Art. 3(3)(f) the user needs to know how he or she can request that the data are shared with a third-party, and, where applicable, the end of the data sharing. The wording "where applicable" indicates that a reference to the right to end data sharing is only required if data sharing is already taking place or is at least intended. However, this approach is not entirely convincing, since it is already of considerable relevance – for the decision to share data – to know that the sharing can also be ended at any time. In addition, at the time the information is provided, permission to share the data will not have been granted yet in most cases. Therefore, it should always be informed about the existence of both rights. As in the case of Art. 3(2)(c) (and Art. 3(3)(a) and (b)), the user must be informed, on the one hand, about the abstract existence of the right to share data as well as the right to end data sharing and, on the other hand, about its concrete exercise.[206] Practicable ways of dealing with both Art. 3(2)(c) and Art. 3(3)(f) have yet to emerge in practice. However, also in the context of Art. 3(3)(f), it is advisable to briefly explain the content of the right to

203 At least for Art. 13(1)(a) GDPR Schwartmann, R. / Jaspers, A. / Thüsing, G. / Kugelmann, D. / Schwartmann, R. / Schneider, A., DS-GVO, 2nd ed. 2020, Art. 13 n. 35.

204 Article 29 Data Protection Working Party, WP 260 – Guidelines on transparency under Regulation 2016/679, 31; Paal, B. / Pauly, D. / Paal, B. / Hennemann, M., DS-GVO BDSG, 3rd ed. 2021, Art. 13 n. 14.

205 Ebner, G., *ZD* 2022, 364 (369); Ehmann, E. / Selmayr, M./ Knyrim, R., DS-GVO, 3rd ed. 2024, Art. 13 n. 44; Auernhammer, H. / Eßer, M., DS-GVO, 7th ed. 2020, Art. 13 n. 24.

206 Ebner, G., *ZD* 2022, 364 (369).

share as well as the right to end the sharing and then provide a link to a corresponding portal through which data share can be initiated.[207]

According to Art. 3(2)(g) the user shall be informed about his or her right to lodge a complaint alleging an infringement of the provisions of Chapter II with the competent authority designated pursuant to Art. 37. As in the context of Art. 13(2)(d) GDPR, the current wording of lit. g raises the question of whether the regulation only requires information on the existence of the right to lodge a complaint or also the naming of a specific competent supervisory authority referred to in Art. 37.[208] Even if the Hungarian data protection authority made a contrary decision[209], it seems favourable that the providing party does not have to designate a specific competent authority. This is already necessary because it will not always be possible to name a competent authority before the contract is being concluded.[210] Ultimately, the wording of lit. g can also be interpreted in such a way that the words "with the competent authority designated pursuant to Art. 37" are to be concluded in the actual notice.[211]

According to Art. 3(3)(h) the user must be informed whether a prospective data holder is the holder of trade secrets contained in the data that is accessible from the connected product or generated during the provision of a related service, and, where the prospective data holder is not the trade secret holder, the identity of the trade secret holder. According to Art. 2(19) "trade secret holder" means a trade secret holder as referred to in Article 2, point (2) of Directive (EU) 2016/943. "Trade secret", therefore, means information which meets all the requirements of Art. 2(1) Directive (EU) 2016/943 (cf. Art. 2(18)). Lit. h generally applies only if the data likely to be accessed by the user contain a trade secret. If the data holder is the owner of the trade secret, only this must be confirmed. If a third party is the owner of the trade secret, its identity must be stated as described above (Art. 3(3)(d)). Generally, the value added of lit. h for the user is questionable.

According to Art. 3(3)(i) the user shall receive information regarding the duration of the contract between the user and the prospective data holder, as well as the arrangements for terminating such an agreement. This

207 Ebner, G., *ZD* 2022, 364 (369).

208 Cf. Ebner, G., *ZD* 2022, 364 (369).

209 The decision can be found at https://www.naih.hu/files/NAIH-2020-2000-hatarozat.pdf, see especially p. 8.

210 See already for Art. 13(2)(d) GDPR Bräutigam, P. / Schmidt-Wudy, F., *CR* 2015, 56 (61).

211 Ebner, G., *ZD* 2022, 364 (369).

refers to the agreement according to Art. 4(13) Sentence 1. The meaning of lit. i may be disputed, since in case of doubt the agreement is concluded after the information according to Art. 3(3). Individual arrangements on the duration of the agreement can therefore not be known at the time of the information according to Art. 3(3)(i). Information about the concrete duration of the agreement is insofar not possible. However, this might not be the case for standard contracts. In this respect, the exact duration of the agreement as well as any conditions to which the duration is linked and the termination modalities must be described in detail. With regard to the termination modalities, a reference to the minimum contract term (if any) and to form requirements (e-mail, verbal, etc.) should be adequate.

Waivability

The information obligations guarantee the transparency of the data generated, enhance easy access for the user[212] and thus also form the basis for the effective exercise of their rights. Taking into account these important functions, the information duties of Art. 3(2) and Art. 3(3) may not be waived.

Enforcement

In the event of an infringement of Art. 3(2) or Art. 3(3), the validity of the contract remains unaffected.[213] If the manufacturer, seller or lessor concludes a contract, the infringement of Art. 3(2) or Art. 3(3) may be categorised as a lack of conformity of the product. This applies in any case in the context of consumer contracts, see Art. 7(1)(d) of the Sales of Goods Directive. Furthermore, there is much to suggest that an infringement is also regarded as lack of conformity of the product in b2b-relationships. According to Art. 8(1)(b) Digital Content Directive, an infringement can also be seen as deception in the contract negotiations. In Germany, at least, private enforcement by competitors should be possible on the basis of the principles of unfair competition law.[214]

212 Cf. rec. 24.

213 Hennemann, M. / Steinrötter, B., *NJW* 2022, 1481 (1483).

214 Appropriate Metzger, A. / Schweitzer, H., *ZEuP* 2023 42 (55).

In addition, natural persons must also have an opportunity to enforce their right to the provision of information. In this respect, it can be argued that Art. 3(2) and Art. 3(3) already provide the necessary statutory basis. In Germany, at least a claim under Sec. 823 para. 2, Sec. 249 para. 2 German Civil Code in conjunction with Art. 3(2) or Art. 3(3) would also be an option. In addition, a claim under Sec. 280 para. 1, Sec. 311 para. 2, Sec. 241 para. 2 German Civil Code (*culpa in contrahendo*) in conjunction with Sec. 249 para. 1 German Civil Code is also conceivable.[215]

This notwithstanding, natural persons and legal persons have in the event of infringements of Art. 3(1) pursuant to Art. 38(1) the right to lodge a complaint, individually or, where relevant, collectively, with the relevant competent authority in the member state of their habitual residence, place of work or establishment if they consider that their rights under this Regulation have been infringed.

215 Cf. in the context of Art. 13 GDPR already Ebner, G., Weniger ist Mehr?, 2022, pp. 155 et seq. with further evidence.

V. Data Licence Agreement and User's Right of Access (Art. 4)

Fundamentally, the Data Act provides new access rights with respect to data generated by the use of a product of the user. Users may access data in the realm of the data holder and also request a sharing to third parties.[216] Conversely, limitations are placed on data holders and data recipients when it comes to the (secondary) use of the data.

Definition of User and Data Holder

According to Art. 2(12) user means a natural or legal person that owns a connected product or to whom temporary rights to use that connected product have been contractually transferred, or that receives related services. Rec. 8 clarifies that users include data subjects.

Uncertainties in the definition of the draft Data Act whether the user is defined by the contractual relationship (lease, rent) or by an actual legal position (ownership)[217] were clarified by the final version's reference to "contractually transferred rights". Although the contractual transfer of a legal position is prerequisite for the application of Chapter II,[218] it remains an open question whether 'problems' within the contractual relation or with regard to the fulfilment of contractual obligations are relevant for the applicability of Chapter II. Examples include cases in which a void contract is nevertheless fulfilled or where a product is used after the termination of an underlying rental agreement.[219]

Rec. 18 additionally reads:

> "The user of a product should be understood as the legal or natural person, such as a business or consumer, but also a public sector body, that is either the owner of a connected product, or someone that has received certain temporary rights, for example by means of a rental

216 For further details cf. Hennemann, M. / Steinrötter, B., *NJW* 2022, 1481 (1483).

217 Bomhard, D. / Merkle, M., *RDi* 2022, 168 (170); Max Planck Institute for Innovation and Competition, Position Statement, 2022, p. 24 n. 59 et seq.; Cf. for a detailed discussion Specht-Riemenschneider, L., *MMR-Beil.* 2022, 809 (813 et seq.).

218 Schmidt-Kessel, M., *MMR-Beil.* 2024, 75 (77).

219 Schmidt-Kessel, M., *MMR-Beil.* 2024, 75 (77).

> or lease agreement, to access or use data obtained from the connected product, or that receives related services for the connected product. Those access rights should in no way alter or interfere with the rights of data subjects, who may be interacting with connected product or related service, to personal data generated by the connected product or during the provision of the related service. Such user bears the risks and enjoys the benefits of using the connected product and should enjoy also the access to the data it generates. The user should therefore be entitled to derive benefit from data generated by that product and any related service. An owner, renter or lessee should equally be considered as user, including when several entities can be considered as users. In the context of multiple users, each user may contribute in a different manner to the data generation and can have an interest in several forms of use, e.g. fleet management for a leasing company, or mobility solutions for individuals using a car sharing service."

While rec. 18 clarifies that multiple persons can be considered as users, it remains unclear how to deal with these scenarios where different persons are to be considered as users (e.g. owner, lessor, driver, regular driver etc. for a smart car).[220]

While the definition for "user" is relied upon at various points throughout the Data Act, it is used particularly often in the context of user-held access and sharing rights under Chapter II.

Definition of Data Holder

According to Art. 2(13) data holder means a natural or legal person that has the right or obligation, in accordance with the Data Act, applicable Union law or national legislation adopted in accordance with Union law, to use and make available data, including, where contractually agreed, product data or related service data which it has retrieved or generated during the provision of a related service.

220 Cf. in this regard below sub IV. 1. and Bomhard, D. / Merkle, M., *RDi* 2022, 168 (170).

The definition "who has the right or obligation to make available data" is circular as according to Art. 4(1) the data holder is obliged to make data available.[221]

It is not clear whether the actual data access is a prerequisite for being a data holder. It is argued that not any obstacle in accessing the data should exclude the applicability of Art. 4-7.[222] The data holder might even evade the access obligations by deleting the data in question.[223] Consequently, it is partly argued that the user shall be notified before deletion and granted a possibility to access the data.[224]

Rec. 30 additionally points to the fact that users after having exercised its right to access might become a data holder themselves[225]:

> "It should be understood that such a user, once data has been made available, may in turn become a data holder, if they meet the criteria under this Regulation and thus become subject to the obligations to make data available under this Regulation."

Whereas the definition of "user" requires a contractually transferred legal position, the data holder is not necessarily the user's contractual partner. Nevertheless, the Art. 4-7 design the relation between data holder and user mainly as a contractual one.[226]

---

221 Cf. Bomhard/Merkle RDi 2022, 168 (169); Schmidt-Kessel, M., *MMR-Beil.* 2024, 75 (77).

222 Schmidt-Kessel, M., *MMR-Beil.* 2024, 75 (77).

223 Specht-Riemenschneider, L., *MMR-Beil.* 2022, 809 (815).

224 See Specht-Riemenschneider, L., *MMR-Beil. 2022*, 809 (815). Cf. also Max Planck Institute for Innovation and Competition, Position Statement, 2022, p. 25 n. 62.

225 In addition, data holder and user might be joint controllers according to Art. 26 GDPR, cf. rec 30.

226 Schmidt-Kessel, M., *MMR-Beil.* 2024, 75 (77).

1. Data Licence Agreement; Use by the Data Holder (Art. 4(13) and (14))

Data Licence Agreement

Art. 4(13) Sentence 1 is a true (but slightly hidden) 'revolution' introduced by the Data Act.[227] It limits the data holder's ability to use the data in question and empowers the user to market the data on his terms.[228]

The scope of the norm is limited to non-personal data (diverging from the general approach of the Data Act, but in order not to interfere with / to touch data protection law) that is 'readily available'. According to Art. 2(17) 'readily available data' "means product data and related service data that a data holder lawfully obtains or can lawfully obtain from the connected product or related service, without disproportionate effort going beyond a simple operation"; while 'product data' "means data generated by the use of a connected product that the manufacturer designed to be retrievable, via an electronic communications service, physical connection or on-device access, by a user, data holder or a third party, including, where relevant, the manufacturer" (Art. 2(15)). 'Related service data' refers to "data representing the digitisation of user actions or of events related to the connected product, recorded intentionally by the user or generated as a by-product of the user's action during the provision of a related service by the provider" (Art. 2 (16)).

The heavily debated and criticised[229] Art. 4(13) Sentence 1 stipulates that the data holder generally requires a contractual agreement with this user in order to use respective *non-personal* data. Rec. 25 confirms and adds:

> "This Regulation should not be understood to confer any new right on data holders to use product data or related service data. Where the manufacturer of a connected product is a data holder, the basis for the manufacturer to use non-personal data should be a contract between

227 Hennemann, M. / Steinrötter, B., *NJW* 2022, 1481 (1483) with further references. Cf. also Leistner, M. / Antoine, L., IPR and the use of open data and data sharing initiatives by public and private actors, 2022, p. 92: "crucial change".

228 Wiebe, A., *GRUR* 2023, 227.

229 E.g., Bomhard, D. / Merkle, M., *RDi* 2022, 168 (174); Leistner, M. / Antoine, L., IPR and the use of open data and data sharing initiatives by public and private actors, 2022, pp. 92 et seq.; Max Planck Institute for Innovation and Competition, Position Statement, 2022, pp. 19 et seq. n. 45 et seq.; Schweitzer, H. / Metzger, A. / Blind, K. / Richter, H. / Niebel, C. / Gutmann, F., The legal framework for access to data in Germany and in the EU, BMWK, 2022, pp. 215 et seq.; Schweitzer, H. / Metzger, A., *GRUR-Int.* 2023, 337.

> the manufacturer and the user. Such a contract could be part of an agreement for the provision of the related service, which could be concluded together with the purchase, rent or lease agreement relating to the connected product."

The Data Act does not provide specific rules for the agreement according to Art. 4(13) (but see Art. 13).[230] Different follow-on problems result from this fact.[231] It is, for example, unclear under which conditions the data licence agreement may be terminated.[232]

The provision of Art. 4(13) raises further questions, for example with regard to the consequences of a rejection by a user or with regard to an amendment of the agreement.[233]

The user on the other hand can use the data for any lawful purpose (as rec. 30 confirms). It is another heavily debated question whether and in which setting users will actually negotiate and / or value the Art. 4(13)-agreement in practice.[234] There are strong concerns that the user will not be aware of the (additional) agreement which might even be concluded implicitly.[235] However, demands to combine Art. 4(13) with a 'bundling' prohibition to hinder a "Total-Buy-Out" were not integrated in the final Data Act.[236]

Specific Limits of the Use of the Data Holder

According to Art. 4(13) Sentence 2 the data holder's use is limited in specific scenarios in which the data holder might "derive insights about the

230 Bomhard, D. / Merkle, M., *RDi* 2022, 168 (174).

231 Max Planck Institute for Innovation and Competition, Position Statement, 2022, p. 21 n. 52.

232 Hennemann, M. / Steinrötter, B., *NJW* 2022, 1481 (1484).

233 Krämer, J. et al. Data Act: Towards a balanced EU data regulation, CERRE report, March 2023, p. 41.

234 Strong doubts by Leistner, M. / Antoine, L., IPR and the use of open data and data sharing initiatives by public and private actors, 2022, p. 93; Specht-Riemenschneider, L., *MMR-Beil.* 2022, 809 (816 et seq.). Cf. also Podszun, R. / Pfeifer, C., *GRUR* 2022, 953 (956); Heinzke, P., *BB* 2023, 201 (208).

235 Leistner, M. / Antoine, L., IPR and the use of open data and data sharing initiatives by public and private actors, 2022, p. 93; Schwamberger, S., in Bernzen, A.K. / Grisse, K. / Kaesling, K. (ed.), Immaterialgüter und Medien im Binnenmarkt: Europäisierung des Rechts und ihre Grenzen, Nomos 2022, pp. 107 et seq.; Steinrötter, B., *GRUR* 2023, 216 (219).

236 Specht-Riemenschneider, L., *MMR-Beil.* 2022, 809 (817).

economic situation, assets and production methods of or the use by the user in any other manner that could undermine the commercial position of that user on the markets in which the user is active".

Rec. 27 points to cases that

> "involve using knowledge about the overall performance of a business or a farm in contractual negotiations with the user on potential acquisition of the user's products or agricultural produce to the user's detriment, or for instance, using such information to feed in larger databases on certain markets in the aggregate ([e].g. databases on crop yields for the upcoming harvesting season) as such use could affect the user negatively in an indirect manner."[237]

The wording "such data" indicates that Art. 4(13) Sentence 2 is referring to non-personal data covered by Art. 4(13) Sentence 1. Furthermore, having the different parallel norm of Art. 5(6) in mind, it is unclear whether the limitations set by Art. 4(13) Sentence 2 are subject to a disposal of the parties.[238]

Making data available to third parties

The data holders should not make non-personal data generated by the use of the product or related service available to third parties for any purposes other than the fulfilment of their contract with the user, Art. 4(14) sent 1. Data holders should also contractually bind third parties to not further share data received from them, Art. 4(14) sent. 2. This ensures that product or related service data is only made available to a third party at the request of the user (rec. 31) and solidifies the central position of the user.

It is however highly doubted whether this control of the user will foster the aim of the Data Act to enable independent innovation and competition in aftermarkets and complementary markets or if it will in fact hinder it massively.[239] Especially, where the user is a consumer, the effective availabil-

237 Rec. 25 further states that "[t]he user should be given the necessary technical interface to manage permissions, preferably with granular permission options (such as "allow once" or "allow while using this app or service"), including the option to withdraw permission."

238 Hennemann, M. / Steinrötter, B., *NJW* 2022, 1481 (1484).

239 Schweitzer, H./Metzger, A., *GRUR Int.* 2023, 337; Kerber, W., Towards a dynamic concept of competition that includes innovation, OECD 2023, 42, p. 17.

ity of the data on the market is questionable. However, the user is free to market the data, including to give the right to market the data contractually to a third party, such as data intermediation services according to the Data Governance Act.[240]

De facto-Control by Agreement?

The requirement of a data licence agreement does not depend on the right to access (and use) according to Art. 4(1) – or its exercise. Rather this requirement of an agreement has the severe consequence that the data holder may not process non-personal data without a respective contractual agreement. This is a 'revolution' with regard to non-personal data.[241] Art. 4(13) and Art. 4(14) lead to the surprising result that the processing of non-personal data is subject to stricter rules than the processing of personal data.[242] However, it has also been questioned whether this will have actual impact in practice.[243] On the one hand, concerning the data licence agreement a "Total-Buy-Out" is possible,[244] on the other hand Art. 4(14) additionally limits the data holder's possibility to make the data available to third parties regardless of the data licence agreement. So, while the actual control over the use of data given to users by Art. 4(13) depends on their bargaining power,[245] Art. 4(14) clearly empowers the user to control the making available of non-personal data. This shows that the Data Act follows a different concept compared to the GDPR, as it is not about the

240 Cf. Hennemann, M./ Steinrötter, B., *NJW* 2024, 1 (7).

241 Henneman, M. / Steinrötter, B., NJW 2022, 1481(1483).

242 Bomhard, D. / Merkle, M., RDi 2022, 168 (174); Max Planck Institute for Innovation and Competition, Position Statement, 2022, p. 20 n. 49; Schweitzer, H. / Metzger, A. / Blind, K. /Richter, H. / Niebel, C./ Gutman, F.; The legal framework for access to Data in Germany and in the EU, BMWK, 2022, p. 216; Specht-Riemenschneider, L., MMR 2022, 809 (816).

243 Schwamberger, S., Der Datenzugang im Data Act: Fortschritt oder Rückschritt?, in: Bernzen, A. K. et al., Immaterialgüter und Medien im Binnenmarkt, Nomos 2022, 88 (107 et seq.); Steinrötter, B., GRUR 2023, 2016 (219).

244 Schwamberger, S., Der Datenzugang im Data Act: Fortschritt oder Rückschritt?, in: Bernzen, A. K. et al., Immaterialgüter und Medien im Binnenmarkt, Nomos 2022, 88 (107 et seq.); Steinrötter, B., GRUR 2023, 2016 (219).

245 Grapentin, S., *RDi* 2023, 173 (179); Krämer, J. et al. Data Act: Towards a balanced EU data regulation, CERRE report, March 2023, p. 41.

protection of data but about the control over the use and making available of data.[246]

As the data licence agreement leads to a control option for the user, it could be seen as (contractually) attributing the right to use and share non-personal data to the user.[247] Otherwise, some understand the access regulation of the Data Act as a manifestation of the technical-factual 'rule' of the data holder who 'only' might have to grant access to data 'under his control'.[248] To the same end, others emphasise the co-generation of data by the data holder and the user.[249] Some commentators associate such a co-generation with the idea of a 'co-property' (Miteigentum) leading to a general 'right' of both the data holder and the user to use the respective non-personal data.[250]

It is generally – and beyond Art. 4(13) – heavily debated whether and to what extent the data access regime introduces and / or paves the way for some type of 'absolute' / 'IP-like' right regarding non-personal data.[251] This debate has to be seen against the background that on the basis of the current law non-personal data (if one has access and notwithstanding trade secret law) can be used freely and without some form of consent and / or agreement by the 'producer'.

Understanding the rights conferred to the user as "absolute" is contradicted by the fact that they only apply in relation to the data holder and that

246 Wienroeder, M., PinG 2024, 103 (106).

247 Cf. also Bomhard, D. / Merkle, M., RDi 2022, 168 (174); Max Planck Institute for Innovation and Competition, Position Statement, 2022, p. 19 n. 45.

248 Kerber, W., Governance of IoT Data: Why the EU Data Act Will not Fulfill Ist Objectives, 2022, https://doi.org/10.1093/grurint/ikac107, p.p. 5et seq.; Specht-Riemenschneider, L., MMR 2022, 809 (818). Cf. Also the proposal of a new Art. 4(4a) by Council Presidency 2022/0047 (COD) – 15035/22, p. 44 in this regard.

249 Schweitzer, H. / Metzger, A. / Blind, K. / Richter, H. / Niebel, C. / Gutmann, F., The legal framework for access to data in Germany and in the EU, BMWK, 2022, p. 219; Metzger, A. / Schweitzer, H., ZEuP 2023, 42; as well as Leistner, M. / Antoine, L.; IPR and the use of open data and data sharing initiatives by public and private actors, 2022, pp. 85 et seq., 93 et seq.

250 Schweitzer, H. / Metzger, A. / Blind, K. / Richter, H. / Niebel, C. / Gutmann, F., The legal framework for access to data in Germany and in the EU, BMWK, 2022, p. 216; Metzger, A. / Schweitzer, H., ZEuP 2023, 42; as well as Leistner, M. / Antoine, L.; IPR and the use of open data and data sharing initiatives by public and private actors, 2022, pp. 80.

251 See in detail Max Planck Institute for Innovation and Competition, Position Statement, 2022, pp. 19 et seq. n. 44 et seq.

the attribution of rights is completely contractual.[252] Furthermore Art. 4(14) sent. 2 would not be necessary if the user had an absolute right.[253]

Despite the fact that the Data Act does not introduce any 'absolute' rights, this attribution of control to the user requires a careful evaluation – also with regard to its economic consequences.[254]

It is questioned whether this control option of the user in relation to the data holder is justified. It is pointed to the fact that the 'generation' of data takes regularly place incidentally and is not connected to any specific efforts of the user.[255] Thus, the 'co-generation' of data serves as the reason that both user and data holder should be able to use the data without the approval of the other party but cannot justify the control-option of the user.[256] Others argue that it is compatible with the general legislative approach which gives the right to use a product and its advantages to the buyer or lessee.[257]

Unfair Terms Control

A data licence agreement is generally subject to the unfair terms control according to Art. 13. This is justified as in some scenarios the user might even have more bargaining power than the data holder and may be in the position to 'dictate' the conditions of the licence agreement.[258] However, Art. 13 does only apply to business-to-business scenarios.[259]

However, rec. 25 might be regarded as a "minimum line" in this regard (also in b2c-scenarios). Rec. 25 combines in a rather confusing way elements of Art. 3(2)[260] and substantial elements:

> "Any contractual term in the agreement stipulating that the data holder may use the data generated by the user of a product or related service should be transparent to the user, including as regards the purpose for

252 Cf. Heinzke, P., BB 2023, 201 (207 et seq.); Schmidt-Kessel, M., MMR-Beil. 1/2024, 75 (78).

253 Schmidt-Kessel, M., MMR-Beil. 1/2024, 75 (78).

254 Hennemann, M. / Steinrötter, B., NJW 2022, 1481 (1486).

255 Funk, A., CR 2023, 421 (425).

256 Cf. Metzger, A. / Schweitzer, H., ZEuP 2023, 42 (54 et seqq.).

257 Schmidt-Kessel, M., MMR-Beil. 1/2024, 75.

258 Grapentin, S., *RDi* 2023, 173 (179); Krämer, J. et al. Data Act: Towards a balanced EU data regulation, CERRE report, March 2023, p. 41.

259 See below VII.

260 See above IV. 3.

> which the data holder intends to use the data. (...) This Regulation should not prevent contractual conditions, whose effect is to exclude or limit the use of the data, or certain categories thereof, by the data holder."

2. *The Right to Access according to Art. 4(1))*

Economic Setting and Assumptions

Art. 4(1) stipulates the Act's key instrument to the benefit of the user, a statutory right to get access to readily available data (along with the relevant set of metadata that is necessary to interpret and use those data). Recognising that these data are "an important input for aftermarket, ancillary, and other services" (rec. 6), the legislator hopes to unlock data silos hitherto controlled exclusively by the data holder and to decrease transaction costs in data-rich markets.[261]

Rec. 15 underlines:

> "[Respective] data are potentially valuable to the user and support innovation and the development of digital and other services protecting the environment, health and the circular economy, in particular though facilitating the maintenance and repair of the products in question."[262]

From a Law & Economics perspective, the data access right introduced by Art. 4(1) has been the subject of intense scrutiny. It is highly debated whether and to what extent the right sets functionally calibrated, sensible, and thought-through parameters and incentives.[263] Whilst there seems to be a general consensus that an information-only / transparency-only approach (cf. Art. 3(2)) would have been insufficient[264], it was and is variously argued that the construction of the right does not go far enough to achieve the stated goals and fulfil the aforementioned aspirations.

261 Paal, B. / Fenik, M., ZfDR 2023, 249 (253 et seq.); Heinzke, P., *BB* 2023, 201 (203).

262 This phrase had first been suggested by Council Presidency 2022/0047(COD) – 15035/22, p. 11.

263 Cf. in this regard Kerber, W., *GRUR Int.* 2023, 120 (128); Krämer, J., Improving The Economic Effectiveness of the B2B and B2C Data Sharing Obligations in the Proposed Data Act, CERRE, 2022; Schweitzer, H. / Metzger, A. / Blind, K. / Richter, H. / Niebel, C. / Gutmann, F., The legal framework for access to data in Germany and in the EU, BMWK, 2022, p. 212.

264 Cf. Krämer, J., Improving The Economic Effectiveness of the B2B and B2C Data Sharing Obligations in the Proposed Data Act, CERRE, 2022, p. 10.

The criticism pertains, first, to which kind of data shall be made accessible, and especially takes issue with the exclusion of derived or inferred data as well those datasets aggregated from multiple sensors and data points.[265]

Second, commentators point out that the user's claim to data access does not alter the technical 'rule' of the data holder, who still might be the only one being able to access the respective product in a *de facto* sense.[266] For instance, Art. 4(11) presupposes that the technical infrastructure storing and variously processing the data at issue is not currently accessible to the user, whereas rec. 22 accepts a computing instance of the manufacturer (i.e., data holder) as a viable gateway for access.

In opposition of the one size fits all-framework constructed by the Act, sectoral approaches have been put forth as an alternative.[267] Similarly, a general set of rules for b2b and b2c scenarios alike is not considered the appropriate regulatory course of action.[268]

Other critiques turn to the user-centricity of the access right[269] and discuss whether collecting data sets from every user individually and not receiving bulk data is economically feasible and / or sensible – also with regard to SMEs.[270] Significant doubts are cast on the practical success of the user activation upon which the access right rests at a foundational level.[271]

---

265 Cf. in this regard Krämer, J., Improving The Economic Effectiveness of the B2B and B2C Data Sharing Obligations in the Proposed Data Act, CERRE, 2022, pp. 12 et seq.; Max Planck Institute for Innovation and Competition, Position Statement, 2022, pp. 10 et seq. n. 20 et seq.

266 *Ex multis*, Finck, M. / Mueller, M-S., 35 (2023) *Journal of Environmental Law* 109 (125).

267 Max Planck Institute for Innovation and Competition, Position Statement, 2022, p. 3 n. 3.

268 Kerber, W., *GRUR-Int.* 2023, 120 (134).

269 Dismissed as a useful premise by Funk, A., *CR* 2023, 421 (425 et seq.).

270 Cf. Krämer, J., Improving The Economic Effectiveness of the B2B and B2C Data Sharing Obligations in the Proposed Data Act, CERRE, 2022, p. 20 as well as Bomhard, D. / Merkle, M., *RDi* 2022, 168 (173); Leistner, M. / Antoine, L., IPR and the use of open data and data sharing initiatives by public and private actors, 2022, pp. 78, 100 et seq.; Max Planck Institute for Innovation and Competition, Position Statement, 2022, p. 9 n. 19.

271 Cf. e.g., Podszun, R. / Pfeifer, C., *GRUR* 2022, 953 (956).

A Remedy for Lack of Data Accessibility-by-Design under Art. 3(1)

Apart from its debatable (behavioural and competition) economic foundations, the right of access raises doctrinal questions. Perhaps the most important one concerns the interplay with the accessibility-by-design[272] demand of Art. 3(1) – both provisions being geared towards the relationship between user and data holder as well as to readily available data.[273]

Access rights seem to be superfluous where the user can access the data sets in question for themselves without further ado[274], but the issue is complicated by vague statutory wording. Namely, under Art. 4(1) the right's availability is conditional upon a situation "[w]here data cannot be directly accessed by the user from the connected product or related service", thus giving precedence to Art. 3(1).[275] Direct accessibility in the way of network access to on-device data storage or via a remote server (cf. rec. 22) is subject to the decisive *caveat* that such access mechanisms must turn out as "relevant and technically feasible". The dual requirement of relevance and technical feasibility (re-appearing in Art. 4(1) and Art. 5(1)) is not explained by the legislator and hence remains woefully unclear.[276] Ultimately, this could become a matter for evaluation of the Act under Art. 49(1)(c).

Manufacturers failing to make product data and related services data directly accessible in violation of Art. 3(1) is the second scenario that will trigger the access right.[277] *Schmidt-Kessel* argues that, in this case, manufacturers as data holders are barred from invoking defences under Art. 4 (notably, regarding trade secrets) as they could otherwise circumvent

---

272 Despite Art. 3(1) being phrased in the latter way, the label "accessibility by design" more precisely captures the technicalities of product design when compared to "access by default"; both terms could also be linked, cf. Paal, B. / Fenik, M., *ZfDR* 2023, 249 (255).

273 Schwamberger, S., in Bernzen, A. K. / Grisse, K. / Kaesling, K. (ed.), Immaterialgüter und Medien im Binnenmarkt: Europäisierung des Rechts und ihre Grenzen, Nomos 2022, p. 101.

274 Specht-Riemenschneider, L., *MMR-Beil.* 2022, 809 (815); Heinzke, P., *BB* 2023, 201 (207).

275 Schmidt-Kessel, M., *MMR-Beil.* 2024, 75 (79).

276 Max Planck Institute for Innovation and Competition, Position Statement, 2022, p. 30 n. 73; Specht-Riemenschneider, *MMR-Beil.* 2022, 809 (815); Podszun, R. / Pfeifer, C., *GRUR* 2022, 953 (956) (opining - with reference to the initial Commission Proposal - that criteria for judging the relevance and appropriateness of direct accessibility should be easy to develop); further, cf. sub IV.2.

277 Max Planck Institute for Innovation and Competition, Position Statement, 2022, p. 32 n. 79; Specht-Riemenschneider, *MMR-Beil.* 2022, 809 (815).

Art. 3(1) to their benefit. This viewpoint can mainly draw on the initial part of Art. 4(1) and the underlying "remedial" nature of the right to access, ensuring specific performance of access to data where accessibility-by-design is lacking.[278]

Effect of the Right: In-Situ Access, Data Retrieval and / or Usage?

Rec. 30 stipulates:

> "The user should be free to use the data for any lawful purpose. This includes providing the data the user has received exercising the right under this Regulation to a third party offering an aftermarket service that may be in competition with a service provided by a data holder, or to instruct the data holder to do so."

In terms of when data sets have been received by, that is made "accessible to the user"[279] pursuant to Art. 4(1), the debate spills over from Art. 3(1)[280]. Can the data holder resort to granting "simple access"[281], i.e. by only allowing processing of (or even less invasive, read-only access to) the data on infrastructure it controls (*in situ*)? Independently from one another, rec. 8 and rec. 22 raise a strong inference that such *in-situ* access could be sufficient:[282]

> "Taking into account the state of the art, all parties to data sharing, including data sharing falling within scope of this Regulation, should implement technical and organisational measures to protect those rights. Such measures include not only pseudonymisation and encryption, but also the use of increasingly available technology that permits algorithms to be brought to the data and allow valuable insights to be derived

278 Schmidt-Kessel, M., *MMR-Beil.* 2024, 75 (80).

279 Further ambiguities between Art. 3(1) and Art. 4(1) are found in the German-language version (*Zugriff* vs. *Zugang*); cf. Podszun, R. / Pfeifer, C., *GRUR* 2022, 953 (957).

280 Cf. sub IV.2.

281 ALI-ELI Principles for a Data Economy, Pr. 8 cmt. a coin this term (as opposed to transfers); cf. Schwamberger, S., in Bernzen, A. K. / Grisse, K. / Kaesling, K. (ed.), Immaterialgüter und Medien im Binnenmarkt: Europäisierung des Rechts und ihre Grenzen, Nomos 2022, p. 105 n. 69.

282 In detail: Kerber, W., *GRUR-Int.* 2023, 120 (124); with respect to rec. 22, cf. also Specht-Riemenschneider, L., *MMR-Beil.* 2022, 809 (816).

> *without the transmission between parties or unnecessary copying of the raw or structured data themselves.*" (rec. 8, emphasis added)

> "Connected products may be designed to permit the user or a third party to process the data on the connected product, *on a computing instance of the manufacturer* or within an information and communications technology (ICT) environment chosen by the user or the third party." (rec. 22, emphasis added)

Upon closer analysis, rec. 8 does not specifically address the right under Art. 4(1) but touches upon adjacent matters. *In-situ* access is recommended[283] (not: mandated) as a technical protection measure in the context of Art. 11, chiefly to prevent unauthorised access and to operationalise the requirements of Art. 4 et seq.[284] In the same breath, Art. 11(1) prescribes limitations to technical protection measures taken by the data holder which "shall not (...) hinder a user's right to obtain a copy of, retrieve, use or access data, to provide data to third parties pursuant to [Art.] 5 (...)". By eliminating the reference to Art. 5, the power to "obtain a copy of, retrieve, use or access data" has to be seen as describing the varied contents of the right granted by Art. 4(1), thereby surpassing mere *in-situ* access.

In contrast, the wording of rec. 22 covers the access regime from Art. 3(1) through to Art. 5(1) ("user or a third party").[285] Given that the notion of processing is mentioned here, rec. 22 can however not be construed to advocate for read-only access as the mere inspection of the data in question does not amount to an operation performed on them (Art. 2(7); cf. Art. 4(2) GDPR).[286] The assumption of a data holder's discretion to simply allow for processing *in situ* without having to migrate the data is refuted by a contextual interpretation of Art. 4(1). For example, the prohibition on ensuing usage in Art. 4(10) only becomes significant if the user is allowed to download or otherwise retrieve the data while observing Art. 4(11).[287] More generally, sole *in-situ* access would run afoul of the Act's broader objectives

283 Kerber, W., *GRUR-Int.* 2023, 120 (124).
284 On the exclusionary relationship between Art. 11 and Art. 3(1), cf. Steege, H., *MMR-Beil.* 2024, 91 (92) and the section devoted in this work to Art. 11 (VI.6.).
285 Specht-Riemenschneider, L., *ZEuP* 2023, 638 (669).
286 Steinrötter, B., *GRUR* 2023, 216 (222); in apparent disagreement: Specht-Riemenschneider, L., *ZEuP* 2023, 638 (669).
287 Correctly, Steinrötter, B., *GRUR* 2023, 216 (222).

to break up data silos and let users share in on the economic benefits of data generation (cf., e.g., rec. 2 and rec. 6).[288]

Ultimately, Art. 4(1) should be understood as implying data retrieval *ex situ*, not least because rec. 22 factors in an ICT environment *chosen by the user* as a viable gateway for access. Structurally, the right then draws inspiration from the right to indirect personal data portability pursuant to Art. 20(1) GDPR – despite key differences in scope (cf. rec. 35).[289] This conclusion does not remove *in-situ* access entirely from consideration, but might relegate it to a defence where data transfers would compromise the confidentiality of trade secrets.[290] In some cases, *in-situ* access may also be preferred by users from a data protection and security viewpoint.[291]

Mandatory Nature of Art. 4; No Circumvention through 'Dark Patterns' (Art. 4(4))

As it is the case with other user rights of Chapter II, Art. 7(2) codifies the semi-mandatory[292] nature of the right to access. Private-law arrangements may not derogate from, let alone contract away the conditions or effects of the right to the detriment of the user. Importantly, this is not to deny the data holder's varied statutory defences pursuant to Art. 4(2), (7), (8), and (11) (which are analysed in-depth in the following section).

The semi-mandatory conception has seen criticism from *inter alia* an Economics perspective.[293] Introducing an element of waivability may however risk defeating the very goals of the Act's data access regime, namely to

288 Heinzke, P., *BB* 2023, 201 (206); Schwamberger, S., in Bernzen, A. K. / Grisse, K. / Kaesling, K. (ed.), Immaterialgüter und Medien im Binnenmarkt: Europäisierung des Rechts und ihre Grenzen, Nomos 2022, p. 105.

289 Concurringly, Geiregat, S., 'The Data Act: Start of a New Era for Data Ownership?' 2022, p. 21 at para. 20 ("conceptual likeness"); Richter, S., *MMR* 2023, 163 (165); Callewaert, C., Data Act und Datenportabilität - Lesson Learned?, in Heinze, C. (ed.), Daten, Plattformen und KI als Dreiklang unserer Zeit, DSRI, 2022, p. 422; Steinrötter, B., *GRUR* 2023, 216 (220-221) agrees in principle, but – supported by Art. 1(5) – also points out a close resemblance to Art. 15(3) GDPR.

290 Paal, B. / Fenik, M., *ZfDR* 2023, 249 (261).

291 Hennemann, M. / Steinrötter, B., *NJW* 2024, 1 (3).

292 Schmidt-Kessel, M., *MMR-Beil.* 2024, 75 (77).

293 E.g., by Schweitzer, H. / Metzger, A. / Blind, K. / Richter, H. / Niebel, C. / Gutmann, F., The legal framework for access to data in Germany and in the EU, BMWK, 2022, p. 219.

counteract data silos and to enable competition in aftermarkets.[294] Instead, a (time-limited) revocable waiver has been favoured both to incentivise long-term investments by a data holder exploiting a data resource exclusively and to allow users to participate *ex post* in previously unforeseen value creation with product and related services data.[295]

It is worth recalling that the non-waivability of the access right does not extend to the use of the data after obtaining access. In line with Art. 4(13), the data licensing agreement concluded between the data holder and the user may provide for a "Total Buy-Out" clause.[296] Rec. 25 bears this in mind for b2b constellations, stating that "[the Act] does not prevent users, in the case of business-to-business relations, [...] from being compensated proportionately, for example in exchange for waiving their right to use or share such data."

On a related note, Art. 4(4) is best understood as preventing circumvention of and manipulation away from the mandatory access right, chiefly in b2c-contexts. According to this provision, "data holders shall not make the exercise of choices or rights under [Art. 4] by the user unduly difficult, including by offering choices to the user in a non-neutral manner or by subverting or impairing the autonomy, decision-making or choices of the user via the structure, design, function or manner of operation of a user digital interface or a part thereof".[297] As rec. 38 clarifies, so-called 'dark patterns' in the design of digital interfaces – defined as "design techniques that push consumers or deceive consumers into decisions that have negative consequences for them" – are outlawed as a result. Rec. 38 further mentions (manipulative) persuasion, nudging, and introducing bias to the decision-making of users as examples. *Martini et al.* interpret this approach to cover well-known design techniques like nagging, forced enrolment, misdirection, obstruction, and bait and switch.[298] Other recently enacted bans on dark patterns found in Art. 5, Art. 13(6) DMA, Art. 25 DSA, as

294 Schweitzer, H. / Metzger, A., 'Shaping Markets: A Critical Evaluation of the Draft Data Act', *ZEuP* 2023, 42 (57); Paal, B. / Fenik, M., *ZfDR* 2023, 249 (259).

295 In-depth Schweitzer, H. / Metzger, A., *ZEuP* 2023, 42 (56 et seqq.).

296 See the discussion sub V.1. above; additionally, cf. Kerber, W., *GRUR-Int.* 2023, 120 (132); Specht-Riemenschneider, L., *MMR-Beil.* 2022, 809 (817); Steinrötter, B., *GRUR* 2023, 216 (219).

297 First proposed by Council Presidency 2022/0047(COD) – 15035/22, p. 44.

298 Martini, M. / Kramme, I. / Kamke, A., *MMR* 2023, 399 (401 et seq.).

well as in Art. 5(1)(a) of the AI Act[299], tend to be more comprehensive and extend to further instances of dark patterns.[300]

Modalities under which Access is Granted as per Art. 4(1)

Once the access right is deemed applicable, the modalities of how and when data sets have to be made accessible come into play. Art. 4(1) lists extensive requirements, namely that access has to be granted "without undue delay, of the same quality as is available to the data holder, easily, securely, free of charge, in a comprehensive, structured, commonly used and machine-readable format and, where relevant and technically feasible, continuously and in real-time."[301]

What qualifies as 'undue delay' is determined by Union, not by member state law.[302] The same language in Art. 12(3) GDPR is interpreted as the shortest amount of time needed to supply the requested data.[303] Taken to the extreme, this could coincide with real-time access under Art. 4(1) and hence be a matter of mere seconds.[304] It should be pointed out that in contrast, Art. 12(3) GDPR sets the maximum time frame at one month (possibly lengthened by another two months). In case personal data is concerned, frictions between Art. 20 GDPR and Art. 4(1) as well as Art. 5(1) will result, the resolution of which may depend on the declared intent of the data subject / user.[305]

Similar frictions are bound to arise where data subjects as users submit overly repetitive requests, i.e. those exceeding reasonable intervals.[306]

---

299 European Parliament legislative resolution of 13 March 2024 on the proposal for a regulation of the European Parliament and of the Council on laying down harmonised rules on Artificial Intelligence (Artificial Intelligence Act) and amending certain Union Legislative Acts, p. 181.

300 Martini, M. / Kramme, I. / Kamke, A., *MMR* 2023, 399 (399 et seq.).

301 Most of these requirements stem from Council Presidency 2022/0047(COD) – 15035/22, p. 44 – also tackling criticism of the original proposal of Art. 4(1), cf. e.g., Krämer, J., Improving The Economic Effectiveness of the B2B and B2C Data Sharing Obligations in the Proposed Data Act, CERRE, 2022, p. 7.

302 Schmidt-Kessel, M., *MMR-Beil.* 2024, 75 (79).

303 EDPB, 'Guidelines 01/2022 on data subject rights - Right of access', 28 March 2023, p. 50 n. 158.

304 Hartmann, B. / McGuire, M. / Schulte-Nölke, H., *RDi* 2023, 49 (53).

305 Richter, S., *MMR* 2023, 163 (166).

306 Rec. 63 GDPR with guidance by EDPB, 'Guidelines 01/2022 on data subject rights - Right of access', 28 March 2023, p. 56 n. 183 et seq.

Whereas access remains 'free of charge' under Art. 4(1), the data holder (viz. controller) could charge for access and indirect portability pursuant to Art. 12(5) GDPR.[307] Making access 'free of charge' does not prohibit data holders from pricing in the related costs as service fees.[308] According to rec. 28, it does however preclude tying access to unfair contractual terms within the meaning of Directives 93/13/EEC and 2005/29/EC where the user is a consumer. Rec. 28 extends this to b2b scenarios involving enterprises (cf. Art. 2(24)) as users, rendering such terms unenforceable across the board.[309]

Turning to the option of *continuous and in real time access*, the already familiar hurdle of relevance and technical feasibility must be cleared, which should be the case where the connected product actually stores data on end and in real time.[310] In practice, data holders will invoke this exception by discharging their notice obligation pursuant to Art. 3(2)(b). Continuous and real-time data transfers represent perhaps the most significant advance over one-off (*ad hoc*) downloads in the context of Art. 20(1) GDPR since they best capture the value of data stemming from its immediate availability.[311] What is more, the technical tools necessary to enable real-time access, namely application programming interfaces (APIs), will be conducive to interoperability.[312] The like-minded rule targeting participants in data spaces (Art. 33(1)(c)), which alludes to connected products, should be read as part of the requirements under Art. 4(1).[313]

As for the *quality* in which data has to be made accessible, it is not unheard of that data holders unwilling to share certain datasets will deliber-

307 Steinrötter, B., *GRUR* 2023, 216 (221).

308 As is noted by Funk, A. *CR* 2023, 421 (426).

309 It stands to reason that unfair terms would also materially alter and therefore derogate from the user's access right in contravention of Art. 7(2) (as reiterated towards the end of Art. 8(2)).

310 Geiregat, S., 'The Data Act: Start of a New Era for Data Ownership?' 2022, p. 21 at para. 21.

311 Krämer, J., Improving The Economic Effectiveness of the B2B and B2C Data Sharing Obligations in the Proposed Data Act, CERRE, 2022, p. 7; Schwamberger, S., in Bernzen, A. K. / Grisse, K. / Kaesling, K. (ed.), Immaterialgüter und Medien im Binnenmarkt: Europäisierung des Rechts und ihre Grenzen, Nomos 2022, p. 94.

312 Krämer, J., Improving The Economic Effectiveness of the B2B and B2C Data Sharing Obligations in the Proposed Data Act, CERRE, 2022, p. 7; further, cf. sub IX.9.

313 To that effect: Schweitzer, H. / Metzger, A., *ZEuP* 2023, 42 (72); cf. sub IX.10.

ately degrade their – otherwise constant – quality.[314] Reinforced by unfair terms control for unilaterally imposed standards of data quality pursuant to Art. 13(5)(g)[315], Art. 4(1) makes sure that the quality does not dip below the level available to the data holder. Rec. 30 expands on which criteria pertain to this assessment:

> "Data holders should ensure that the data made available to the third party is as accurate, complete, reliable, relevant and up-to-date[316] as the data the data holder itself may be able or entitled to access from the use of the connected product or related service."

Rec. 30 mistakenly refers only to "data made available to the third party". From the positioning and content of rec. 30 on the whole, however, it can be deduced that the elements of data quality mentioned also apply to the access of the user as such.

The obligation to maintain data quality is likewise placed under the *caveat* of relevance and technical feasibility, the reason being that the individual needs of a user may call for a different presentation of the data at issue.[317]

Following suggestions from academia[318], the requirements of a *structured, commonly used, and machine-readable format* are lifted verbatim from Art. 20(1) GDPR. Yet in doing so, the well-known uncertainties of this phrase are reproduced. According to (inconclusive) guidance, the term "structured" should be interpreted with a view to how easily the data can be re-used at the destination[319], which would likely exclude PDF and HTML files in IoT contexts.[320] The notion of machine-readability is susceptible to

314 Krämer, J., Improving The Economic Effectiveness of the B2B and B2C Data Sharing Obligations in the Proposed Data Act, CERRE, 2022, p. 19; cf. Paal, B. / Fenik, M., *ZfDR* 2023, 249 (253).

315 Cf. sub VII, below.

316 Similarly, Max Planck Institute for Innovation and Competition, Position Statement, 2022, p. 43 n. 116; for a different view of which factors make up data quality, cf. von Lewinski, K. / Hähnle, J., *DuD* 2021, 686 (687) (adding usability and presentation quality / readability).

317 Schmidt-Kessel, M., *MMR-Beil.* 2024, 75 (80).

318 E.g., by Schweitzer, H. / Metzger, A., *ZEuP* 2023, 42 (72).

319 Article 29 Working Party, 'Guidelines on the right to data portability' WP 242 rev.01 (5 April 2017) p. 18.

320 Cf. Dix, A., 'DSGVO Art. 20 Recht auf Datenübertragbarkeit', in Simitis, S. / Hornung, G. / Spiecker gen. Döhmann, I. (ed.), Datenschutzrecht: DSGVO mit BDSG, Nomos 2019, para. 11.

wildly diverging interpretations, from OCR-readable paper formats on one end[321] to autonomously machine-readable formats on the other (thereby excluding most text- and image-based files).[322] A format is commonly used where it is widely accepted in the relevant market, with open formats such as XML, JSON, and CSV being recommended in the context of Art. 20 GDPR.[323] The additional insistence on a *comprehensive* format prohibits the data holder from relying, to the detriment of users, on a blend of multiple formats for the same access request.

Data in Scope of the Access Right

Per Art. 4(1), "readily available data, as well as the relevant metadata necessary to interpret and use those data" has to be made accessible to the user. Because Art. 2(17) defines 'readily available data' as the umbrella term for product data and related service data, Art. 4(1) uses practically the same language as Art. 3(1). Logically sound, the scope of the data coming within the access right corresponds to the extent of accessibility-by-design. In particular, inferred and derived data are excluded (rec. 15).[324] From a different angle, the breadth of data covered under the right goes as far as is permissible in accordance with data protection law.[325] Rec. 35 highlights how the user-held access right thereby seeks to improve upon Art. 20(1) GDPR (apart from the aforementioned continuous and real-time access):

> "This Regulation grants users the right to access and make available to a third party any product data or related service data, irrespective of their nature as personal data, of the distinction between actively provided or passively observed data, and irrespective of the legal basis of processing."

---

321 Hennemann, M., *PinG* 2017, 5 (7).

322 Geiregat, S., 'The Data Act: Start of a New Era for Data Ownership?' 2022, p. 36 at para. 36.

323 Article 29 Working Party, 'Guidelines on the right to data portability' WP 242 rev.01 (5 April 2017) p. 18; for JSON and fitness tracking apps, this has recently been affirmed in a decision by the Austrian Federal Administrative Court (ECLI:AT:BVWG:2023:W211.2261980.1.00 at para 3.3.2).

324 Cf. IV.2 and the beginning of this section.

325 Bomhard, D. / Merkle, M., *RDi* 2022, 168 (169).

Identification of the Requesting User (Art. 4(5))

According to its second sentence, the right under Art. 4(1) is exercised via "a simple request through electronic means where technically feasible". Rec. 29 adds that "[i]n the case of personal data processed by a processor on behalf of the controller, data holders should ensure that the access request is received and handled by the processor."

The user does not have to observe a specific form and can submit the request at any given time.[326] Delaying the access request is not advisable however because data holders are not expected, let alone required to store the data generated by connected products indefinitely. Instead, rec. 24 vaguely stipulates that a reasonable data retention policy must be implemented by the data holder (balancing storage limitation under Art. 5(1)(e) GDPR and the effectiveness of access rights). While immediate deletion upon generation would clearly violate accessibility-by-design (Art. 3(1))[327], data holders may subsequently choose to rid themselves of data sets they have already analysed – along with the associated obligations under Art. 4 et seq.[328] No matter how long data is being retained, the duration must be communicated to the user under Art. 3(2)(c) and Art. 3(3)(a)-(b) in order not to undermine the concept of access upon request.[329]

Art. 4(5) tackles the question of how data holders know whether the 'correct' user is requesting access. By limiting the data holder to information that is necessary to verify the user, the principles of purpose limitation and data minimisation as per Art. 5(1)(b) and (c) GDPR are unnecessarily duplicated.[330]

No information on the requested access shall be kept that is not "necessary for the sound execution of the user's access request and for the security and the maintenance of the data infrastructure" (Art. 4(5) Sentence 2). Not least by singling out log data (recording changes to and retrieval of elements in a database[331]), it becomes apparent that the legislator intended for the user and for third parties to use the data without being obliged

326 Specht-Riemenschneider, L., *MMR-Beil.* 2022, 809 (815); Heinzke, P., *BB* 2023, 201 (206).
327 Schweitzer, H. / Metzger, A., *ZEuP* 2023, 42 (52).
328 Bomhard, D. / Merkle, M., *RDi* 2022, 168 (174).
329 Further, cf. IV.3, above.
330 Hennemann, M. / Steinrötter, B., *NJW* 2024, 1 (3).
331 Butterfield, A. / Ngondi, G.E. / Kerr, A. (ed.), A Dictionary of Computer Science, s.v. "log file", 7th edn, OUP 2016.

to reveal to the data holder their (competitively relevant) business plans with regard to specific data sets.[332] As rec. 21 puts it, no "examination or clearance [of the request] by the manufacturer or data holder" should be needed.

Additionally, rec. 21 concedes (and does not attempt to change) the fact that use of a connected product or related service will typically entail setting up a user account. This has been criticised as effectively barring anonymous usage of IoT products, including access requests.[333]

3. *Limitations of and Defences to the User's Right of Access*

The remaining parts of Art. 4 turn to the interests of data holders in two ways: first, by establishing defences[334] against the user's access right concerning matters of cybersecurity (Art. 4(2)), confidentiality of trade secrets (Art. 4(6)-(9)), and data protection (Art. 4(12)); and second, by establishing loyalty obligations of users[335] towards data holders in accordance with Art. 4(10)-(11).

No 'Right to Hack'[336] (Art. 4(11))

Even prior to access, Art. 4(11) articulates a duty of loyalty in denying users a 'right to hack'. Coercive means may not be used, gaps in the technical infrastructure may not be abused (even if they are widely known). The user accordingly cannot 'self-remedy' refusals or delays on the part of the data holder and take the access 'into their own hands' by penetrating the IoT-product through exploits not foreseen / enabled by the data holder. Art. 4(11) is considered as tightening the previously discussed *de facto* technical control attributed to the data holder.[337]

---

332 Schweitzer, H. / Metzger, A., *ZEuP* 2023, 42 (55).

333 Podszun, R. / Pfeifer, C., *GRUR* 2022, 953 (961); Specht-Riemenschneider, L., *ZEuP* 2023, 638 (663 et seq.).

334 Cf. Hennemann, M. / Steinrötter, B., *NJW* 2024, 1 (4).

335 Schmidt-Kessel, M., *MMR-Beil.* 2024, 75 (81) ("*Schutz- und Treuepflichten*").

336 Specht-Riemenschneider, L., *MMR-Beil.* 2022, 809 (823) (with regard to the parallel norm in Art. 5(5)).

337 Kerber, W., *GRUR-Int.* 2023, 120 (124 et seq.); cf. sub 2.

Security of the Connected Product (Art. 4(2))

It is possible to restrict access to, (further) use or sharing of the data at the outset. Art. 4(2) stipulates that users and data holders can contractually restrict (or even prohibit *in toto)* such processing that "could undermine security requirements of the connected product, as laid down by Union or national law, resulting in a serious adverse effect on the health, safety or security of natural persons".

Added as a result of the trilogue, the provision seems geared towards upcoming cybersecurity legislation targeting connected products (cf. rec. 115). Art. 4(2) may therefore have been inserted specifically to anticipate the essential cybersecurity requirements for the design of "products with digital elements" pursuant to Art. 13 and Annex I of the Cyber Resilience Act as passed on 12 March 2024 (including regular security updates, amongst other safeguards).[338]

Where the data holder refuses access, this shall be reported to the competent authority in accordance with Art. 37. In light of the comparatively less invasive restriction of access or prohibition of further use, the outright refusal of access must be understood as a last resort given particularly grave health and safety implications. Overall, the reference to "a serious adverse effect on the health, safety or security of natural persons" is indicative of clauses under Art. 4(2) being the strict exception.

Art. 4(3) furnishes the user with instruments of redress (complaints / dispute resolution) in the event they disagree with the data holder on matters connected to the contractual restrictions or prohibitions that have been made pursuant to Art. 4(2).

Access to Lawfully Processed Personal Data Only (Art. 4(12))

Access to personal data entails their disclosure to the user, typically by way of transmission – and therefore qualifies as processing of personal data according to Art. 4(2) GDPR.[339] To accommodate the ramifications under

338 Commission, Proposal for a Regulation of the European Parliament and of the Council on horizontal cybersecurity requirements for products with digital elements and amending Regulation (EU) 2019/1020, COM(2022) 454 final.

339 *In situ*-access by way of a query on the data holder's server infrastructure would also fall within Art. 4(2) GDPR, specifically as data that have been otherwise made available (cf. Roßnagel, A., 'DSGVO Art. 4 Nr. 2 Begriffsbestimmung "Verarbeitung"',

data protection law, a non-dispositive legal barrier to the right to access is set by Art. 4(12). The rule focuses on the scenario where the user is not the data subject whose personal data is being requested. Accordingly, "a valid legal basis under Article 6(1) [GDPR] and, where relevant, the conditions of Article 9 [GDPR] and Article 5(3) [ePrivacy-Directive]"[340] must be shown. As rec. 7 stresses generally, such a legal basis is not found in the fulfilment of the access right itself. *Specht-Riemenschneider* contests this finding based on a contextualisation of Art. 4(12) with Art. 1(5). The former provision would be rendered mostly symbolic if it simply reiterated the continued importance of data protection rules. It is therefore argued that the access right can amount *eo ipso* to a justification of processing, namely to a "legal obligation" as cited by Art. 6(1)(c) GDPR.[341]

Vice versa, should the user happen to be the data subject for the personal data being requested, their consent to processing pursuant to Art. 6(1)(a) and 7 GDPR is implicitly given along with the request for access.[342] The same inference of consent can be drawn with respect to Art. 5(3) ePrivacy-Directive, which may also govern access to data sets generated by connected products due to these products being classed as 'terminal equipment'[343] (rec. 36).

Rec. 34 elaborates on the role of users that are not the data subjects at issue. Where they act as enterprises (cf. Art. 2(24), including sole traders) and unless shared household use of the connected product is concerned, these users are considered controllers in the sense of Art. 4(7) GDPR. The burden of demonstrating a valid legal basis for processing would then rest with the user – most likely alongside the data holder, triggering the requirements for joint controllership stated in Art. 26 GDPR.[344] Assuming a kinship with the household exemption under Art. 2(2)(c) GDPR, 'shared

---

in Simitis, S. / Hornung, G. / Spiecker gen. Döhmann, I. (ed.), Datenschutzrecht: DSGVO mit BDSG, Nomos 2019, para. 26.

340 First suggested by Council Presidency 2022/0047(COD) – 15035/22, pp. 45 et seq.

341 Specht-Riemenschneider, L., *ZEuP* 2023, 638 (665 et seq.).

342 *Ex multis*, Hennemann, M. / Steinrötter, B., *NJW* 2024, 1 (4); Steinrötter, B. *GRUR* 2023, 216 (223); Specht-Riemenschneider, *MMR-Beil.* 2022, 809 (810).

343 See guidance by EDPB, 'Guidelines 2/2023 on Technical Scope of Art. 5(3) of ePrivacy Directive' (14 November) para. 16 ("for example, smartphones, laptops, connected cars or connected TVs, smart glasses").

344 Paal, B. / Fenik, M., *ZfDR* 2023, 249 (256).

household use' would for instance not cover company-issued 'smart' wristbands being worn in an employment context.[345]

Especially with respect to Art. 4(12), the Data Act will not ease, let alone resolve the inherent tension between data economy and data protection law by "slicing the Gordian knot"[346] in which both fields of law are entangled. Art. 4(12) presents data holders with dilemmatic choices of immense significance in terms of compliance. They must now find – a nearly impossible mission – the 'correct' boundary between non-personal data and personal data. Failing to provide non-personal data (due to a 'wrong' classification as personal data) could elicit a fine under Art. 40 (and respective national law); providing personal data in breach of data protection law (due to a 'wrong' classification as non-personal data) could likewise result in a fine under Art. 83 GDPR *and* under Art. 40 (if Art. 4(12) is seen as more than a declaratory reference to data protection law[347]). Rec. 34 is of some assistance in this regard by incorporating the rule for so-called mixed data sets as per Art. 2(2) of Regulation (EU) 2018/1807: "Processing of (...) data is subject to the rules established under [the GDPR], including where personal and non-personal data in a data set are inextricably linked."[348]

Even setting aside the quandary of labelling data sets as personal or non-personal, Art. 4(12) requires users that are not a natural person (mostly, enterprises) to evaluate their (subsequent) processing of personal data. Because Art. 6(1)(f) GDPR in particular leaves enormous room for debate[349], users will prefer collecting consent declarations from the data subjects at stake. It is unlikely however that respective users will always be in a *de facto* position to contact data subjects – thus being dependent on the data holder's willingness to intermediate. Data holders, in turn, will also face difficulties in identifying affected data subjects where they diverge from the (enterprise) user – a problem which the Act attempts to remedy

345 Cf. Heinzke, P., *BB* 2023, 201 (205).

346 Hennemann, M. / Steinrötter, B., *NJW* 2022, 1481 (1482); Hennemann, M. / Steinrötter, B., *NJW* 2024, 1 (5).

347 Richter, S., *MMR* 2023, 163 (165); Steinrötter, *GRUR* 2023, 216 (223) (noting the accumulated risk of fines).

348 For information on what is meant by the 'inextricably linked' criterion, see Commission, 'Guidance on the Regulation on a framework for the free flow of non-personal data in the European Union', COM(2019) 250 final, p. 10.

349 See however the suggestion by Specht-Riemenschneider, *ZEuP* 2023, 638 (666) that compliance with the Art. 4(1) access right should influence the weighing of interests under Art. 6(1)(f) GDPR *a priori*.

by recommending "separate accounts for individual [natural] persons" by design (rec. 24).[350]

Trade Secrets (Art. 4(6)-(9))

Per se, the protection of certain data as trade secrets of the data holder does not trump the user's right of access. In no uncertain manner, rec. 31 maintains: "[d]ata holders cannot, in principle, refuse a data access request under this Regulation solely on the basis that certain data is considered to be a trade secret, as this would subvert the intended effects of this Regulation." Sensibly, the Act seeks to balance the competing interests of users and data holders by enabling the disclosure of data to users while "preserv[ing] the protection afforded to trade secrets under [the Trade Secrets Directive]" (rec. 31). Still, it is the user on whose side the chosen legislative approach favouring disclosure errs in Art. 4(6), with the data holder having to show circumstances that legitimise the various defences under Art. 4(7)-(8).[351] Some commentators have gone so far as to describe the user-friendly approach as a system of compulsory licensing to effectuate the access right.[352]

According to the general rule established in the first sentence of Art. 4(6), trade secrets "shall be disclosed only where the data holder and the user take all necessary measures prior to the disclosure to preserve their confidentiality", also and "in particular regarding third parties". By implying that trade secrets shall *only* be disclosed if the necessary measures are taken, Art. 4(6) is formulated in a rather confusing way.[353] The provision should be read with an emphasis on when measures become "necessary". Considering Art. 4(3)(c) of the Trade Secrets Directive, a data holder that is not simultaneously the relevant trade secret holder (cf. Art. 2(19)) has to implement such measures. Should the data holder fail to take necessary

---

350 Further, cf. Heinzke, P., *BB* 2023, 201 (205).

351 Cf. Macher, E. / Ballestrem, J., *GRUR-Prax* 2023, 661 (661) with details on the legislative history.

352 Max Planck Institute for Innovation and Competition, Position Statement, 2022, p. 101 n. 286 et seq.; cf. Heinzke, P., *BB* 2023, 201 (206).

353 Cf. for a discussion of Art. 4(6) in detail Leistner, M. / Antoine, L., IPR and the use of open data and data sharing initiatives by public and private actors, 2022, pp. 86 et seq.

precautions to preserve confidentiality, the disclosure of the trade secrets represented within the data at issue will be deemed unlawful.[354]

The second sentence of Art. 4(6) specifies that the necessary measures taken by the data holder comprise proportionate technical and organisational measures (TOM)[355], which are exemplified by model contractual terms (cf. Art. 41), confidentiality agreements, strict access protocols, technical standards (cf. Art. 11) and the application of codes of conduct. Most notably, non-disclosure agreements (NDAs) with penalty clauses in the event of a breach of confidentiality are bound to play a pivotal rule.[356] Even though NDAs may form part of the data licensing agreement with the user, this further layer adds to the complexity of the general contractual setting, especially vis-à-vis consumers.[357]

Perhaps most importantly, in its second sentence, Art. 4(6) places the data holder (or a divergent trade secret holder) under the obligation "to identify the data which are protected as trade secrets, including in the relevant metadata". The atypical assessment of trade secrecy *ex ante*, i.e. before the data holder has sued for infringement, presents the data holder with considerable leeway in negotiating the NDA because they can make sweeping claims about data sets containung trade secrets.[358] In line with Art. 9(1) of the Trade Secrets Directive, the onus of trade secrets being affected is namely met if the risk of disclosure is demonstrated to be more likely than not.[359]

To discourage strategic "overclaiming"[360], *Schmidt-Kessel* argues that the data holder – representing the user's interests in a quasi-fiduciary capacity – should separate out data sets involving trade secrets from the outset to the best of their abilities for Art. 4(6)-(8) so as not to obstruct the user's access

354 Cf. Schweitzer, H. / Metzger, A., *ZEuP* 2023, 42 (75).

355 Hennemann, M. / Steinrötter, B., *NJW* 2024, 1 (4).

356 Bomhard, D. / Merkle, M., *RDi* 2022, 168 (171).

357 Hennemann, M. / Steinrötter, B., *NJW* 2022, 1481 (1484); Paal, B. / Fenik, M., *ZfDR* 2023, 249 (258).

358 Max Planck Institute for Innovation and Competition, Position Statement, 2022, p. 101 n. 280 et seq.; in agreement: Kerber, W., *GRUR-Int.* 2023, 120 (126); Ducuing, C. / Margoni, T. / Schirru, L. (ed.), *CiTiP Working Paper* 2022, pp. 81 et seq. (noting the more serious consequences in the context of Art. 5(9)).

359 Pauly, D.A. / Wichert, F. / Baumann, J., *MMR* 2024, 211 (212) with further references.

360 Wiebe, A., *GRUR* 2023, 227 (234).

right.[361] Crucially, this could be accomplished at the level of product design so that these data do not become readily available data in the first place.[362]

At any rate, leaving the process of identifying trade secrets in the IoT-generated data to the data holder *ex ante* is consequential. Whereas derived or inferred data (cf. rec. 15) are excluded from consideration, other IoT-generated data sets are capable of trade secret protection within the meaning of Art. 2(1) of the Trade Secrets Directive.[363] In particular, the curation and aggregation (cf. rec. 33) of "raw" sensor data from multiple data points prior to further analysis may reveal not generally known and therefore commercially valuable information about the functionalities and design of a connected product.[364] It seems plausible however that this would not include the mere prospect or probability of aggregation between a plurality of users' data at the hands of a third party.[365] From a practical perspective, close evaluation of the trade secrets regime interacting with the access right pursuant to Art. 49(1)(f) will be needed.

Art. 4(7) addresses the potential failures of disclosing trade secrets pursuant to Art. 4(6). Failures can arise from (1) no agreement on the necessary measures preserving confidentiality having been reached, (2) the user not having implemented the measures or (3) the user undermining the confidentiality of the trade secrets (e.g., by violating Art. 4(11)). Under these circumstances, the data holder is given a right of retention[366]: they can withhold or (apparently in the case of continuous access) suspend sharing "data identified as trade secrets" with the user. The duly substantiated decision must be provided to the user in writing without undue delay while specifying which of the above scenarios (no agreement / failure of implementation / undermining user behaviour) applies.[367] Additionally, the data holder has to notify the competent authority (cf. Art. 37), an obligation

361 Schmidt-Kessel, M., *MMR-Beil.* 2024, 75 (81) ("*Trennungsgebot*").

362 Macher, E. / Ballestrem, J., *GRUR-Prax* 2023, 661 (662).

363 This was prominently denied for raw machine-generated data by the Commission, 'Building a European Data Economy' Commission, COM(2017) 9 final, p. 10.

364 In-depth: Grapentin, S., *RDi* 2023, 173 (174 et seq.); similarly, Wiebe, A., *GRUR* 2023, 227 (232); Heinzke, P., *BB* 2023, 201 (206); Hartmann, B. / McGuire, M. / Schulte-Nölke, H., *RDi* 2023, 49 (54) contend that aggregated data are of no concern in the context of Art. 5(9) due to purpose-specificity, thereby overlooking Art. 4(6).

365 Grapentin, S., *RDi* 2023, 173 (177).

366 Schmidt-Kessel, M., *MMR-Beil.* 2024, 75 (79) ("*Zurückbehaltungsrechte*").

367 Pauly, D.A. / Wichert, F. / Baumann, J., *MMR* 2024, 211 (213).

which could make data holders more reluctant to exercise the right of retention.[368]

Art. 4(8) considers the situation that despite the implementation of measures in line with Art. 4(6), the data holder may exceptionally face a high likelihood of "serious economic damage" due to the disclosure of trade secrets to the user. Here, the data holder is entitled to refuse an access request entirely, but only if they can substantiate that serious economic damage is likely to occur based on "objective elements". Even with the three examples for such objective elements given in the second sentence of Art. 4(8), demonstrating that one user's request has such dire consequences for the data holder will be virtually impossible *in praxi*[369] and should be weighed against the interests of the user in obtaining the data.[370] Again, bringing this defence against the user's request for access is conditional upon notifying the competent authority (cf. Art. 37).

Should the user wish to challenge the defences invoked with reference to the two preceding paragraphs, Art. 4(9) furnishes them with redress mechanisms (complaints / dispute resolution).

Restrictions on Onward Usage: Non-Compete (Art. 4(10)) and Sharing with Gatekeepers (Art. 5(3)(c))

When compared to the position of data holders (restricted by Art. 4(13)-(14) and the data licensing agreement made thereunder), the user is – at least by default – largely free to use the data as they see fit.[371] Having obtained access, the user must however accept two noteworthy restrictions to this relative freedom of usage.

First, Art. 4(10) stipulates a non-compete obligation of the user.[372] In a regulatory effort to avert outright duplication of the connected product by competitors in the same product (not: geographical) market[373], the user may not use the (personal or non-personal) data made available to them to

368 Hennemann, M. / Steinrötter, B., *NJW* 2024, 1 (4).
369 Grapentin, S., *RDi* 2023, 173 (176 et seq.).
370 Heinzke, P. / Herbers, B. / Kraus, M., *BB* 2024, 649 (653).
371 Schmidt-Kessel, M., *MMR-Beil.* 2024, 75 (81); on (total) buy-out clauses, cf. sub 2 of this section.
372 *Ex multis*, Paal, B. / Fenik, M., *ZfDR* 2023, 249 (258).
373 Bomhard, D., MMR-Beil. 2024, 71 (73) ("*Nachahmungsschutz*"); Heinzke, P. / Herbers, B. / Kraus, M., *BB* 2024, 649 (654).

> "develop a connected product that competes with the connected product from which the data originate, nor share the data with a third party with that intent and shall not use such data to derive insights about the economic situation, assets and production methods of the manufacturer or, where applicable, the data holder."

Rec. 32 reveals a two-fold underpinning: the aim is to "avoid undermining investment incentives" of the data holder into a connected product, which would happen if competitors were free to develop a "product which is considered to be interchangeable or substitutable by users". At the same time, it is the stated intention of the legislator to stimulate the development of entirely novel (complementary) *services* as well as innovation on aftermarkets (cf. the second sentence of rec. 30). The focus on aftermarket promotion also explains why 'related services' were omitted from the non-compete rule under Art. 4(10) in the Act's final version.[374] Moreover it is solely[375] in an aftermarket context that rec. 32 declares permissible reverse engineering the characteristics of a connected product from the data obtained, namely for maintenance and analytics purposes. Overall, the distinction between substitutes and (aftermarket) complements within the non-compete rule has been criticised for lacking a comprehensive economic justification.[376] In particular, the rule is called into question for overlooking the (not infrequent) value creation by data holders through the provision of related services[377] and for effectively hindering users to switch to a competing product manufacturer.[378] Lastly, the consequences of *the user* violating Art. 4(10) remain unclear.[379]

Second, the user is barred from sharing the data they have obtained under Art. 4(1) with a third party designated as a gatekeeper pursuant to Art. 3 DMA. Misplaced in Art. 5(3)(c), this prohibition concerns the user's

374 By contrast, related services had formed part of prior (pre-trilogue) versions of the non-compete rule, but not of the initial Commission proposal; cf. Schweitzer, H. / Metzger, A., *ZEuP* 2023, 42 (61).

375 Unclear on this aspect: Heinzke, P. / Herbers, B. / Kraus, M., *BB* 2024, 649 (654).

376 Cf. Krämer, J., Improving The Economic Effectiveness of the B2B and B2C Data Sharing Obligations in the Proposed Data Act, CERRE, 2022, pp. 23 et seq.; Leistner, M. / Antoine, L., IPR and the use of open data and data sharing initiatives by public and private actors, 2022, pp. 88 et seq.

377 Heinzke, P. / Herbers, B. / Kraus, M., *BB* 2024, 649 (654).

378 Schweitzer, H. / Metzger, A., *ZEuP* 2023, 42 (61).

379 Hennemann, M. / Steinrötter, B., *NJW* 2022, 1481 (1484); for violations by the data recipient, cf. Art. 6(2)(e), read jointly with Art. 11(2) and (3)(b).

freedom of onwards usage and should hence be merged with a discussion of Art. 4(10).[380]

380 Similarly, Schmidt-Kessel, M., *MMR-Beil.* 2024, 75 (79).

VI. Right to Share Data with Third Parties (Art. 5-6) and FRAND Obligations for Data Holders When Providing Access (Art. 8-12)

The Data Act aims to break down data silos in order to make them usable for different parties. This is why Art. 5 provides the user with the option to grant a third party access vis-à-vis the data holder. Such an access raises follow-up questions, *inter alia* with respect to the compensation of the data holder, the "how" of granting access and the technical protection measures to be taken. These topics are regulated by Art. 8-12.

1. The Right to Share Data with Third Parties (Art. 5)

Art. 5(1) broadens the user's options. Next to or instead of requesting access according to Art. 4(1), the user has the right to demand access in favour of a third party.

As far as the user's position is concerned, the right resembles Art. 20(2) GDPR.[381] The user may 'port' applicable data sets directly to a third-party entity of their choice. However, the right introduced by Art. 5(1) represents a significant advance over Art. 20 GDPR. The obligations arising between this third party and the data holder are governed in detail through a variety of rules in Art. 6 (and, for data recipients, Art. 8 and 9).[382] At the same time, rec. 25 underlines that the Data Act does not bar voluntary data sharing arrangements emanating from a data holder. This means that in contrast to Art. 20 GDPR, often four or more entities (e.g., data holders other than the party selling or leasing a connected product to the user) will legitimately participate in the sharing of readily available data.[383] Due to multiple actors being involved, the right has also been likened to the transit of goods sold to the "end user" within a complex supply chain.[384]

381 Hennemann, M. / Steinrötter, B., *NJW* 2024, 1 (3).

382 Max Planck Institute for Innovation and Competition, Position Statement, 2022, p. 28 n. 70.

383 Schweitzer, H. / Metzger, A., *ZEuP* 2023, 42 (51).

384 Schmidt-Kessel, M., *MMR-Beil.* 2024, 75 (75).

The right granted in Art. 5(1) faces much of the same criticisms as the access right pursuant to Art. 4(1), not least because it is not an independent right of the third party, but is dependent on the user's exercise (and discretion)[385] and, as a result, equally relies on the much-debated premise of user-initiated data flows.[386] While the third party can set financial incentives in order to 'activate' the user respectively, they potentially encounter 'double pricing' with respect to the compensation to be paid to the data holder according to Art. 9(1).[387] To achieve user empowerment more reliably, the legislator acknowledges in rec. 27 that "sector-specific needs and objectives" must be addressed by regulation, building on initiatives such as the Code of Conduct for agricultural data sharing by contractual agreement.[388]

In addition, it is questioned whether the exclusion of gatekeepers as eligible third parties in Art. 5(3) is serving innovation and the common wealth.[389] Specifically, the agglomeration of readily available data driven by market power is a concern that can manifest itself outside the realm of core platform services according to Art. 2(2) Digital Markets Act.[390] The design of Art. 5 may even give rise to (non-gatekeeper) specialised third parties aggregating data sets from the user base of a connected product.[391]

---

385 Cf. Bomhard, D. / Merkle, M. *RDi* 2022, 168 (171) (*„nutzerakzessorischer Datenzugang"*).

386 Kerber, W., *GRUR-Int.* 2023, 120 (125).

387 See below VI. 4. as well as Krämer, J., Improving The Economic Effectiveness of the B2B and B2C Data Sharing Obligations in the Proposed Data Act, CERRE, 2022, pp. 15, 21. Cf. also Specht-Riemenschneider, L., *MMR* 2022, 809 (823); Max Planck Institute for Innovation and Competition, Position Statement, 2022, pp. 27 et seq. n. 69 et seq.

388 For an in-depth analysis of the ramifications of the Data Act for precision farming and agricultural data, cf. Atik, C., 'Data Act: Legal Implications for the Digital Agriculture Sector', 2022 (SSRN pre-print).

389 Krämer, J., Improving The Economic Effectiveness of the B2B and B2C Data Sharing Obligations in the Proposed Data Act, CERRE, 2022, pp. 25 et seq.

390 For agriculture, e.g., Atik, C., 'Data Act: Legal Implications for the Digital Agriculture Sector', 2022 (SSRN pre-print), p. 16.

391 Kerber, W., *GRUR-Int.* 2023, 120 (130 n. 80).

Significant Overlaps Between the Regulatory Architectures of User and Third-Party Access

With respect to the parameters of access, Art. 5(1) largely follows the design of Art. 4(1)[392] ("without undue delay, of the same quality as is available to the data holder, easily, securely, free of charge to the user, in a comprehensive, structured, commonly used and machine-readable format and, where relevant and technically feasible, continuously and in real-time") – albeit with two notable differences. First, by referencing Art. 9 in its second sentence, Art. 5(1) highlights that (enterprise) third parties – unlike users – have to remunerate the data holder in exchange for access.[393] Second, the requirement of access "without undue delay" must be understood as applying if negotiations over the FRAND conditions of access have concluded – the possible failure of which is foreseen by Art. 5(8).[394] In this case, rec. 42 maintains that "the right to share data with third parties is enforceable in national courts or tribunals", meaning that the lack of an agreement can be overcome.[395]

The process of verifying the relevant user whose readily available data is being requested for sharing is identical between Art. 4(5) and Art. 5(4). Probably by mistake, the low threshold for a valid request ("simple request through electronic means, where technically feasible") has not been incorporated from Art. 4(1).

Eligible Third Parties / Data Recipients (Art. 2(14))

In light of the manifold similarities, Art. 5 mainly diverges from Art. 4 when it comes to the beneficiary of the right. According to rec. 33, eligible third parties encompass, *inter alia,* "an enterprise, a research organisation or a not-for-profit organisation." The third party does not have to be established in the European Union.[396] Natural persons might also qualify as third parties, provided that they are "acting for purposes which are related to [their] trade, business, craft or profession". Consumers (cf. Art. 2(23)) therefore should not fall within this definition.

392 Cf. above V. 2; other complementary provisions are found in Art. 6(2)(e) and Art. 6(2)(f).

393 Heinzke, P., / Herbers, B. / Kraus, M., *BB* 2024, 649 (655).

394 Paal, B. / Fenik, M., *ZfDR* 2023, 249 (257).

395 Antoine, L., *CR* 2024, 1 (7).

396 Antoine, L., *CR* 2024, 1 (7).

Third parties, in turn, form part of the broader notion of data recipients, which is used throughout Chapter III (Art. 8-12) of the Act. The statutory definition in Art. 2(14) reads:

> "data recipient means natural or legal person, acting for purposes which are related to that person's trade, business, craft or profession, other than the user of a connected product or related service, to whom the data holder makes data available, *including a third party following a request by the user to the data holder* or in accordance with a legal obligation under Union law or national legislation adopted in accordance with Union law" (emphasis added)

By focusing on commercial characteristics ("trade, business, craft, or profession"), it appears that the definition has primarily been devised with enterprises (cf. Art. 2(24)) in mind as third-party recipients. Nonetheless, Art. 9(4) demonstrates that not-for-profit research organisations are liable to give a (reduced) compensation to the data holder.[397]

In Particular: Gatekeepers (Art. 5(3))

Bearing one of goals of the Data Act in mind, breaking up data silos, the often criticised[398] Art. 5(3) stipulates that designated gatekeepers according to Art. 3 DMA are *not* eligible third parties. Apparently, this prohibition stands even where the data holder has been designated as a gatekeeper themselves.[399] Art. 6(2)(d) further reinforces the rule by outlawing onwards sharing by the third party to a gatekeeper.

To avoid user activation to the benefit of gatekeepers, they are not allowed to

- "solicit or commercially incentivise a user in any manner, including by providing monetary or any other compensation, to make data available

397 Cf. below VI. 4.

398 IMCO, PE736.701, pp. 27 et seq. proposed to delete Art. 5(3) entirely; *ex multis,* Krämer, J., Improving The Economic Effectiveness of the B2B and B2C Data Sharing Obligations in the Proposed Data Act, CERRE, 2022, pp. 25 et seq.; Martens, B., 'Pro- and anti-competitive provisions in the proposed European Union Data Act', 2022, pp. 14 et seq.; with a positive view on Art. 5(3): Max Planck Institute for Innovation and Competition, Position Statement, 2022, p. 34 n. 91.

399 Voicing doubts over this ambiguity: Martens, B., 'Pro- and anti-competitive provisions in the proposed European Union Data Act', 2022, p. 15.

to one of its services that the user has obtained pursuant to a request under Article 4(1)" (Art. 5(3)(a))
- "solicit or commercially incentivise a user to request the data holder to make data available to one of its services pursuant to paragraph 1 of this Article" (Art. 5(3)(b))
- "receive data from a user that the user has obtained pursuant to a request under Article 4(1)" (Art. 5(3)(c))[400]

Rec. 40 points to the legislator's motivation for excluding gatekeepers from the data access regime established by the Act:

> "Start-ups, small enterprises, enterprises that qualify as a medium-sized enterprises [...] and enterprises from traditional sectors with less-developed digital capabilities struggle to obtain access to relevant data. This Regulation aims to facilitate access to data for those entities, while ensuring that the corresponding obligations are as proportionate as possible to avoid overreach. At the same time, a small number of very large enterprises have emerged with considerable economic power in the digital economy through the accumulation and aggregation of vast volumes of data and the technological infrastructure for monetising them. Those very large enterprises include undertakings that provide core platform services controlling whole platform ecosystems in the digital economy and which existing or new market operators are unable to challenge or contest."

Importantly, rec. 40 goes on to clarify that gatekeepers still have the option (within the limits of purpose / contract specificity set by Art. 4(14)) to obtain data by contractual arrangements with data holders:

> "As voluntary agreements between gatekeepers and data holders remain unaffected, the limitation on granting access to gatekeepers would not exclude them from the market or prevent them from offering their services."

In Particular: Data Intermediaries

Pursuant to Art. 5(1), a request to share data with a third party does not need to be made by the user, but can also be submitted by a party acting on the behalf of the user. Rec. 30 explain that this includes data intermediation

400 On Art. 5(3)(c) and its misplaced position in the statutory text, cf. already sub V.3.

services within the meaning of Art. 2(11) DGA (cf. Art. 2(10)). Rec. 33 elaborates on the catalysing role of data intermediaries:

> "Business-to-business data intermediaries and personal information management systems (PIMS) [pursuant to Art. 10(a) and (b) DGA] may support users or third parties in establishing commercial relations with an undetermined number of potential counterparties for any lawful purpose falling within the scope of this Regulation. They could play an instrumental role in aggregating access to data so that big data analyses or machine learning can be facilitated, provided that users remain in full control of whether to provide their data to such aggregation and the commercial terms under which their data are to be used."

Against this backdrop, it is conceivable that data intermediaries could help groups of users commercialise readily available data by aggregating and forwarding them to (other) third parties in return for payment of an appropriate fee.[401] Such a form of monetisation is more likely to succeed if the user does not merely authorise the data intermediary to make the sharing request on their behalf, but if they cede their access and sharing rights (with regard to non-personal data).[402]

Exemption for the Testing of Products not yet Placed on the Market (Art. 5(2))

Art. 5(2) stipulates that the right to third-party access does not apply where "readily available data in the context of the testing of new connected products, substances or processes that are not yet placed on the market unless their use by a third party is contractually permitted." According to Art. 2(22), the relevant "placing on the market" relates to the first time the connected product has been made available on the Union market.

The provision somewhat resembles Art. 31(2), which exempts non-production versions of data processing services from falling under the scope of the switching-related rights and obligations.

---

401 Richter, H., *GRUR-Int.* 2023, 458 (469) (discussing the original draft of Art. 6(2)(c)).

402 On that prospect, cf. Wiebe, A., *GRUR* 2023, 1569 (1572); cf. also Hennemann, M. / Steinrötter, B., *NJW* 2024, 1 (6).

Data Protection Law (Art. 5(7)-(8), Art. 5(13))

The interface of the right to third-party access with data protection law is covered by Art. 5(7), (8) and (13).

Art. 5(7) is drafted in parallel to Art. 4(12).[403] Consequently, the sharing of personal data is contingent upon a valid legal basis for processing in line with Art. 6 GDPR (and, if applicable, Art. 9 GDPR or Art. 5(3) of the ePrivacy Directive, cf. rec. 36).

Art. 5(8) confirms that the Act does not touch the exercise of rights of the data subject under the GDPR, especially the right to have one's personal data ported to another controller pursuant to Art. 20(2) GDPR.[404] The provision thereby expands on the juxtaposition of Art. 20 GDPR and the data access regime offered by the Act that is laid down in Art. 1(5).

Art. 5(13) (additionally) confirms that the right according to Art. 5(1) "shall not adversely affect data protection rights of others pursuant to the applicable Union and national law on the protection of personal data". Some commentators had favoured a broader exception modelled after Art. 15(4) GDPR and Art. 20(4) GDPR, namely that rights and freedoms (i.e., beyond a data protection context) should not be adversely affected.[405]

Trade Secrets (Art. 5(9)-(11))

The data holder can raise the protection of trade secrets as a defence in almost the same way as under Art. 4(6)-(8).[406] However, Art. 5(9) differs in that it limits disclosure of applicable data sets "to the extent that such disclosure is strictly necessary to fulfil the purpose agreed between the user and the third party."

This rule has been widely criticised for creating legal uncertainty.[407] It is unclear from the outset how and why the data holder should be aware of the purpose laid down in a contract that they are not part of. One might read into the norm that the user has the obligation to disclose the purpose to the data holder. In addition, Art. 5(10) rightly seems to assume that there

403 See above V.3.
404 Cf. above V.3. and rec. 35 for a legislative account reflecting on the exact scope of Art. 20 GDPR.
405 E.g. Specht-Riemenschneider, L., *MMR-Beil.* 2022, 809 (819).
406 Cf. above V.3.
407 E.g. Schweitzer, H. / Metzger, A., *ZEuP* 2023, 42 (76).

will always be – in line with Art. 8 – a contractual agreement (including a non-disclosure agreement) between data holder and data recipient and therefore a point of contact to clarify the purpose. In order not to thwart the limitation under Art. 5(9) to the detriment of data holders, the purpose in the agreement between users and third parties must be specific to a sufficient degree.[408] Because the data holder is not privy to this agreement as the "other contracting party", unfair terms control pursuant to Art. 13(5)(b) will be effective if the purpose has been disclosed to or is incorporated in the NDA with the data holder.[409]

Implicit (Second) Data License Agreement

The exercise of the right to third-party access goes along with a contractual agreement (a second data license agreement between the user and the third party regarding the use of the data according to Art. 6(1)[410])) – and which might be accompanied by an NDA pursuant to Art. 5(9).

Art. 5 does not clearly state how access (and / or the data license agreement) can be terminated. Rec. 38, however, spells out that "[i]t should be as easy for the user to refuse or discontinue access by the third party to the data as it is for the user to authorise access."

2. Obligations of Third Parties (Art. 6)

Art. 6 spells out the obligations of data recipients which receive data on the basis of Art. 5(1). These are partly linked to an agreement between the user and the data recipient (Art. 6(1) implicitly highlights the fact (or better: the necessity) of an agreement between user and data recipient); partly, the obligations are to be committed independently of an / the agreement. Many aspects of Art. 6 are related to the user's right of access under Art. 4, therefore some conflicts can be considered (and resolved) in parallel.[411]

---

408 Pauly, D.A. / Wichert, F. / Baumann, J., *MMR* 2024, 211 (214).

409 Further, including on the interplay with Sec. 307 German Civil Code, cf. Graf von Westphalen, F., *BB* 2024, 515 (520).

410 Heinzke, P., / Herbers, B. / Kraus, M., *BB* 2024, 649 (650).

411 Schmidt-Kessel, M., *MMR-Beil. 2024*, 75 (80 et seq.).

Non-Exclusivity

With or without an agreement, the data recipient shall not – according to Art. 6(2)(h) – "prevent the user that is a consumer (...) from making the data it receives available to other parties". Doubts from an Economics perspective have been brought forward whether and to what extent the non-exclusivity does set negative incentives for data brokers.[412] The wording "that is a consumer", which was added only in the trilogue, is an expression of the intended protection of consumers, who are to be guarded in their decisions to switch between services and products.[413]

Limited Use / Non-Compete / Security

According to Art. 6(1), a third party may only use the data made available (1) for the purposes and under the conditions agreed with the user and (2) subject to Union and national law on the protection of personal data including the rights of the data subject (Art. 12 et seq. GDPR) insofar as personal data are concerned.[414] The wording does not clearly state whether the purpose must be agreed between the user and the data holder or between the user and the third party. However, it must be based on the agreement between the user and the third party, as otherwise it would be a contract to the disadvantage of third parties.[415]

Under Art. 6(2)(b), the data recipient may not "use the data it receives for the profiling, unless it is necessary to provide the service requested by the user".[416] Rec. 39 seems to be even stricter when referring to "processing activities [that] are strictly necessary to provide the service requested by the user, including in the context of automated decision-making".[417]

---

412 Krämer, J., Improving The Economic Effectiveness of the B2B and B2C Data Sharing Obligations in the Proposed Data Act, CERRE, 2022, p. 21.

413 Cf. rec. 38 and 40.

414 Rec. 37 is even narrower: "In order to prevent the exploitation of users, third parties to whom data has been made available at the request of the user should process those data only for the purposes agreed with the user and share them with another third party only with the agreement of the user to such data sharing."

415 Schmidt-Kessel, M., *MMR-Beil. 2024*, 75 (80).

416 The wording "(...) for the profiling of natural persons (...) [Art. 4(4) GDPR] (...)" provided for during the procedure did not come to be adopted in the final version.

417 Cf. also Council Presidency 2022/0047(COD) – 15035/22, p. 46 in this regard.

According to the highly debated[418] Art. 6(2)(e), the data recipient may not use the received data to develop a competing product or share the data with another third party for that purpose. In addition, third parties shall not use any product data to derive insights about the economic situation, assets and production methods of, or use by, the data holder. However, the third party is allowed to develop a non-competing new and innovative product or related service (rec. 39). This is one of the aforementioned aims of the Act, namely to drive innovation in the aftermarket.

Third parties are not permitted to use the data in a manner that has an adverse impact on the security of the connected product or related service (Art. 6(2)(f)). The provision, which was added in the final version, is not explained in detail in the recitals. What exactly "the security" of the product or service constitutes remains unclear, but is likely targeted at the security of the product or service itself.

In addition, Art. 6(2)(g) stipulates that a data recipient shall not disregard the specific measures agreed with a data holder or with the trade secrets holder pursuant to Art. 5(9).

Passing-On of Data

Art. 6 also regulates the passing-on of received data by third parties. This is not permitted in principle. However, it is possible if it has been contractually agreed with the user (Art. 6(2)(c)). This indicates that the user and the third party might also agree on a general passing-on to a third party, e.g., for a 'sale' of the data.[419] In addition, the third party must take all measures to protect trade secrets.

As outlined above, Art. 5(3) excludes the transfer of data to gatekeepers as third parties. As a consistent continuation, Art. 6(2)(d) prohibits the transfer of data by third parties to gatekeepers.

418 Cf. Krämer, J., Improving The Economic Effectiveness of the B2B and B2C Data Sharing Obligations in the Proposed Data Act, CERRE, 2022, pp. 13 et seq., 23 et seq.; Max Planck Institute for Innovation and Competition, Position Statement, 2022, p. 35 n. 94.

419 Max Planck Institute for Innovation and Competition, Position Statement, 2022, p. 7 n. 14. Cf. also Leistner, M. / Antoine, L., IPR and the use of open data and data sharing initiatives by public and private actors, 2022, p. 98.

Erasing Data

Above the aforementioned limitations is the general requirement for third parties to erase[420] the data received if it no longer fulfils the agreed purpose. This can also be waived by agreement with the user.[421] Rec. 39 clarifies that this duty "complements the right to erasure of the data subject pursuant to [Art. 17 GDPR]".

Impairing Decision-making

Art. 6(2)(a) provides for particularly far-reaching protection of the user's autonomy. According to this provision, the exercise of the user's choices or rights under Art. 5 and 6 must not be made excessively difficult. In this regard, users must not be offered choices in a non-neutral manner or be deceived, coerced or manipulated. When exactly this is the case will have to be determined by jurisdiction in each individual case. The Data Act uses the term 'dark patterns' in this context, which are defined as design techniques that pressure or deceive consumers into making decisions that have negative consequences for them (rec. 38). However, common and legitimate business practices should not be regarded as dark patterns. The distinction will also have to be made on a case-by-case basis.

3. Conditions between Data Holder and Data Recipient

Complementing the access rights and the aforementioned material restrictions, Chapter III sets out requirements concerning the contractual content of data sharing agreements. The provisions of the chapter only apply in business-to-business constellations (Art. 12(1)). The data sharing must be based on FRAND principles (Art. 8) and compensations should be agreed fairly and transparently (Art. 9). Chapter III also sets out a (more or less concrete) system for alternative dispute resolution (Art. 10) and deals with secure data transmission through technical standards (Art. 11).

420 Until shortly before finalisation, the provision spoke of "to *delete*".
421 This again demonstrates the strong user-centricity of the Data Act.

FRAND-System

In case of a data access in business-to-business-relations under Art. 5 or under other Union law or national legislation adopted in accordance with Union law, Art. 8(1) sets out the principle of a **f**air, **r**easonable **and** **n**on-**d**iscriminatory access (FRAND). The Data Act hereby is seeking to establish a system of fair data sharing.[422] Rec. 42 describes the FRAND-system as "general access rules", which do not apply to obligations regarding data access under the GDPR. Since the FRAND rules represent a link between mandatory access rights and the contractual arrangement, they are an obligation of the data holder.[423] FRAND terms are an already known element in competition law and IP law – and can also be found in Art. 6(11) Digital Markets Act.[424] Despite the restrictive rules, the Data Act recognises the parties' freedom of contract (rec. 43).

Scope of Application

Art. 8 applies to data sharing obligations under Art. 5 or under other applicable Union law or national legislation adopted in accordance with Union law. Further, the indeterminacy of the scope of Chapter III has been criticised, since the "provision of data to a data recipient" can fall under different legal acts of the EU, in particular the DMA.[425] It was therefore proposed to clarify that Chapter III applies to obligations to make data available *only* where a reference to the Data Act is to be found.[426] This does not, however, fulfil the purpose of the Data Act as a horizontal regulation. The opening of the FRAND system is particularly relevant for further sector-specific data provision obligations following the Data Act.[427]

In temporal regard, Art. 50(4) clarifies that Chapter III (and hence also Art. 8) only applies to provision obligations that arise after the date of ap-

422 Cf. rec. 5 and 42.
423 Wiebe, A., *GRUR* 2023, 1569 (1572 et seq.).
424 Cf. Ducuing, C. / Margoni, T. / Schirru, L. (ed.), *CiTiP Working Paper* 2022, 32.
425 Ducuing, C. / Margoni, T. / Schirru, L. (ed.), *CiTiP Working Paper* 2022, 44 et seq.
426 Ducuing, C. / Margoni, T. / Schirru, L. (ed.), *CiTiP Working Paper* 2022, 45; cf. also for further proposals Schweitzer, H. / Metzger, A. / Blind, K. / Richter, H. / Niebel, C. / Gutmann, F., The legal framework for access to data in Germany and in the EU, BMWK, 2022, pp. 224 et seq.
427 Louven, S., *MMR-Beil.* 2024, 82 (83).

plication of the Data Act the 12 September 2025. Data provision obligations that arise before this date are therefore not covered.

Relationship to Art. 13

It is not entirely clear whether the provisions of Art. 8 et seq. alone or also Art. 13 apply in case of data transfer to recipients. Partially, it was considered that Art. 8 et seq. had priority.[428] However, the parallel applicability of both provisions results from the wording of Art. 8(1) and (2).[429] According to the latter provision, a contractual term of an agreement "shall not be binding if it constitutes an unfair contractual term within the meaning of Article 13 (...)".[430]

FRAND Conditions

Art. 8(1) does not establish a contractual obligation to provide data, but presumes it.[431] The rather vague general FRAND conditions from Art. 8(1) initially offer the advantage of flexibility. Yet, it is argued that FRAND terms might not be a sensible solution in many cases covered by the Act.[432] It might prove to be difficult for law enforcers and courts to create general principles in order assess FRAND terms[433], starting by stating a definition for the term 'fair', which is not provided by the proposal.[434] Since FRAND conditions are familiar from European competition and intellectual property law, the principles developed there (by the ECJ) could be transferable to the Data Act. In particular, formal negotiation obligations and obligations to co-operate must be observed, the compliance of which must be examined on a case-by-case basis.[435] FRAND therefore relates more to pro-

428 In this sense Metzger, A. / Schweitzer, H., *ZEuP* 2023, 42 (67).
429 Schwamberger, S., *MMR-Beil.* 2024, 96 (97); cf. also Wiebe, A., *GRUR* 2023, 1569 (1573).
430 See more on this under VII.
431 Louven, S., *MMR-Beil.* 2024, 82 (83).
432 Ducuing, C. / Margoni, T. / Schirru, L. (ed.), *CiTiP Working Paper* 2022, 35.
433 Max Planck Institute for Innovation and Competition, Position Statement, 2022, pp. 36 et seq. n. 99; Metzger, A. / Schweitzer, H., *ZEuP* 2023, 42 (67 et seq.).
434 Vbw, Data Act – Anpassungsbedarf aus Sicht der Bayerischen Wirtschaft, 2022, p. 13.
435 Cf. in detail Louven, S., *MMR-Beil.* 2024, 82 (84).

cedural positions than to material content.[436] *One* basic principle will not be able to cover all constellations. As a result, it will come down to a relative FRAND definition[437], which will also have to be filled in by jurisdiction on a case-specific basis.

Terms to the Detriment of the User

Art. 8(2) stipulates, in addition to the reference to Art. 13, that a contractual term of an agreement "shall not be binding if (...) to the detriment of the user, it excludes the application of, derogates from or varies the effect of the user's rights under Chapter II". The wording of the provision is almost identical to Art. 7(2). Although the provision does not explicitly stipulate it, it only refers to the provision of data in accordance with Art. 5 or a provision of data in accordance with another Union provision, but not to the provision of data on a voluntary basis.[438] This follows from its systematic position under Art. 8(1), which only refers to these forms of data provision.

Prohibition of Discrimination

Art. 8(3), which is modelled on Art. 102 TFEU[439], states that a data holder is not allowed to discriminate "between comparable categories of data recipients, including partner enterprises or linked enterprises..." (this formulation raises ambiguities[440]). When a data recipient asserts a term to be discriminatory, the data holder shall without undue delay[441] provide the data recipient, upon its reasoned request, with information showing

436 Wiebe, A., *GRUR* 2023, 1569 (1572 et seq.).
437 Louven, S., *MMR-Beil.* 2024, 82 (84).
438 Specht-Riemenschneider, L., *MMR-Beil.* 2022, 809 (820).
439 Picht, P.G., Caught in the Acts – Framing Mandatory Data Access Transactions under the Data Act, further EU Digital Regulation Acts, and Competition Law, 2022, 21.
440 Weizenbaum Institute for the Networked Society, Position paper regarding Data Act, 2022, p. 15.
441 The temporal component was included during the procedure, cf. Council Presidency 2022/0047(COD) – 13342/22, p. 45; ITRE PE732.704, p. 41. It remains questionable whether the passage achieves the intended purpose, because it does not contain any further information on what specific information must be shared.

that there has been no discrimination (Art. 8(3)). This burden of proof rule results from the consideration that the data recipient generally has no insight into the structures of the data holder and therefore does not know whether conditions are discriminatory.[442] In contrast to Art. 9(7), this also means that the data recipient must proactively point out the possibility of discrimination.[443] The use of different conditions for different data recipients may be justified if there are objective reasons (rec. 45).

It was objected that the formulation of the FRAND concept as a unilateral obligation (of the data holder) could gain the risk of a superior standing of the data recipient.[444] Therefore, in the legislative process it was proposed to reformulate the rule as mutual obligation of both parties, so private law courts and the dispute settlement bodies of Art. 10 could enforce the FRAND concept also against the data recipient where it is needed.[445] However, the proposal was finally not considered.

Provision Only at the User's Request

According to Art. 8(4)[446], a data holder shall not make data available to a data recipient, including on an exclusive basis, unless otherwise requested by the user under Chapter II. The word "including" was not initially intended and was only added in the final version. As a result, the purpose of the provision is not entirely clear.[447] While Art. 8(1) used to be a pure prohibition of exclusive access to data (which should strengthen the broad provision of data intended by the Data Act)[448], it now provides for a general ban unless permission is granted. This means that any provision of data without a user request is unlawful.

442 Cf. rec. 45.
443 Louven, S., *MMR-Beil.* 2024, 82 (84).
444 Max Planck Institute for Innovation and Competition, Position Statement, 2022, p. 39 n. 103.
445 Max Planck Institute for Innovation and Competition, Position Statement, 2022, p. 39 n. 103.
446 ITRE PE738.548, p. 67 sought to delete the entire paragraph.
447 Cf. in detail Louven, S., *MMR-Beil.* 2024, 82 (84 et seq.).
448 Hennemann, M. / Steinrötter, B., *NJW* 2022, 1481 (1484); Specht-Riemenschneider, L., *MMR-Beil.* 2022, 809 (822).

More Information than Necessary

According to Art. 8(5), data holders and data recipients shall not be required to provide more information than necessary in order to be compliant with the terms agreed or their obligations under the Data Act or other applicable Union law or national legislation adopted in accordance with Union law. The exact information that may be requested is not specified and depends on the individual case. Furthermore, it remains unclear whether the provision only addresses the contractual parties or also law enforcement or courts.[449]

Respect of Trade Secrets

The highly debated Art. 8(6) states that unless otherwise provided by Union law, including Art. 4(6) and 5(9)[450] or by national legislation adopted in accordance with Union law, an obligation to make data available to a data recipient shall not oblige the disclosure of trade secrets (within the meaning of Directive (EU) 2016/943).[451]

In the legislative process it has been critically emphasised that Art. 8(6) handles trade secrets, which should be left to the legal systems of the member states.[452] Therefore, it was argued to delete Art. 8(6) completely (which, however, was not successful).[453]

In principle, it must be examined carefully whether data contain a trade secret.[454] However, it has been criticised that Art. 8(6) could "invite" data holders not to share data arguing that otherwise trade secrets would be

449 Max Planck Institute for Innovation and Competition, Position Statement, 2022, p. 39 n. 105.

450 The Council Presidency and the Committee on Industry, Technology and Energy (ITRE) have proposed the harmonisation of Art. 4(3) and Art. 5(8) with Art. 8(6) in order to clarify that there is no obligation to share trade secrets with a data recipient except in the cases expressly provided by law, cf. Council Presidency 2022/0047(COD) – 13342/22, p. 45; ITRE PE732.704, p. 41.

451 Directive (EU) 2016/943 of the European Parliament and of the Council on the protection of undisclosed know-how and business information (trade secrets) against their unlawful acquisition, use and disclosure.

452 Max Planck Institute for Innovation and Competition, Position Statement, 2022, p. 102 n. 284.

453 Max Planck Institute for Innovation and Competition, Position Statement, 2022, p. 39 n. 106.

454 For the German GeschGehG cf. Heinzke, P., *BB* 2023, 201 (205 et seq.).

revealed.[455] In that case, the Art. 5 et seq. are in danger to miss their objectives as data holders could try to blur data extensively. As a minimum, it can be expected that the general conditions for the existence of a trade secret must be stated or explained.

Specht-Riemenschneider has criticised the general priority of trade secrets in Art. 8(6) and Art. 5(9). The protection of trade secrets could also be ensured by blacking out or pseudonymising sensitive data, without completely refraining the sharing of non-personal data.

4. Compensation

The data economy is rarely characterised by altruistic motives, but (like other markets) by profit interests. The Data Act pushes data flows between data holder and data recipient under strict conditions by the Art. 5 and 6. The closely related question of whether data holders can demand compensation for this obligation is answered in Art. 9. The provision presupposes the possibility of agreeing compensation and makes specifications for their structure.[456] The Data Act does not stipulate that this must be a monetary compensation.[457] Other forms of remuneration are therefore also possible.

To avoid compensation, the Data Act does not hinder the user to request the data free of charge according to Art. 4(1) by himself – and then forward the data on to third parties.[458] This 'easy way out' has been widely criticised.[459] The way is, however, only 'easy' if the user takes the technical burden – and has the technical capabilities – to access, store, and forward the respective data. Especially in the consumer segment, this will regularly not be the case.

455 Max Planck Institute for Innovation and Competition, Position Statement, 2022, p. 39 n. 106; Krämer, J., Improving The Economic Effectiveness of the B2B and B2C Data Sharing Obligations in the Proposed Data Act, CERRE, 2022, p. 21.

456 Cf. also rec. 46.

457 Louven, S., *MMR-Beil.* 2024, 82 (85).

458 Bomhard, D. / Merkle, M., *RDi* 2022, 168 (171).

459 Krämer, J., Improving The Economic Effectiveness of the B2B and B2C Data Sharing Obligations in the Proposed Data Act, CERRE, 2022, pp. 16 et seq.; Max Planck Institute for Innovation and Competition, Position Statement, 2022, p. 29 n. 72.

General Provisions

Art. 9(1) states that any "compensation agreed upon between a data holder and a data recipient for making data available in business-to-business relations shall be non-discriminatory and reasonable and may include a margin".

The key terms are not further defined. Initially, it is not clear what exactly 'reasonable' means. The provision does not state calculation methods or examples. This was the subject of lively debates during the legislative process.[460] From a practical and an Economics perspective it has been argued that it will be difficult to determine a respective compensation – and that corresponding lengthy negotiations and / or court proceedings are highly likely.[461] To counterbalance respective challenges, a rebuttable presumption of a zero-access price was proposed in the literature.[462]

Notably, Art. 9 does not define an upper or lower limit for compensation, meaning that it is possible for compensation to be as high as possible, but also close to zero.[463] Although Art. 9(2) contains general criteria that must be taken into account with regard to compensation (see below), it will primarily be the dispute settlement bodies under Art. 10 and courts that will be concerned with respective questions and will draw up guidelines.[464] To determine reasonableness, comparable market prices or market-orientated approaches from market practice could, however, serve as a basis.[465] In this context, it is important to emphasise the prohibition of overcompensation. This results from the (admittedly vaguely formulated) parameters of Art. 9. The compensation can be demanded therefore *only* for the provision.[466]

---

460 Cf. ITRE PE739.548, pp. 69 et seq.; LIBE PE737.389, p. 46; ITRE PE738.548, pp. 69 et seq.; ITRE PE738.548, p. 70; ITRE PE738.548, p. 72.

461 Krämer, J., Improving The Economic Effectiveness of the B2B and B2C Data Sharing Obligations in the Proposed Data Act, CERRE, 2022, pp. 15 et seq.

462 See Krämer, J., Improving The Economic Effectiveness of the B2B and B2C Data Sharing Obligations in the Proposed Data Act, CERRE, 2022, p. 24. Cf. also Max Planck Institute for Innovation and Competition, Position Statement, 2022, p. 29 n. 72.

463 Louven, S., *MMR-Beil.* 2024, 82 (85).

464 Max Planck Institute for Innovation and Competition, Position Statement, 2022, p. 37 n. 101.

465 Cf. in detail Louven, S., *MMR-Beil.* 2024, 82 (85 et seq.).

466 Cf. in detail Louven, S., *MMR-Beil.* 2024, 82 (86).

Furthermore, it is unclear what 'non-discriminatory' means in the context of Art. 9. It is worth considering whether the criteria from Art. 8 can be transferred.[467]

Finally, the Act makes a crucial distinction between the costs of providing data and a margin. The data holder may therefore make a profit from the provision of data.[468] Such profit is first of all limited by the criteria 'reasonable' and, second, can be limited or completely excluded by Union regulations, Art. 9(6).[469]

Compensation Factors

Art. 9(2) specifies concrete details on how the compensation can be determined. Firstly, the "costs incurred in making the data available, including, in particular, the costs necessary for the formatting of data, dissemination via electronic means and storage" should be considered (Art. 9(2)(a)).[470] Furthermore, investments in the collection and production of data should be taken into account and the fact whether other parties contributed to obtaining, generating or collecting the data in question (Art. 9(2)(b)). A compensation can also depend on the volume, format and nature of the data (Art. 9(3)). According to the wording, the enumeration is neither obligatory nor exhaustive. It is therefore imaginable that other costs and circumstances on the part of the data holder may also have an impact on the compensation.[471]

Micro, Small, And Medium-Sized Enterprises

The Data Act recognises an increased need for the protection of SME.[472] Therefore, Art. 9(4) states that they shall not be charged a margin or other compensation in excess of the directly related costs of providing the data as described in Art. 9(2)(a). This also applies to non-profit organisations.

467 In favour of this Louven, S., *MMR-Beil.* 2024, 82 (85).
468 Louven, S., *MMR-Beil.* 2024, 82 (85).
469 See below for the requirements.
470 This wording is partly based on the amendment proposed by the Council Presidency, cf. Council Presidency 2022/0047(COD) – 13342/22, p. 45.
471 Cf. Louven, S., *MMR-Beil.* 2024, 82 (85).
472 Cf. rec. 49.

Specht-Riemenschneider concludes from this that the compensations should not be understood as payment for the concrete data, but as an actual "equalisation" for the costs incurred and investment required for making the data available.[473]

The limitation set by Art. 9(4) can put large companies at a massive disadvantage and is consequently criticised on this ground.[474] On the other hand, it was argued that the cost-based approach was more in line with the objectives of the Data Act and that the limitation should be applied to all types of data recipients.[475]

Art. 9 does not provide for any special rules for cases in which SMEs themselves are data holders. This has been criticised because, if SMEs share data with each other, no profit can be made and the growth of the company may suffer as a result.[476]

Due to the increased relevance of data intermediaries in the supply of data, it was partially proposed (but not adopted) to put data intermediaries with regard to compensations on the same level as SME.[477] This would have been in line with the DGA's aim to promote data intermediaries (cf. rec. 27 DGA).

Guidelines on the Costs

The Commission shall adopt guidelines on the calculation of reasonable compensation (Art. 9(5)). In doing so, it shall recognise the advice of the EDIB (cf. Art. 42).

It is not fully clear to which compensations these guidelines relate. The open wording suggests that the guidelines refer to all compensation within the meaning of Art. 9, whereas the systematic position of the paragraph suggests that they refer only to Art. 9(4), i.e. to the compensation of SMEs and non-profit research organisations.

---

473 Specht-Riemenschneider, L., *MMR-Beil.* 2022, 809 (822).

474 BDI Stellungnahme zum Legislativvorschlag des EU-Data Act, 2022, p. 16.

475 ITRE PE739.548, p. 74 therefore wanted to change the wording to „Any reasonable compensation(…)".

476 Vbw, Data Act, Anpassungsbedarf aus Sicht der Bayerischen Wirtschaft, 2022, p. 18; Bitkom, 'Bitkom Position Paper EU Data Act Proposal' (19 April 2022), 2022, p. 6.

477 MyData Global response of the Data Act, 2022, p. 5.

Exclusion of Compensation

Art. 9(6) allows Union law or national legislation adopted in accordance with Union law to exclude compensation for making data available or providing for lower compensation. For these cases, rec. 50 sets up higher requirements for compensations, namely the need to ensure consumer participation and competition or to promote innovation in certain markets.[478] Thus, rec. 50 underlines that compensation should generally be negotiated by the parties themselves. Their regulation shall be the exception.

Information

To ensure the compliance of compensation terms with the paras. 1 to 4, Art. 9(7) stipulates an obligation for the data holder to provide the data recipient with information containing the calculation of the compensation in a sufficiently detailed form.[479] Rec. 51 underlines the principle of transparency respectively.

Calculation

In the Commission's proposal, neither the text of the regulation nor the recitals provided concrete calculation criteria, which was heavily criticised.[480] Although there are quite concrete factors for the calculation, it might remain difficult to 'find' a respective compensation in dispute settlement scenarios or before courts.[481] A major hurdle in the calculation of the consideration is especially the "convertibility" of the data. The costs of

478 The ITRE Draft Report proposed to delete Art. 9(6) in its entirety to ensure a coherent structure of the Data Act as a horizontal framework; cf. ITRE PE732.704, pp. 42 et seq.

479 While the Commission's draft spoke of the data recipient's possibility "to verify that the requirements of para. 1 and, where applicable, para. 2 are met" the Council Presidency proposed to use a more neutral wording that states the data recipient's possibility to "assess whether the requirements of..." cf. Council Presidency 2022/0047(COD) – 15035/22, p. 49.

480 Cf. e.g. Gerpott, T., *CR* 2022, 271 (279) or Leistner, M. / Antoine, L., IPR and the use of open data and data sharing initiatives by public and private actors, 2022, p. 104.

481 Leistner, M. / Antoine, L., IPR and the use of open data and data sharing initiatives by public and private actors, 2022, p. 104.

collecting and transmitting the data are typically relatively low, while the collected data later have a high commercial value.[482] In this regard, it is considered whether a complete waiver or a flat-rate reimbursement in the amount of a few Euros would be more expedient than concrete calculation in individual cases, particularly in order to avoid the disruptive potential of concrete cost calculation.[483]

5. Dispute Settlement

In case of disagreements regarding the sharing of data in accordance with Art. 4 et seq. or the FRAND conditions in Art. 8 or with regard to compensations, the parties under the Data Act are at free rein to consult (state) courts for dispute resolution.[484] However, these classic contradictory processes could be connected with practical difficulties in enforcement and intensive (and costly) measures, which are not always intended. The Data Act therefore introduces the idea of independent dispute settlement bodies to which the Act's actors can turn. This alternative (and therefore simpler) way to resolve disputes should benefit data holders and data recipients and thereby strengthen trust in data sharing (rec. 52). The dispute settlement bodies should offer simple, fast and low-cost ways to do this. There is neither an obligation of the member states to establish dispute settlement bodies (rec. 52) nor an obligation of the authorised parties to use them (rec. 53). This dispute settlement system is regulated in Art. 10 and will be discussed in the following.[485]

From the start of the legislative process, Art. 10 has contained a number of gaps and ambiguities, particularly with regard to the practical implementation of the procedures.[486] Even though details have changed in the course of the legislative process (particularly with regard to the personal scope of application), many of the identified weaknesses remained, such as inadequate rules on international jurisdiction, a lack of procedural rules or harmonisation requirements.

---

482 Podszun, R., Der EU Data Act und der Zugang zu Sekundärmärkten am Beispiel des Handwerks, 2022, p. 52.

483 Podszun, R., Der EU Data Act und der Zugang zu Sekundärmärkten am Beispiel des Handwerks, 2022, pp. 54 et seq.

484 Cf. Art. 4(3), 4(9) or 5(12).

485 For a deep insight cf. Weiß, R., *MMR-Beil.* 2024, 101.

486 Cf. especially Niedermaier, T. / Picht, P., FRAND ADR under the Data Act and the SEP Regulation, 2022.

Personal Scope

Art. 10(1) states that "[u]sers, data holders and data recipients shall have access to a dispute settlement body (...) to settle disputes pursuant to [Art.] 4(3) and (9) and [Art.] 5(12) as well as disputes relating to the fair, reasonable and non-discriminatory terms and conditions for, and transparent manner of, making data available in accordance with this Chapter and Chapter IV".[487]

An access to dispute resolution bodies for the user was added in the final version. However, the idea that the interests of the user require an equal level of protection is not new. At an earlier stage of the legislation, it was proposed that the data recipient (who were already authorised in the Commission version) should act as the user's legal representative.[488] Art. 4(3) and (9) were added as a consequence of the inclusion of the user. Art. 4(3) emphasises unrestricted access to courts in case of a dispute with the data holder about an agreement under Art. 4(2). In addition, the user may bring the complaint to the competent authority in accordance with Art. 37 (Art. 4(3)(a)). Furthermore, there is the aforementioned possibility of dispute resolution in accordance with Art. 10(1). The user has the same rights if the data holder refuses access in accordance with Art. 4(7) and (8) (Art. 4(9)).

Art. 5(12) extends these possibilities to third parties if these seek to challenge a data holder's decision to refuse or to withhold or suspend data sharing pursuant to Art. 5(10) and (11).

Art. 10(4) further expands the group of persons entitled to settlement access to customers and providers of data processing services to settle disputes relating to breaches of the rights of customers and the obligations of providers of data processing services, in accordance with Art. 23 to 31.

---

487 In the Commission proposal, Art. 10 was limited to Art. 8 (FRAND-terms), which was criticised, cf. Gerpott, T., *CR* 2022, 271 (279); Max Planck Institute for Innovation and Competition, Position Statement, 2022, p. 40 n. 108; Cf. ITRE PE739.548, p. 79 with the propose to take in Art. 13 in the wording. Later on, Chapter IV (Art. 13) was also included, cf. Council Presidency 2022/0047(COD) – 15035/22, p. 49.

488 IMCO PE736.701, p. 29.

Material Scope

In substance, the dispute settlement body can decide on the existence of a claim for data provision, its conditions and compensation.[489] The 'if' and 'how' of data provision are therefore reviewable.[490] The settlement bodies can decide on FRAND terms and conditions as well as on the other provisions of Chapter II (compensation and technical protection measures). Moreover, the bodies serve to determine whether contractual terms are unfair within the meaning of Art. 13.

Fees

Knowing how high the costs of proceedings under Art. 10 are plays a major role in the question of whether to pursue alternative dispute resolution. Art. 10 therefore also addresses the fees for dispute settlement. According to Art. 10(2) dispute settlement bodies shall make the fees, or the mechanisms used to determine the fees, known to the parties concerned *before* those parties request a decision. This can be particularly important for counselling practice to be able to predict the risks and benefits of alternative dispute resolution.

The question of who has to bear which costs is of particular importance. This is regulated in Art. 10(3). If the dispute settlement body decides in favour of the user or of the data recipient, the data holder has to bear all the fees charged by the dispute settlement body. Further, he has to reimburse that user or that data recipient for any other reasonable expenses that it has incurred in relation to the dispute settlement. On the other hand, if the dispute settlement body decides in favour of the data holder, the user or the data recipient has *not* to reimburse any fees or other expenses that the data holder paid or is to pay in relation to the dispute settlement, unless the dispute settlement body finds that the user or the data recipient manifestly acted in bad faith. This rule underlines the guiding principle of the Data Act according to which users and data recipients are structurally weaker and therefore worth protecting (unless they are acting "in bad faith"). However, alternative dispute resolution is intentionally not made attractive

489 In the Commission's version, the dispute settlement body's review was limited to the "how" of provision.

490 Weiß, R., *MMR-Beil.* 2024, 101.

for the data holder. This raises the question of how often settlement bodies are actually called upon in practice.[491]

Certification

Dispute settlement bodies must be certified by the member state in which they are located (Art. 10(5)). The bodies are private, state-established bodies are not intended (in contrast to the Commission draft).[492] To be certified, the body must fulfil a number of requirements. The body has to demonstrate that it is impartial and independent, and it will issue its decisions in accordance with clear, non-discriminatory and fair rules of procedure (Art. 10(5)(a)). It further must have the necessary expertise, in particular in relation to fair, reasonable and non-discriminatory terms and conditions, including compensation, and on making data available in a transparent manner (Art. 10(5)(b)). It is, however, criticised that too little expertise actually exists in this regard.[493] In addition, there is no or hardly any case law on this topic in the EU. Art. 10 also does not contain any requirements regarding the professional qualification of such settlement bodies.[494] Finally, from a technical and formal point of view, the settlement body has to enable easy access through electronic communication technology (Art. 10(5)(c)) and issue its decisions in a swift, efficient and cost-effective manner and in at least one official language of the Union (Art. 10(5)(d)).

Apart from these conditions, the Data Act does not specify further requirements. However, the member states are free to adopt more detailed provisions themselves, which also regulate questions relating to the expiry and re-certification (rec. 52).

The certified dispute settlement bodies shall be notified to the Commission (Art. 10(6)). The certified and notified dispute settlement bodies should be listed on a dedicated and updated website by the Commission.

The Commission's proposal stipulated that – in case there is no certified dispute settlement body in a member state by the 12 September 2025 – the respective state should establish and certify a settlement body which fulfils the aforementioned conditions. This provision was deleted.

---

491 Weiß, R., *MMR-Beil.* 2024, 101 (104).

492 Weiß, R., *MMR-Beil.* 2024, 101 (102).

493 Max Planck Institute for Innovation and Competition, Position Statement, 2022, p. 42 n. 113.

494 Max Planck Institute for Innovation and Competition, Position Statement, 2022, p. 42 n. 113.

Refusing Disputes / International Jurisdiction

According to Art. 10(7) dispute settlement bodies shall refuse a request to resolve a dispute, when the concerning dispute has already been brought before another dispute settlement body or before a court or a tribunal of a member state. The term "of a member state" will not only refer to the body that has been called upon, but to all other bodies in all member states.[495]

It has been criticised that the Art. 10 does not regulate its international jurisdiction (and rec. 52 does not either elaborate on this matter).[496] However, rec. 53 was added in the course of the legislation, which, in addition to the voluntary nature of the procedure, also clarifies that the parties may submit disputes to any dispute resolution body, whether in their own member state or in another. This right to choose freely among the settlement bodies in the EU could lead to conflicts, not at least because a party might prefer to start the conflict in the country of its domicile.[497] This again brings up the unanswered question of the application of Art. 4(1) Regulation (EU) 1215/2012 (Brussels I-bis Regulation)[498], which states the obligation to sue another party in the courts of the state of the defendant's domicile.[499] However, even when Brussels I-bis Regulation is applicable, there is a high chance that not all member states have certified settlement bodies, which raises the question, to which settlement body a dispute should be brought.[500] Due to these uncertainties, it might eventually be the wiser option to bring the dispute to a member state Court directly.[501]

495 Weiß, R., *MMR-Beil.* 2024, 101 (102).

496 Max Planck Institute for Innovation and Competition, Position Statement, 2022, pp. 40 et seq. n. 111.

497 Max Planck Institute for Innovation and Competition, Position Statement, 2022, pp. 40 et seq. n. 111.

498 Regulation (EU) 1215/2012 of the European Parliament and of the Council on jurisdiction and the recognition and enforcement of judgments in civil and commercial matters.

499 Max Planck Institute for Innovation and Competition, Position Statement, 2022, pp. 40 et seq. n. 111.

500 Max Planck Institute for Innovation and Competition, Position Statement, 2022, pp. 40 et seq. n. 112.

501 Max Planck Institute for Innovation and Competition, Position Statement, 2022, pp. 40 et seq. n. 112.

Competences of the Settlement Bodies

Art. 10 does not define the concrete competences of the settlement bodies. This leads to significant uncertainty. In many cases, the bodies must be able to clarify both facts and legal issues, for example whether technical protection measures within the meaning of Art. 11 have been implemented or circumvented (fact) and at the same time whether these unlawfully discriminate against the data recipient (legal question).[502] As no clear limits were set in the final version either, it can be assumed that the dispute settlement bodies have a broad decision-making competence within the scope of Art. 10(1). This ranges from simple recommendations to the parties to concrete measures, such as deciding on the (non-)binding nature of a contractual term.

Rules of Procedure

Art. 10(8) states that the parties must be granted a reasonable period of time to demonstrate their point of view on matters the parties have brought before the settlement bodies and ensures the right to a fair trial under Art. 6(1) ECHR.[503] The undefined legal term of a "reasonable period of time" will have to be clarified. The parties shall also be provided with the submissions of the other party and any statement made by experts. In that context, the parties shall also be granted the possibility to comment on those submissions and statements.

A dispute settlement body shall adopt its decision within 90 days after the request pursuant to Art. 10(1) and (4). The decision has to be in writing or on a durable medium and shall be supported by a statement of reasons (Art. 10(9)).

Art. 10 does not contain any further specifications regarding the form or the procedure. Even if it is not expressly laid down, it seems possible and useful for the member states or the dispute settlement body itself to create its own rules or internal statutes that specify the procedure.

502 Niedermaier, T. / Picht, P., FRAND ADR under the Data Act and the SEP Regulation, 2022, pp. 4 et seq.

503 Weiß, R., *MMR-Beil.* 2024, 101 (103).

Annual Activity Reports

In order to create uniform 'case law' and comparability, Art. 10(10) provides that the dispute settlement bodies shall draw and make publicly annual activity reports. Those reports shall include, in particular, an aggregation of the outcomes of disputes, the average time taken to resolve and the most common reasons for disputes. To avoid unnecessary exchange of information and disputes, Art. 10(11) states that the annual reports may include recommendations as to how the respective problems can be avoided or resolved. The provision therefore does not include any coordination of the dispute resolution bodies, which would, however, be desirable in order to create a level playing field, standardised decisions and thus greater legal certainty.[504]

Decision Effects / Enforcement / Interplay with Judicial Clarification

According to Art. 10(12), the decision of the dispute settlement body only binds the parties if they have explicitly consented to its binding nature before the start of the dispute settlements proceedings. It is likely that many disputes are not brought before a dispute resolution body in the first place.[505]

Rec. 56 stipulates that the parties shall not be prevented to exercise their fundamental rights to an effective remedy and to a fair trial. In this respect, Art. 10(13) states that Art. 10 does not affect the right of the parties to seek an effective remedy before a court or tribunal of a member state. The wording "remedy" in Art 10(13) could be understood to suggest that dispute settlement has priority over state court proceedings and that only the decision of the dispute settlement body is subject to review.[506] However, it would then be unclear why the Data Act emphasises so strongly at other points that the right to make use of state courts remains unaffected (Art. 4(3) and (9), 5(12), rec. 56 second sentence).

504 Weiß, R., *MMR-Beil.* 2024, 101 (102).

505 Max Planck Institute for Innovation and Competition, Position Statement, 2022, p. 42 n. 114.

506 Apparently in this sense Weiß, R., *MMR-Beil.* 2024, 101 (103).

6. Technical Protection

Technical protective measures to be used when transferring data are addressed by Art. 11.[507] The data holder is given far-reaching (technical) protection options with equally far-reaching enforcement and intervention options in case of unauthorised use by the data recipient. This gives the data holder the *de facto*-possibility to restrict the use of the data in a selective and targeted manner. This form of 'exclusivity' has already been recognised in the literature as a construct that comes close to unintended data ownership.[508] It is not clear whether the user has a legal claim against the data holder to the implementation of technical protection measures.[509]

Art. 11 is not related to or linked to Art. 3.[510] Although both provisions deal with technical requirements in the broadest sense, the provisions regulate different complexes. Art. 11 does not impose obligations on the manufacturer, but on the data holder (which can, but does not need to the same person). Also, Art. 3 DA only addresses product data and related services data, while Art. 11 gives the data holder the possibility to protect all data by technical protection measures.

Protection Measures

Art. 11(1) "allows" for technical protection measures to prevent unauthorised access to data and to ensure compliance with Art. 4, 5, 6, 8 and 9 and the agreed contractual terms for making data available. Examples of protection measures include smart contracts and encryption, including metadata. The data holder is not obliged to use protection measures. Rather, Art. 11 sets limits for the use of respective measures.[511]

According to Art. 11(1) the implementation of the technical protection measures must fulfil three requirements. First, the measures must be "appropriate". The question of when a measure is appropriate is difficult to answer in abstract terms and depends significantly on the type and extent of the data provision. A case-by-case assessment is necessary here.[512]

507 For a deep insight cf. Steege, H., *MMR-Beil.* 2024, 91.
508 Steege, H., *MMR-Beil.* 2024, 91.
509 Ducuing, C. / Margoni, T. / Schirru, L. (ed.), *CiTiP Working Paper* 2022, 38.
510 For the following, cf. Steege, H., *MMR-Beil.* 2024, 91 (92).
511 Specht-Riemenschneider, L., *MMR-Beil.* 2022, 809 (823).
512 Steege, H., *MMR-Beil.* 2024, 91 (93).

Second, the measures shall not discriminate between data recipients. Similar to Art. 9, the question arises as to whether definitions and principles (yet to be developed) from Art. 8 are transferable for the understanding of this term. Neither Art. 11(1) nor the correlating rec. 57 explain whether and when discrimination can be justified in individual cases.[513]

Third, the measures shall not hinder a user's right to obtain a copy of, retrieve, use or access data, to provide data to third parties pursuant to Art. 5 or any right of a third party under Union law or national legislation adopted in accordance with Union law. On the one hand, it is questionable at what point the user is prevented from exercising the aforementioned rights. From the open wording, it could be concluded that an obstacle already exists if the measures are only capable of preventing the rights.[514] On the other hand, it is unclear at what level a security measure is considered to be obstructive and whether the subjective knowledge and skills of the user or those of an objective average user should be used as a yardstick.[515]

Finally, the third sentence of Art. 11(1) states that users and third parties shall not alter or remove the technical protection measures unless agreed by the data holder. Any circumvention of protection measures is unlawful. Even if it is not clear from the wording of Art. 11(1), this authorisation must be given at the time of the circumvention.[516] According to the broad wording, it also seems possible that the data holder might authorise a circumvention retrospectively.[517]

Conditions and Consequences

Art. 11(2) and (3) address the consequences for data recipients and third parties in specific scenarios. The scenarios are defined in Art. 11(3). The provision conclusively lists five settings. Art. 11(3)(a) refers to the case that a third party or a data recipient has "provided false information to a data holder, deployed deceptive or coercive means or abused gaps in the technical infrastructure of the data holder designed to protect the data" to obtain data. The broadly worded provision is (partially) focused on

513 Steege, H., *MMR-Beil.* 2024, 91 (94) raising the problem.
514 In favour of this cf. Steege, H., *MMR-Beil.* 2024, 91 (94).
515 Password protection alone will not be enough to hinder the user's rights, cf. Steege, H., *MMR-Beil.* 2024, 91 (94 et seq.).
516 Steege, H., *MMR-Beil.* 2024, 91 (93).
517 Steege, H., *MMR-Beil.* 2024, 91 (94).

the *technical* circumvention of established protective measures. Rec. 57 specifies that "misleading the data holder by providing false information with the intent to use the data for unlawful purposes" falls under the provision. However, details are not specified. Hence, it remains unclear when information is "false" or when exactly gaps have been "abused". Another technical aspect is mentioned by Art. 11(3)(d). It refers to a setting in which the technical and organisational measures agreed in accordance with Art. 5(9) have not been maintained. In the form of a general clause, Art. 11(3)(e) refers to Art. 11(1) and an alternation or removal of technical protection measures without the agreement of the data holder.

In contrast, Art. 11(3)(b) and (c) refer to unauthorised use of *the data*. According to the provisions data recipients may not use "the data made available for unauthorised purposes, including the development of a competing connected product within the meaning of [Art. 6(2)(e)]" and may not "unlawfully disclose data to another party". It is not clarified what "unlawfully" means. This will depend on the contractual agreement between the data holder and the data recipient.

It is not explicitly stated who has to *prove* whether one of the settings defined in Art. 11(3) are fulfilled.[518]

The consequences of the settings defined in Art. 11(3) are stipulated in Art. 11(2). The provision specifies – also conclusively – four measures with which the data recipient or the third party must comply if requested by the data holder, the holder of the trade secret, or the user. Art. 11(5) states that the user shall have the same rights according to Art. 11(2) if a data recipient infringes Art. 6(2)(a) or (b).

Art. 11(2)(a) and (b) refer to the erasure of the data and the termination of all activities made possible by the data. All data and copies thereof must be deleted (Art. 11(2)(a)). In addition, the data recipient can be obliged "to end the production, offering or placing on the market or use of goods, derivative data or services produced on the basis of knowledge obtained through such data, or the importation, export or storage of infringing goods for those purposes, and destroy any infringing goods, where there is a serious risk that the unlawful use of those data will cause significant harm to the data holder, the trade secret holder or the user or where such a measure would not be disproportionate in light of the interests of the data holder, the trade secret holder or the user" (Art. 11(2)(b)).

518 Cf. Gerpott, T., *CR* 2022, 271 (279).

Furthermore, the data recipient or the third party might have "to inform the user of the unauthorised use or disclosure of the data and of the measures taken to put an end to the unauthorised use or disclosure of the data" (Art. 11(2)(c)). However, the provision does not specify in detail how the user must be informed and what information is included. For example, the wording does not indicate whether it must be informed about when the data was disclosed or which parties were involved. A narrow interpretation would potentially undermine the purpose of the provision. The user should in any case be aware of the general circumstances of the "data leak" and whether these have been solved. This refers in particular to the question of *which* data is affected, *when* the incident took place, *why* the data was disclosed and *where* the data flowed to.

Finally, the data recipient or the third party might have to compensate the party suffering from the misuse or disclosure of the unlawfully accessed or used data (Art. 11(2)(d)). Excessive requests from the data holder or third parties are limited by rec. 57, according to which all requests from harmed parties shall "be assessed in the light of their proportionality in relation to the interests of the data holder, the trade secret holder or the user". This exemption is not further defined or explained.

The obligations under Art. 11(2) must be fulfilled without delay. As already outlined above, the term 'undue delay' is to be determined by union law.[519]

Altering or Removing Technical Protection by the User and others

Art. 11(4) extends the personal scope of Art. 11(2). According to the provision, also the user may neither alter nor remove the technical protection measures taken by the data holder. This also applies to the measures taken to protect trade secrets. In addition, any other party that receives data from the user violating provisions of the Data Act is subject to the obligations under Art. 11(2).

Art. 11(4) clarifies that there is no 'right to hack' for the user and can furthermore be seen as a "small crack" in the principle of user-centricity in favour of the data holder.

519 See sub. V.

Enforcement

Art. 11 does not contain any information on private enforcement (the Data Act focuses more on public enforcement (cf. Art. 40)).[520] However, Art. 11(2) (also in favour of the cases regulated by Art. 11(4) and (5)) seems to establish respective claim enforceable before a court.

Disputes under Art. 11 may be brought before a dispute resolution body within the meaning of Art. 10(5). Art. 11 is not explicitly mentioned in Art. 10(1), but is covered by the "making data available in accordance with (...) Chapter [III]" of that very provision.

7. Common Standards for Smart Contracts (Art. 36)

Hailed for their "potential to facilitate automated data sharing and pooling at scale while enforcing usage restrictions"[521], so-called smart contracts had been floated by the Commission as a high-level technical tool since the outset of the Data Act initiative. The main use case manifesting in the Act's final version concerns long-term arrangements (put differently, data licensing agreements[522]) between data holders and data recipients regularly sharing data; in these settings, smart contracts are envisioned to decrease transaction costs (rec. 47).

Smart contracts are chiefly mentioned (and put into concrete terms) by Art. 36. They also appear in two other regulatory contexts: first, in Art. 11(1) as a protective measure against unauthorised disclosure when implementing the sharing of readily available data pursuant to Art. 4 et seq.; and second, as objects of interoperability requirements to enable the automatic execution of data licensing agreements within data spaces pursuant to Art. 33(1)(d).

The Notion of Smart Contracts

According to Art. 2(39), "smart contract" means a computer program used for the automated execution of an agreement or part thereof, using a

520 Cf. for the German private law Steege, H., *MMR-Beil.* 2024, 91 (95).
521 Commission, 'Inception Impact Assessment: Data Act', Ares(2021)3527151, p. 3.
522 Siglmüller, J., *MMR-Beil.* 2024, 112 (115).

sequence of electronic data records and ensuring their integrity and the accuracy of their chronological ordering. To some extent, the definition picks up on the classical conceptualisation by *Nick Szabo,* who in 1994 had defined smart contracts as computerised transaction protocols that execute the terms of a contract.[523] Where prior versions had tied the notion of smart contracts to the use of electronic ledgers and thus, the Distributed Ledger Technology (DLT), Art. 2(39) has rightfully abandoned the DLT and its popular epithet – the blockchain – as a necessary vehicle for smart contracts.[524] Instead, rec. 104 affirms the principle of technical neutrality, which does not preclude that smart contracts *can* be connected to an electronic ledger. Viewing smart contracts through the lens of computer programs exclusively can still be regarded, however, as a violation of technological neutrality.[525]

Essential Requirements for Smart Contracts (Art. 36(1))

When it comes to the technicalities of smart contracts, Art. 36(1) deems essential five characteristics: robustness, safe termination and interruption, data archiving and continuity, access control, and consistency with the data sharing agreement the smart contract executes. Rec. 104 clarifies that these requirements only apply to vendors of smart contracts, except where they develop smart contracts in-house exclusively for internal use. Judging from the juxtaposition in Art. 36(2), Art. 36(3), and Art. 36(9) of vendors and other persons whose business involves the deployment of smart contracts for others, it appears that vendors are indeed identified by the sale of such computer programs.

Looking at the above requirements, (rigorous) access control mechanisms feature twice in Art. 36(1)(a) and Art. 36(1)(d), which is probably due to poor drafting. Robustness under Art. 36(1)(a) is lauded in principle as the capacity to avoid functional errors and withstand third-party manipulation, but its suitability to address well-known vulnerabilities of smart contracts in practice is called into question (at least in the absence of

523 Cit. per Max Planck Institute for Innovation and Competition, Position Statement, 2022, p. 84 n. 234; for other definitions of the term, cf. Mik, E., *EuCML* 2024, 1 (1) (lamenting a “medley of inconsistent approaches”).

524 Siglmüller, J., *MMR-Beil.* 2024, 112 (116).

525 Max Planck Institute for Innovation and Competition, Position Statement, 2022, p. 84 n. 234.

harmonised standards under Art. 36(5)).[526] The possibility to interrupt and safely terminate the execution of the self-executing protocol underlying the smart contract (Art. 36(1)(b)) is indispensable to allow for amendments to the otherwise immutable contract.[527] However, this goal clashes with the characteristic integrity and consistency of smart contracts (Art. 36(1)(e)) as well as their auditability (Art. 36(1)(c)), which could be thwarted should a "kill switch" become necessary to avoid future accidental executions of the protocol.[528] More generally, the consistency between the smart contract and the agreement it is meant to execute can be hard to verify from the rules as transcribed into source code.[529]

Declaration of Conformity (Art. 36(2) and (3))

Vendors of smart contracts or, failing that, persons whose business involves the deployment of smart contracts for others in the context of executing an agreement to make data available shall perform a conformity assessment to ascertain that the essential requirements under Art. 36(1) are met. Per rec. 105, the conformity assessment should observe the general principles of the Accreditation Regulation (EC) No. 765/2008. Upon a positive result of the assessment, the vendor or trader shall issue a so-called EU declaration of conformity, which pursuant to Art. 36(3) triggers their responsibility for compliance with Art. 36(1). Art. 36(3) does little in the way of linking this responsibility to (private) enforcement, nor does it specify the details of the declaration (conversely, see Annex V of the AI Act).

As for the enforceability of smart contracts themselves, there is broad consensus that the current member state law on contracts is reasonably well-equipped to accommodate smart contracts in much the same way as conventional agreements.[530]

---

526 Casolari, F. / Taddeo, M. / Turillazzi, A. / Floridi, L., 'How to Improve Smart Contracts in the European Union Data Act' 2:9 (2023) *Digital Society* 3.

527 Id. at 2.

528 Max Planck Institute for Innovation and Competition, Position Statement, 2022, p. 85 n. 235.

529 Mik, E., *EuCML* 2024, 1 (3).

530 Siglmüller, J., *MMR-Beil.* 2024, 112 (115 n. 27); cf. Casolari, F. / Taddeo, M. / Turillazzi, A. / Floridi, L., 2:9 (2023) *Digital Society* 4.

Harmonised Standards (Art. 36(4) and (5))

In accordance with Art. 36(5), the Commission shall request one or more of the three European standardisation organisations (CEN, Cenelec, and ETSI[531]) to draft harmonised standards on the matter of essential requirements for smart contracts raised by Art. 36(1). With some degree of redundancy, harmonised standards are defined in Art. 2(43) by reference to Art. 2(1)(c) Regulation (EU) No. 1025/2012 as European standards adopted on the basis of a request made by the Commission for the application of Union harmonisation legislation. Once adopted by the standardisation organisation, the Commission shall assess the harmonised standards per Art. 36(10).

Art. 36(4) creates a presumption of conformity with the essential requirements prescribed by Art. 36(1) if the vendor of a smart contract can show compliance with the relevant parts of the harmonised standards. Unlike in the case of Art. 13(5), jointly read with rec. 62, this favourable presumption is arguably non-rebuttable.

Common Specifications (Art. 36(6) to (9))

Where the Commission's request under Art. 36(5) has not been accepted by the European standardisation organisation in question, or where the harmonised standards are not delivered within the applicable deadline or within the parameters of the request, the Commission may intervene in the absence of harmonised standards published in the Official Journal and adopt so-called common specifications. By this rather generic term, Art. 2(42) "means a document, other than a standard, containing technical solutions providing a means to comply with certain requirements and obligations established under [the Data Act]".

Rec. 103 is adamant to express the underpinning consideration that these common specifications "should be adopted only as an *exceptional fall-back solution* to facilitate compliance with the essential requirements of this Regulation" (emphasis added). The political struggle over who can claim the authority to determine essential requirements for smart contracts has thus been decided in favour of the European standardisation organisations.[532]

---

531 Annex I of Regulation (EU) No. 1025/2012.
532 Siglmüller, J., *MMR-Beil.* 2024, 112 (116).

With common specifications ranking below harmonised standards, the Commission must, in accordance with Art. 36(7), inform a dedicated committee under Art. 22 Regulation (EU) No. 1025/2012 before commencing the drafting process. Likewise, the Commission should first hear the advice of the EDIB, specifically of its sub-group on standardisation, interoperability, and portability.[533]

Like Art. 36(4), Art. 36(9) attributes to the common specifications a (non-rebuttable) presumption of conformity with the essential requirements for smart contracts. Unlike with harmonised standards, however, member states can notify the Commission that common specifications do not align with the essential requirements (Art. 36(11)).

8. *Scope of Obligations*

The scope of application of Chapter III is regulated in an unusual way at the end in Art. 12. The provisions apply accordingly where, in business-to-business-relations, a data holder is obliged under Art. 5, or under Union law or national legislation adopted in accordance with Union law, to make data available to a data recipient.[534]

According to Art. 12(2), an agreement that – to the detriment of a party or the user – derogated from the provisions of Chapter III is not binding in their respect. The rules of Art. 8-11 DA are therefore conceived as (partially unilateral) mandatory law.[535]

Art. 12 does not contain any statements on the relationship to the GDPR. To ensure the observance of the GDPR, one proposal was to add another paragraph that would have stated:

> "Any contractual term in a data sharing agreement between data holders and data recipients which, to the detriment of the data subjects undermines the application of their rights to privacy and data protection,

---

533 Established under Art. 29(2)(b) DGA; cf. Hennemann, M., in Specht-Riemenschneider, L. / id. (ed.), *Data Governance Act,* Nomos 2023, Art. 29 mn. 22.

534 The ITRE Draft Opinion proposed to add an Art. 12(1)(a) that would state: "The obligations set out in this Regulation do not preclude a reciprocity of data sharing between a data recipient, user and data holder agreed in contracts.", cf. ITRE PE739.548, p. 87.

535 Hennemann, M. / Steinrötter, B., *NJW* 2022, 1481 (1485).

> derogates from it, or varies its effect, shall not be binding on that party".[536]

However, the proposal was not included in the final version.

536 ITRE PE739.548, p. 88.

VII. Unfair Terms for Data Access and Use between Enterprises (Art. 13)

Chapter IV ('Unfair Terms Related to Data Access and Use Between Enterprises', Art. 13) addresses unfair contractual terms in data sharing contracts (only) between businesses, where unequal bargaining power[537] might be used to impose unilaterally a contractual term on another enterprise. If found to be unfair, such a term will not be binding (Art. 13(1)).[538]

Despite far-reaching amendments in the course of the legislation, the basic structure of Art. 13 has not changed. The provisions include absolute and relative clause bans recognisable from the Unfair Terms Directive (and national law, e.g. Sec. 308, 309 German Civil Code).[539] However, Art. 13 is limited to the unfairness of terms and, unlike the Unfair Terms Directive, does not deal with the transparency of contract terms (as known from Unfair Terms Directive).[540]

With regard to the temporal scope of application, Art. 13 generally applies to contracts that are concluded 20 months after the Data Act comes into force (Art. 50(5)).

Personal Scope

In the draft version of the Commission proposal, the scope of Art. 13 was limited to micro, small or medium-sized enterprise as defined in Article 2 of the Annex to Recommendation 2003/361/EC.[541] It was assumed that the Data Act would not see any need for protection in contracts between large(r) companies.[542] This gave rise to follow-up questions, such as wheth-

537 Cf. rec. 58.

538 Cf. in detail on Art. 13 DA Hennemann, M. in: Lohsse, S. / Schulze, R. / Staudenmayer, D. (ed.), Private Law and the Data Act, Nomos 2024 (forthcoming).

539 Council Directive 93/13/EEC.

540 Cf. Staudenmeyer, D., *EuZW* 2022, 596 (602) arguing that, consequently, there is no control of the main subject matter even if this subject matter is drafted in an opaque way.

541 Commission, COM(2022) 68 final Explanatory Memorandum, p. 15.

542 Staudenmeyer, D., *EuZW* 2022, 596 (600).

er the unfairness test also would apply if the imposing party were itself a micro, small or medium-sized enterprise. This raised the consequential question of the protective purpose of an unfairness test between two small companies.[543]

The legislator therefore refrained from implementing the original limitation in the final version. Art. 13 therefore applies to *any* enterprise. One possible explanation for this quite radical change could be the criticism raised early that the protection of companies in the area of data trading does not depend on the size of the company, but on the degree of data dependency, so a possible imbalance is not related to the size of a company.[544]

Consumers, however, are excluded from Art. 13.[545] The fact that Art. 13 does not apply to the benefit of consumers is partly explained by the already comprehensive protection provided by the Unfair Terms Directive and the respective national provisions on standard terms control.[546] Art. 1(9) also states that the Data Act "complements and is without prejudice to Union law which aims to promote the interests of consumers and ensure a high level of consumer protection, and to protect their health, safety and economic interests, in particular Directives 93/13/EEC, 2005/29/EC and 2011/83/EU".

Material Scope

Art. 13 applies (only) to contracts between companies relating to the access and use of data (Art. 1(2)(c)). The provision is not limited to contractual relationships under the Data Act. Rather, the title and the open wording of Art. 13(1) indicate that all data-related contracts between enterprises are covered.[547] Moreover, all *data-related* obligations are included – from the generation of data to the transfer of data to third parties.[548]

543 Weizenbaum Institute for the Networked Society, Position paper regarding Data Act, 2022, pp. 14 et seq.

544 Max Planck Institute for Innovation and Competition, Position Statement, 2022, p. 46 n. 125.

545 Max Planck Institute for Innovation and Competition, Position Statement, 2022, p. 48 n. 129.

546 Bomhard, D. / Merkle, M., *RDi* 2022, 168 (173).

547 Cf. also Hennemann, M. in: Lohsse, S. / Schulze, R. / Staudenmayer, D. (ed.), Private Law and the Data Act, Nomos 2024 (forthcoming).

548 Schwamberger, S., *MMR-Beil.* 2024, 96 (97).

This goes along with rec. 60 which states that the rules of Art. 13 should apply only to those elements of a contract that are related to making data available. That refers to contractual terms concerning access to and use of the data as well as liability or remedies for breach and termination of data related obligations. Other parts of the contract that have no connection to the provision of data remain unaffected.

As laid down above, the relationship between Art. 13 and Art. 8 is debated.[549] According to the concept of Art. 4 et seq., contractual relationships are established between all parties involved. Users enter contractual relationships with the data holder (Art. 4) and, where applicable, with third parties (Art. 5). Third parties have contractual relationships with the user and the data holder. The respective conclusion that Art. 8 and 13 always apply in parallel is also underpinned by Art. 8(1). The provision stresses that third-party access should fulfil the requirements of Art. 8 et seq. *and* Chapter IV.

Unilaterally Imposed

Art. 13 provides a fairness test for contractual terms that have been *imposed unilaterally*. Art. 13(6) explains (more or less) what this exactly refers to. A term shall be considered to be unilaterally imposed if it has been brought into the contract by one contracting party and the other contracting party has not been able to influence its content despite an attempt to negotiate it. Rec. 59 underlines the importance of contractual freedom as an essential concept in B2B-relations. It states that not all contractual terms shall be subject to an unfairness test, but only to those terms that are unilaterally imposed. In contrast, a term that is "simply provided by one party and accepted by the other enterprise or a term that is negotiated and subsequently agreed in an amended way between contracting parties should not be considered as unilaterally imposed". It therefore might be possible to argue that Art. 13 can be excluded via a simple accept button that must be pushed by the other party.[550]

This setting gives rise to numerous delimitation questions. At what point is an attempt to negotiate sufficient? Does one have to communicate expressly that negotiations do take place? Is, for example, the business

549 See above sub VI. 3.
550 Wiebe, A., *GRUR* 2023, 1569 (1575).

response to an offer: "After careful consideration, I agree to your terms" an attempt to negotiate?[551]

The second sentence of Art. 13(6) establishes a burden of proof rule according to which the imposing party must prove that the condition was not imposed unilaterally. This may defuse[552] the questions raised above in practice. However, it is unclear how it would be possible for the imposing party to prove that the other party did not attempt to negotiate the terms.[553] This does potentially run counter to the goal to protect the legally less well-informed companies.[554] In addition, there will be formal or strategic attempts during the negotiation process to escape the scope of the chapter.[555] It is further unclear whether and how Art. 13 applies to global multilateral data agreements; the term and the concept of "unilateral imposition" do not fit in this context.[556]

Mandatory Provisions

By way of clarification, Art. 13(2) provides that contractual terms that reflect mandatory provisions of Union law which would apply if the contractual terms did not regulate the matter, should not be considered unfair and therefore fall outside the scope of application.

Subject Matter of the Contract

Art. 13(8) clarifies that Art. 13 does not apply to contractual terms defining the main subject matter of the contract, i.e., those terms that define the

551 It is precisely this situation that rec. 59 has not considered.

552 Schwamberger, S., *MMR-Beil.* 2024, 96 (98).

553 Hennemann, M. / Steinrötter, B., *NJW* 2022, 1481 (1485).

554 Max Planck Institute for Innovation and Competition, Position Statement, 2022, p. 45 n. 122.

555 Cf. in this regard Max Planck Institute for Innovation and Competition, Position Statement, 2022, p. 45 n. 126; Podszun, R., Der EU Data Act und der Zugang zu Sekundärmärkten am Beispiel des Handwerks, 2022, pp. 56 et seq.

556 Leistner, M. / Antoine, L., IPR and the use of open data and data sharing initiatives by public and private actors, 2022, p. 107.

specific performance[557] or to the adequacy of the price, as against the data supplied in exchange.[558]

Further Aspects

Lastly, Art. 13(6) clarifies that "the party that supplied the contested term may not argue that the term is an unfair contractual term".

According to Art. 13(9), the parties of a contract addressed by Art. 13 shall not exclude the application of Art. 13, derogate from it, or vary its effects.

It is to be added that during the legislative process there was a proposal to include another paragraph that provided for the establishment of guidelines on reasonable prices by the Commission. The provision would have stated:

> "Within 12 months from the entry into force of this Regulation, the Commission shall by means of implementing acts further develop guidelines on the reasonable prices for the compensation for data sharing and measures to prevent and mitigate data market distortion practices provided in Chapters III and IV".[559]

However, the proposal was ultimately not accepted.

Unfairness

If found to be unfair, a term will not be binding (Art. 13(1)). Art. 13(7) clarifies in this regard that other contractual terms shall stay binding when the unfair contractual term is severable from these other terms. To determine the unfairness of a clause, the criteria of Art. 13(4) serves as a "black (clauses) list"[560] and Art. 13(5) serves a "grey (clauses) list"[561]. In addition, Art. 13(3) provides a kind of general clause.

---

557 ECJ ECLI:EU:C:2014:282 = *EuZW* 2014, 506 – Kásler (C-26/13); CEJ ECLI:EU:C:2015:127 = *GRUR Int.* 2015, 471 – Matei (C-143/13).

558 The clarifying half-sentence "nor to the adequacy of the price, as against the data supplied in exchange " was proposed by Council Presidency 2022/0047(COD) – 13342/22, p. 49.

559 ITRE PE739.548, pp. 96 et seq.

560 Gerpott, T., *CR* 2022, 271 (278); Staudenmeyer, D., *EuZW* 2022, 596 (598).

561 Staudenmeyer, D., *EuZW* 2022, 596 (598).

General Unfairness Provision

According to Art. 13(3), a contractual term is unfair if it is of such a nature that its use grossly deviates from good commercial practice in data access and use, contrary to good faith and fair dealing. It is not entirely clear whether a deviation from good commercial practice and a contrast to good faith and fair dealing must occur cumulatively. However, the wording suggests that this is not the case.[562] The language versions are not the same, for example the German version of the Data Act contains the word "oder" (= or).

Specific criteria for a 'good business practice' and a 'gross deviation' from it are not provided and remain unclear.[563] Also, it is questionable what the provision to define 'good' business practice actually is.[564] According to rec. 63, the black and grey lists discussed below can serve as a yardstick when assessing whether a term falls under the general provision of Art. 13(3). Model contract terms according to Art. 41 can also be used for this purpose in future (cf. rec. 62). One present option for interpretation could be found in the ALI-ELI Principles for a Data Economy,[565] which in Principles 7 et seq., contain provisions on contractual data transfer, as well as the "Default rules for data provision contracts" currently being developed by UNCITRAL[566].[567]

'Black' List

A contractual term is unfair according to Art. 13(4) if its object or effect is to "exclude or limit the liability of the party that unilaterally imposed the term

562 Cf. in this sense only Wiebe, A., *GRUR* 2023, 1569 (1575); in contrast Schwamberger, S., *MMR-Beil.* 2024, 96 (98), assuming that a significant deviation from good commercial practice leads to a breach of good faith.

563 BDI Stellungnahme zum Legislativvorschlag des EU-Data Act, 2022, pp. 17 et seq.; Weizenbaum Institute for the Networked Society, Position paper regarding Data Act, 2022, p. 14.

564 Cf. Staudenmeyer, D., *EuZW* 2022, 596 (599).

565 ALI-ELI Principles for a Data Economy: Data Rights and Transactions, 2022, https://principlesforadataeconomy.org/the-project/the-current-draft/.

566 UNCITRAL, Default rules for data provision contracts (first revision) https://documents-dds-ny.un.org/doc/UNDOC/LTD/V23/064/75/PDF/V2306475.pdf?OpenElement.

567 Schwamberger, S., *MMR-Beil.* 2024, 96 (100).

for intentional acts or gross negligence" (Art. 13 (4)(a)). Further, a term is unfair if it excludes the remedies available to the party upon whom the term has been unilaterally imposed in case of non-performance of contractual obligations, or the liability of the party that unilaterally imposed the term in case of breach of those obligations (Art. 13 (4)(b)). At last, a term that gives the party that unilaterally imposed the term the exclusive right to determine whether the data supplied are in conformity with the contract or to interpret any contractual term is unfair (Art. 13 (4)(c)). Despite the fact that Art. 13(4)(a) refers to liability, the provision does not establish a reference for liability.[568]

'Grey' List

In contrast, Art. 13(5) contains criteria that only indicate unfairness which can be rebutted in the case at hand. A term is therefore presumed unfair if it inappropriately limits "remedies in case of non-performance of contractual obligations or the liability in the case of a breach of those obligations, or extend the liability of the enterprise upon whom the term has been unilaterally imposed" (Art. 13 (5)(a)). The provision is sometimes understood as a future ban on 'as is'-clauses, which would lead to an obligation to contractually guarantee data quality.[569]

A term is further presumed to be unfair if the imposing party unilaterally obtains access to the other party's data and this access harms the other party (Art. 13 (5)(b)). A term shall also not prevent or restrict the party on whom the term is imposed and who has provided the data from making appropriate use of that data (Art. 13 (5)(c)). For example, this could include a buy-out of the user by the data holder.[570]

The party on whom the term has been imposed may also not be prevented from terminating the contract within a reasonable period of time (Art. 13 (5)(d)). Equally, a term shall not allow the imposing party to terminate the contract within an unreasonably short period of time, taking into account any realistic possibility for the other party to party to switch to another comparable service and the financial disadvantage caused by the

568 BDI Stellungnahme zum Legislativvorschlag des EU-Data Act, 2022, p. 18.

569 Bomhard, D. / Merkle, M., *RDi* 2022, 168 (173). Differently, Hennemann, M. in: Lohsse, S. / Schulze, R. / Staudenmayer, D. (ed.), Private Law and the Data Act, Nomos 2024 (forthcoming).

570 Wiebe, A., *GRUR* 2023, 1569 (1575).

financial disadvantage caused by the termination, unless there are serious grounds (Art. 13(5)(f)). Furthermore, the party on which the term has been imposed may not be prevented from obtaining a copy of the data provided during the term of the contract or for a reasonable period after the end of the contract (Art. 13(5)(e)).[571]

Lastly, a term may not permit the imposing party to unilaterally change the agreed price or essential conditions relating to the data provided, unless the imposing party is simultaneously given a right of termination in this event (Art. 13(5)(g)). However, according to the provision, terms that provide for the unilateral modification of the conditions of an indeterminate contract by the imposing party are possible if the contract also provides a valid reason for the imposing party to notify the other party of the changes within a reasonable period of time and for the other party to terminate the contract free of charge in this case.

Picking up the idea that users should be able to decide whether they are willing to "sell" data only to the contracting party, i.e., sharing data exclusively with the contracting party and getting compensation for that, one (not successful) proposal has been to change and extend the wording of Art. 13(5)(c) to:

> „prevent the party upon whom the term has been unilaterally imposed from using the data contributed or generated by that party, including data transmitted from a connected product, as defined under Article 3(2a), during the period of the contract, or to limit the use of such data to the extent that that party is not entitled to use, extract, access or control such data or exploit the value of such data in a proportionate manner, unless it has presented that party with an explicit choice between concluding the agreement without limitation to its rights and the option to be compensated proportionately in exchange for foregoing those rights".[572]

The effectiveness of Art. 13(4) and (5) is doubted by some commentators.[573] It is noteworthy that the cases regulated in Art. 13(4) have only a rudiment-

571 It was proposed to further refine the wording "copy of the data", having the debate about the scope of Art. 15(3) GDPR in mind, cf. Leistner, M. / Antoine, L., IPR and the use of open data and data sharing initiatives by public and private actors, 2022, p. 108.

572 ITRE PE739.548, p. 94.

573 Staudenmeyer, D., *EuZW* 2022, 596 (598).

ary reference to data such as Art. 13(4)(c), which speaks of the agreed data quality. Further data reference is contained in Art. 13(5)(b), (c), (d) and (g). In summary, the prohibitions on clauses are rather vague. The model contract terms provided for in Art. 41 by the Commission can and will be helpful in the interpretation of terms in the future (cf. rec. 62).[574]

Enforcement

Unfair terms are not binding according to Art. 13(1). The provision presumes private enforcement which is regulated by the Data Act only to a limited extent.[575] The private enforcement approach is, however, also supported by the non-derogability of Art. 13 according to Art. 13(9).[576] However, the parallel structure of Art. 37 et seq. to Art. 77 et seq. GDPR is sometimes seen as an argument in favour of public enforcement (only).[577]

574 Hennemann, M. / Steinrötter, B., *NJW* 2022, 1481 (1485).
575 Cf. Schwamberger, S., *MMR-Beil.* 2024, 96 (100).
576 Cf. Schwamberger, S., *MMR-Beil.* 2024, 96 (100).
577 Cf. Schwamberger, S., *MMR-Beil.* 2024, 96 (100).

VIII. Making Data Available to Public-Sector Bodies based on Exceptional Need (Art. 14-22)

Chapter V ('Making Data Available to Public Sector Bodies, the Commission, the European Central Bank or Union Bodies based on Exceptional Need', Art. 14-22) creates a framework under which public-sector bodies may request certain data in specific scenarios, especially in the case of public emergencies, such as public health emergencies or major natural or human-induced disasters.[578] These provisions are meant to combat the lack of available data for the use in favour of the public good.[579]

These provisions seem especially relevant and timely after the global pandemic in general and the recent flood disasters in Germany, Austria and Slovenia in particular.[580] The provisions are seen as a "fundamental advancement in the recognition of the public utility of data, and sets proportionate – yet narrow – conditions under which this public utility takes precedence over private interests".[581]

1. Obligation to Make Data Available to Public-Sector Bodies (Art. 14)

Art. 14(1) obliges data holders, upon a duly reasoned request, to make data available to certain eligible bodies, where they demonstrate an exceptional need to carry out its statutory duties in the public interest. Only data holders that are a legal person other than public sector bodies are addressed. However, rec. 63 adds that the notion of data holder may include public undertakings. Eligible bodies include public sector bodies, the Commission, the European Central Bank or a Union body.

578 Commission, COM(2022) 68 final Explanatory Memorandum, p. 15.
579 Höne, M. / Knapp, J., *ZGI* 2023, 168.
580 Schaller, T. / Zurawski, P., *ZD-Aktuell* 2022, 01169.
581 Margoni, T. / Ducuing, C. / Schirru, L., Data property, data governance and Common European Data Spaces, May 2023, v. 0.4, p. 10.

Union and Public Sector Body

Union bodies means Union bodies, offices and agencies set up by or pursuant to acts adopted on the basis of the Treaty on European Union, the TFEU or the Treaty establishing the European Atomic Energy Community, Art. 2(27).

According to Art. 2(28) public sector body refers to national, regional or local authorities of the member states and bodies governed by public law of the member states, or associations formed by one or more such authorities or one or more such bodies. The term "public sector body" is exclusively relevant for Chapter V (Art. 14-22). According to rec. 63 research-performing organisations and research-funding organisations could also be organised as public sector bodies or as bodies governed by public law, thus being entitled to requests according to Art. 14.

It should be noted that this definition of public sector body differs from the definition in Art. 2(17) DGA, where instead of "national authorities" it reads "State". A broader understanding can be explained by the fact that while the DGA obliges the public sector body concerning the reuse of its data, under Chapter V of the Data Act data holders are obliged to make data available to them.

Material Scope of the Obligation to Make Data Available

The provisions establish the right for the public sector bodies to both access and use the data requested.[582] The request also encompasses the metadata necessary to interpret and use those data. In contrast to the user's right to data access in Art. 4(1), which is limited to data generated by the use of a product or related service, the obligations to make data available refer to all types of data.[583]

Rec. 63 further states public emergencies as primary examples for such an exceptional need. It adds that exceptional needs are circumstances which are unforeseeable and limited in time, in contrast to other circumstances which might be planned, scheduled, periodic or frequent. The prerequisites for such an obligation are further defined in the following Art. 15-22.

582 Leistner, M. / Antoine, L., IPR and the use of open data and data sharing initiatives by public and private actors, 2022, p. 109.

583 Regarding the access to and use of personal data it is still debated whether Art. 14 et seqq. fulfil the requirements for a legal basis according to Art. 6(1)(c) and (e) GDPR. (see below VIII.11.).

Rec. 64 justifies the obligation based on the assessment that in such cases of public emergency the public interest "will outweigh the interests of the data holders to dispose freely of the data they hold". However, the interests of data subjects whose personal data is made available are not addressed. Some argue that the rights under Art. 15, 16 and 17 CFREU of the data subjects might be affected.[584]

If data holders do not comply with this obligation, they may face sanctions according to Art. 40.[585]

In the original proposal small and micro enterprises as defined in Art. 2 of the Annex to Recommendation 2003/361/EC were exempted from the obligation to make data available, Art. 14(2). As proposed by the MPIIC Statement, the JURI Draft opinion and the Council Presidency in its compromise text, this exemption was deleted.[586] This change is in line with the aim of this chapter, as public emergencies require broadest possible access to data and in these cases the public interest outweighs the interests of the data holders to dispose freely of the data they hold (rec. 63) as well as the expected burden on small and micro enterprises. However, SMEs are only obliged to provide data in situations of exceptional need to respond to a public emergency, rec. 63 (cf. Art. 15 (a)).

Considering the importance of access to relevant data, it is questionable whether access in cases of public emergencies is sufficient to further the fulfilment of tasks in the public interest.[587] Especially concerning non-personal data, lesser requirements for access rights of public sector bodies are conceivable and should have been considered. However, instead of expanding access rights concerning non-personal data, the scope of Art. 14 was narrowed by limiting scenarios under Art. 15(b) (former Art. 15(b) and (c)) to concern only the making-available of non-personal data. In general, the requirements for the different scenarios of exceptional need are stricter compared to the draft version. Respective amendments reduced the material scope of the obligation drastically.

584 Höne, M. / Knapp, J., *ZGI* 2023, 168, 169.
585 Klink-Straub, J. / Straub, T., *ZD-Aktuell* 2022, 01076.
586 Max Planck Institute for Innovation and Competition, Position Statement, 2022, p. 49 n. 133, JURI PE736.696, pp. 12, 40, https://www.euractiv.com/section/data-privacy/news/swedish-presidency-tries-to-close-in-on-the-data-act/.
587 Specht-Riemenschneider, L., *MMR-Beil.* 2022, 809 (826).

2. Definition of Exceptional Need (Art. 15)

The reference point for the obligation to make data available are the circumstances under which public sector bodies may request data from private data holders. Art. 15(1) defines two scenarios which may constitute an exceptional need, which should be limited in time and scope.

Response to a Public Emergency

According to Art. 15(1)(a), an exceptional need is given where the data requested is necessary to respond to a public emergency and the public sector body is unable to obtain such data by alternative means in a timely and effective manner under equivalent conditions. This means that the request under Art. 14 does not have to be the last resort.[588]

Definition of Public Emergency

According to Art. 2(29) public emergency means an exceptional situation, limited in time which is negatively affecting the population of the Union, a Member State or part of it, with a risk of serious and lasting repercussions on living conditions or economic stability, financial stability, or the substantial and immediate degradation of economic assets in the Union or the relevant Member State(s). Art. 2(29) gives public health emergencies, emergencies resulting from natural disasters, as well as human-induced major disasters, including major cybersecurity incidents as examples for a public emergency.

Like "public sector body", the term "public emergency" is exclusively relevant for Chapter V and is only used in Art. 15, 18, and 20.

It is highly questionable whether providing the examples for public emergencies in the definition additionally to rec. 63 is helpful. It inflates the definition without adding to its understanding, as the examples were already provided in the recital.

Whether such a public emergency exists shall be determined or officially declared "according to the relevant procedures under Union or national law", Art 2(29). This may lead to various different procedures in the member states to determine a public emergency in the individual member states.

588 Schröder, M., *MMR-Beil.* 2024, 104 (105); Höne, M. / Knapp, J., *ZGI* 2023, 168 (169).

Instead, a standard European procedure could lead to more legal certainty regarding the obligation to make data available in cases of exceptional need.

Fulfilling a Specific Task in the Public Interest

An exceptional need may also exist according to Art. 15(1)(b) where the eligible body has identified specific data, the lack of which prevents it from fulfilling a specific task in the public interest, that has been explicitly provided by law, Art. 15 (1)(b)(i). Art. 15(1)(b) further gives official statistics or the mitigation or recovery from a public emergency as examples. In these non-emergency situations only non-personal data can be requested.

Rec. 65 adds that the eligible body should have "identified specific data that could not otherwise be obtained in a timely and effective manner and under equivalent conditions". This further requires that it has exhausted all other means at its disposal to obtain such data, including, but not limited to, purchase of the data on the market by offering market rates or relying on existing obligations to make data available, or the adoption of new legislative measures which could guarantee the timely availability of the data, Art. 15(1)(b)(ii). This requirement might "incentivise data holders to make data available beforehand and systematically".[589] Nevertheless, it remains unclear which efforts the eligible bodies should make before requesting the data.[590]

According to Art. 15(3), the obligation to demonstrate that the public sector body was unable to obtain non-personal data by purchasing them on the market shall not apply where the specific task carried out in the public interest is the production of official statistics and where the purchase of such data is not allowed by national law.

Art. 15(1)(b) does not apply to SMEs, Art. 15(2).

Assessment of the Definitions

While the definition in Art. 2(29) and the scenario of Art. 15(1)(a) seem to give a narrow and strict understanding of an exceptional need, this

589 Krämer, J. et al. Data Act: Towards a balanced EU data regulation, CERRE report, March 2023, p. 63.

590 Cf. Krämer, J. et al. Data Act: Towards a balanced EU data regulation, CERRE report, March 2023, p. 63.

understanding is expanded in Art. 15(b) regarding time as well as intensity.[591] Although this is reflected in the increasing requirements for the data request, some had argued to concretise the conditions for an exceptional need.[592] According to the BDI, the definitions of "public emergency" and also "fulfilling a specific task in the public interest that has been explicitly provided by law" are too broad and lack legal certainty for the data holders, when the obligation to make data available exists.[593]

Regarding the necessary differentiation between Art. 15(1)(a) and (b) in some scenarios of public emergency, for example a pandemic, it might be difficult to effectively distinguish between response, prevention, and recovery.[594] However, this differentiation remains necessary, due to different requirements in paras. (a) and (b) and its link to the possibility to claim compensation, Art. 20. Respective difficulties in the application of Art. 15 could have been minimised by combining the response to a public emergency with the prevention of and recovery from it together in Art. 15(1)(a) as proposed by the JURI Draft Opinion.[595]

Concerning the prerequisites of Art. 15(1)(b)(ii) it remains open, whether "purchasing the data on the market" refers only to data already offered on the market or if the public sector body is also required to individually negotiate with potential data providers, if the needed data has not been offered.[596] It is argued that it should be understood as data that is "actually offered to the public".[597] Furthermore, it should be clarified how to determine the "market rate", as single-source data would be prone to monopoly pricing.[598]

It seems questionable, how the requirement that the exceptional need should be limited in time and scope is consistent with the possibility of existing obligations to make data available or the adoption of new legislative

591 Cf. also Schaller, T. / Zurawski, P., *ZD-Aktuell* 2022, 01169.

592 Cf. also Schaller, T. / Zurawski, P., *ZD-Aktuell* 2022, 01169; Hilgendorf, E. / Vogel, P., *JZ* 2022, 380 (388).

593 BDI Stellungnahme zum Legislativvorschlag des EU-Data Act, 2022, p. 18.

594 Ducuing, C. / Margoni, T. / Schirru, L. (ed.), *CiTiP Working Paper* 2022, 48.

595 JURI PE736.696, p. 40.

596 Max Planck Institute for Innovation and Competition, Position Statement, 2022, pp. 50, 51 n. 137.

597 Krämer, J. et al. Data Act: Towards a balanced EU data regulation, CERRE report, March 2023, p. 63.

598 Max Planck Institute for Innovation and Competition, Position Statement, 2022, p. 51 n. 137; Krämer, J. et al. Data Act: Towards a balanced EU data regulation, CERRE report, March 2023, p. 63.

measures which could guarantee the timely availability of the data, to which Art. 15(1)(b)(ii) refers.

The requirement that the data could not be obtained by measures such as the purchase on the market or the adoption of new legislative measures limits the scope of application of this case of exceptional need drastically.[599]

3. Relationship with Other Obligations to Make Data Available (Art. 16)

Existing Obligations to Make Data Available

According to Art. 16(1) the provisions of Chapter V should not affect existing obligations in Union or national law of reporting and complying with information requests. Rec. 66 explains further that "obligations placed on data holders to provide data that are motivated by needs of a non-exceptional nature, notably where the range of data and of data holders is known and where data use can take place on a regular basis, as in the case of reporting obligations and internal market obligations, should not be affected". The same applies to existing obligations to demonstrate or verify compliance with legal obligations. According to rec. 66 this includes "cases where public sector bodies assign the task of the verification of compliance to entities other than public sector bodies".

These provisions together show that Chapter V only regulates "ad hoc" data access and thus should only pre-empt national legislation concerning ad hoc data access.[600] This is also evident in the first sentence of Art. 15(1).

In addition to Art. 1(6) sent. 1 and Art. 16(1), rec. 66 clarifies that this regulation neither applies to nor pre empts "voluntary arrangements for exchange of data between private and public entities". The provisions do not address the possibility that such voluntary agreements could explicitly rule out the application of the rules under Chapter V.[601]

Art. 16(1) is expanded by rec. 67 which reads that the Data Act complements and is without prejudice to the Union and national laws providing for the access to and enabling to use data for statistical purposes, in partic-

599 Schröder, M., *MMR-Beil.* 2024, 104 (105); similarly also Specht-Riemenschneider, L., *MMR-Beil.* 2022, 809 (824).

600 Max Planck Institute for Innovation and Competition, Position Statement, 2022, p. 53 n. 145.

601 Cf. Krämer, J. et al. Data Act: Towards a balanced EU data regulation, CERRE report, March 2023, p. 67.

ular Regulation (EC) No 223/2009 on European statistics and its related legal acts as well as national legal acts related to official statistics.

The Prevention, Investigation and Prosecution of Criminal and Administrative Offences

Art. 16(2) excludes the prevention, investigation, detection or prosecution of criminal or administrative offences, or the execution of criminal penalties, as well as customs or taxation administration as possible scenarios in which an exceptional need may occur. Therefore, concerning these areas "public sector bodies should rely on their powers under sectoral legislation" (rec. 60).

Correspondingly, the Union and national law applicable in these areas is not affected by Chapter V, as is also stated by Art. 1(4) for the entire Data Act. Art. 16(2), however, adds that applicable law on the prosecution of administrative offences and execution of administrative penalties should not be affected.

Art. 16(2) and Art. 19(1) together ensure the data made available is only used for the intended purposes.[602]

4. Requirements for the Request to Make Data Available (Art. 17 paras. 1 and 2)

Rec. 69 states the necessity for a "proportionate, limited and predictable framework at Union level [...] to ensure legal certainty and to minimise the administrative burdens placed on businesses". Hence, Art. 17 lays down requirements for requests for data to be made available in cases of exceptional need. These provisions ensure that the public sector body has to prove in its request the exceptional need and the conditions of the obligation to make data available.[603] It gives the data holder precise information about the request and thus reduces the data holder's burden.[604] However, the public sector body may face difficulties specifying the data required, as it may

602 Klink-Straub, J. / Straub, T., *ZD-Aktuell* 2022, 01076.

603 Schaller, T. / Zurawski, P., *ZD-Aktuell* 2022, 01169.

604 Leistner, M. / Antoine, L., IPR and the use of open data and data sharing initiatives by public and private actors, 2022, p. 110.

often not know which data private entities hold.[605] As the data holder can decline a request due to unavailability of the data, information imbalances could reduce the effectiveness of this data access right.[606]

Information To Be Provided

The precise information to be given in the context of a request pursuant to Art. 14(1) are according to Art. 17(1):

- specify what data are required, including metadata that is necessary to interpret and use that data (lit. a)
- demonstrate that the conditions necessary for the existence of the exceptional need as referred to in Article 15 for the purpose of which the data are requested are met (lit. b)
- explain the purpose of the request, the intended use of the data requested, including when applicable by a third party in accordance with paragraph 4, the duration of that use, and, where relevant, how the processing of personal data is to address the exceptional need (lit. c)
- specify, if possible, when the data is expected to be deleted by all parties that have access to it (lit. d)
- justify the choice of data holder to which the request is addressed (lit. e)
- specify any other public sector bodies, Union institutions, agencies or bodies and the third parties with which the data requested is expected to be shared with (lit. f)
- where personal data are requested, specify any measures necessary and proportionate to implement data protection principles, data protection safeguards such as the level of aggregation or pseudonymisation, and whether anonymisation can be applied by the data holder before making data available (lit. g)
- state the legal provision allocating to the requesting public sector body or to the Commission, the European Central Bank or Union bodies the specific public interest task relevant for requesting the data (lit. h)
- specify the deadline referred to in Art. 18 and by which the data are to be made available and within which the data holder may request the public

605 Max Planck Institute for Innovation and Competition, Position Statement, 2022, p. 54 n. 148.

606 Max Planck Institute for Innovation and Competition, Position Statement, 2022, p. 54 n. 148; Krämer, J. et al. Data Act: Towards a balanced EU data regulation, CERRE report, March 2023, p. 68.

sector body, the Commission, the European Central Bank or Union body to modify or withdraw the request (lit. i)
- make its best effort to avoid that compliance with the data request results in the data holders' liability for infringement of Union or national law (lit. j)

The provision of Art. 17(1)(j) implies a precedence of the obligation under Art. 14 DA over other legal obligations of the data holder, even if compliance leads to a liability of the data holder.[607]

Further requirements

Beyond these informational duties Art. 17(2) stipulates further requirements for the request. According to Art. 17(2)(a), the request must be made in writing and be expressed in clear, concise, and plain language understandable to the data holder. It must be specific with regards to the type of data requested and correspond to data which the data holder has control over at the time of the request, Art. 17 (2)(b).

According to Art. 17(2)(c), the request must be justified and proportionate to the exceptional need, in terms of the granularity and volume of the data requested and frequency of access of the data requested.

According to Art. 17(2)(d), the request must respect the legitimate aims of the data holder, committing to ensuring the protection of trade secrets in accordance with Article 19(3), and the cost and effort required to make the data available. For example, the deadline referred to in Art. 17(1)(i) must also consider legitimate aims and especially the time and effort needed to protect affected personal data as well as the time needed for its anonymisation and pseudonymisation, as required by Art.18(4).[608]

As the requirement of Art. 17(2)(d) demands subsequently for strong technical and legal safeguards to ensure the effective protection of trade secrets, the Centre for IT & IP Law (CiTiP) of the KU Leuven recommended that the Data Act should have required for public sector bodies to be equipped with the necessary legal, technical, and human resources to comply with these obligations.[609]

Rec. 69 adds that the burden on data holders should be minimised by obliging requesting entities to respect the once-only principle, which

607 Cf. Schröder, M., *MMR-Beil.* 2024, 104 (106).
608 BDI Stellungnahme zum Legislativvorschlag des EU-Data Act, 2022, p. 19.
609 Ducuing, C. / Margoni, T. / Schirru, L. (ed.), *CiTiP Working Paper* 2022, 49.

prevents the same data from being requested more than once by more than one public sector body where those data are needed to respond to a public emergency.

According to *Leistner and Antoine*, Art. 17(2)(c) and (d) ensure that the legitimate interests of the data holder are observed and – consequentially – achieve balanced and proportionate results.[610]

According to Art. 17(2)(e), the request must concern non-personal data, and only if this is demonstrated to be insufficient to respond to the exceptional need to use data, in accordance with Article 15(1)(a), request personal data in aggregated or pseudonymised form and set out the technical and organisational measures that will be taken to protect the data (rec. 72).

According to Art. 17(2)(f), the request must inform the data holder of the penalties that shall be imposed pursuant to Art. 40 by the competent authority referred to in Art. 37 in the event of non-compliance with the request.

According to Art. 17(2)(g) and to ensure transparency (rec. 69), the request should be transmitted to the data coordinator referred to in Art. 37 where the requesting public sector body is established, who shall make the request publicly available online without undue delay unless it considers that this would create a risk for public security. The Commission, the European Central Bank and Union bodies shall make their requests available online without undue delay and inform the Commission thereof.

In case personal data are requested, the request should be notified without undue delay to the independent supervisory authority responsible for monitoring the application of Regulation (EU) 2016/679 in the member state where the data holder is established, Art. 17(2)(i).

According to Art. 17(6) the Commission should develop a model template for requests pursuant to Chapter V. However, it is questionable whether a model template is suitable for the scenarios of exceptional need given in Art. 15, especially those according to lit. a.

5. Reuse of the Data Made Available (Art. 17 (3) and (4))

As the data obtained may be commercially sensitive, it should not be made available for reuse within the meaning of Directive (EU) 2019/1024 (Open

610 Leistner, M. / Antoine, L., IPR and the use of open data and data sharing initiatives by public and private actors, 2022, p. 110.

Data Directive)[611] or the Data Governance Act. Correspondingly, the Open Data Directive and the Data Governance Act shall not apply to the data held by public sector bodies obtained pursuant to Chapter V, Art. 17(3). As not all obtained data will be commercially sensitive, it is questionable why the prohibition should apply to all data, especially since commercially sensitive data would be excluded from the scope of application of the Open Data Directive.[612] According to rec. 65, the data holder can expressly agree for the data to be used for other than the requested purposes. A similar approach, with the application of the Open Data Directive as the default and the possibility of the data holder to deny the re-use or to specify the purposes of the re-use, would have been more favourable.[613]

Nevertheless, as stated in rec. 70, the Open Data Directive is still applicable to the reuse of "official statistics for the production of which data obtained pursuant to this Regulation [the Data Act] was used, provided the reuse does not include the underlying data."

Furthermore, it must be noted that rec. 70 points to the option for public bodies to "[share] the data for conducting research or for the compilation of official statistics, provided the conditions laid down in this Regulation [the Data Act] are met". This is further regulated in Art. 21.

As the Open Data Directive only regulates the re-use of data, but does not provide access to data, access to data is still governed by national rules or sectoral EU or national legislation.[614] Thus, the Data Act does not exclude access of third parties to data obtained under Chapter V under existing legislation.[615] Although Art. 19(2)(b) limits the purposes for which data may be shared, it also indicates that the sharing of data received is not generally excluded.

However, according to Art. 17(4), Art. 17(3) does not preclude the public sector body to exchange the data obtained pursuant to Chapter V with other public sector bodies, in view of completing the tasks in Art. 15, as specified in the request in accordance with Art. 17(1)(f). It may also make

611 Directive (EU) 2019/1024 of the European Parliament and of the Council on open data and the re-use of public sector information.

612 Max Planck Institute for Innovation and Competition, Position Statement, 2022, p. 56 n. 153.

613 Max Planck Institute for Innovation and Competition, Position Statement, 2022, p. 56 n. 153.

614 Max Planck Institute for Innovation and Competition, Position Statement, 2022, p. 57 n. 154.

615 Max Planck Institute for Innovation and Competition, Position Statement, 2022, p. 57 n. 154.

the data available to a third party in cases where it has outsourced, by means of a publicly available agreement, technical inspections or other functions to this third party. It is required to observe Art. 19.

The possibility to exchange data between public sector bodies given in Art. 17(4) is made necessary by the once-only principle according to rec. 69. However, it may lead to a circumvention of the requirements for a request according to Art. 17(1) and may dilute the consideration of the purpose for which the data were requested.[616]

Where a public sector body or a Union institution, agency, or body transmits or makes data available under Art. 17(4), it shall notify the data holder from whom the data was received without undue delay.

Where the data holder considers that its rights under Chapter V have been infringed by the transmission or making available of data, it may lodge a complaint with the competent authority designated pursuant to Art. 37 of the member state where the data holder is established, Art. 17(5).

6. Compliance with Requests for Data (Art. 18)

The data holder should comply with the request without undue delay, taking into account necessary technical, organisational and legal measures (Art. 18(1)). 'Complying' means making the data available, which has been sometimes understood as *in situ* access to the data.[617] Against this interpretation, and in favor of a transfer of the data to the requesting body, speaks the obligation to erase the data, Art. 19(1)(c), as well as the possibility to share it with other public sector bodies, Art. 17(4), and research organisations, Art. 20, which requires prior transfer of the data to the requesting body. *Specht-Riemenschneider* also argues that such an *in situ*-access would not suffice for the purposes of Chapter V.[618]

The data holder may however decline the request or seek its modification under specific circumstances; for example if the data holder does not have control over the data requested (Art. 18(2)(a)) or if the request does not meet the conditions laid down in Art. 17(1) and (2) (Art. 18(2)(c)).

According to Art. 18(2)(b), the data holder may also decline or seek modification of the request if the data holder already provided the reques-

616 Schaller, T. / Zurawski, P., *ZD-Aktuell* 2022, 01169.
617 Schröder, M., *MMR-Beil.* 2024, 104 (106).
618 Specht-Riemenschneider, L., *MMR-Beil.* 2022, 809 (826).

ted data in response to previously submitted request for the same purpose by another public sector body or Union institution agency or body (*once only-principle*) and the data holder has not been notified of the destruction of the data pursuant to Art. 19(1)(c). While this principle is useful to minimise the burden on data holders and may incentivise a better cross-border coordination between public sector bodies, it may come into conflict with the public interest to respond to a public emergency timely and effectively.[619] As the MPIIC has pointed out, there may be cases where the public sector body which originally requested the data is no longer in the possession of the data or where it cannot provide the data in a timely manner to the public sector body in an exceptional need.[620] In these cases, if there is a public emergency according to Art. 15(a) the public interest should prevail over the interest to minimise the burden for data holders.[621]

According to Art. 18(3), a data holder – in the case of Art. 18(2)(b) – shall indicate the identity of the public sector body or Union institution agency or body that previously submitted a request for the same purpose.

Decline or Seek for Modification

According to Art. 18(2) the decline or the seeking of modification must be made without undue delay and not later than within 5 working days in the case of a request for the data necessary to respond to a public emergency (Art. 15(1)(a)). In other cases of exceptional need the data holder should decline or seek modification without undue delay and not later than within 30 working days, Art. 18(2). Furthermore, rec. 71 states that the "data holder (...) should communicate the underlying justification for refusing the request to the" public sector body requesting the data. This requirement seems to only stem from the recitals.

Potential conflicts between the obligation to make data available and the *sui generis* database rights under the Directive 96/6/EC are not expressly addressed in the provisions, e.g., in Art. 18 or Art. 43. In addition, Art. 43 concerns only data obtained from or generated by a connected product or

619 Max Planck Institute for Innovation and Competition, Position Statement, 2022, p. 55 n. 149.

620 Max Planck Institute for Innovation and Competition, Position Statement, 2022, p. 55 n. 149.

621 Max Planck Institute for Innovation and Competition, Position Statement, 2022, p. 55 n. 149.

related service. Regarding the access right under Art. 14 this leads to the questionable result that the applicability of the *sui generis* database rights depends on the way the data was generated. Only rec. 71 states that "where the *sui generis* database rights [...] apply in relation to the requested datasets, data holders should exercise their rights in a way that does not prevent the public sector body [...] from obtaining the data, or from sharing it, in accordance with" the Data Act. The phrasing of the recital corresponds to the provisions regarding the *sui generis* database rights in the Open Data Directive and the Data Governance Act.[622]

Art. 18(5) also states the possibility for the public sector body to challenge the data holder's refusal and the possibility for the data holder to challenge the request, if the matter cannot be solved by an appropriate modification of the request. The competent authority flows from Art. 37. However, the legal nature of this challenge, its procedure and its legal effects are not further specified in the Art. 37-42, though when the data holder refuses a request in cases of public emergencies a timely decision is urgent.[623]

Anonymisation and Pseudonymisation of Personal Data

If the requested dataset includes personal data the data holder shall anonymise it. Where the compliance with the request requires the disclosure of personal data, the data holder should aggregate or pseudonymise the data, Art. 18(4). According to rec. 64 the public sector body should demonstrate the strict necessity to use personal data and the specific and limited purposes for processing. Rec. 72 underlines that the "making available of the data and their subsequent use should be accompanied by safeguards for the rights and interests of individuals concerned by those data". If this provision was understood as regarding all individuals concerned in any way it would be hard to fulfil. A more practical interpretation would be to understand it as referring to data subjects within the meaning of the GDPR.

In cases of exceptional need not related to a public emergency, personal data cannot be requested, Art. 15(1)(b).

---

622 Leistner, M. / Antoine, L., IPR and the use of open data and data sharing initiatives by public and private actors, 2022, p. 110; Max Planck Institute for Innovation and Competition, Position Statement, 2022, p. 59 n. 161.

623 Cf. Schröder, M., *MMR-Beil.* 2024, 104 (106); corresponding changes were suggested by the Max Planck Institute for Innovation and Competition, Position Statement, 2022, p. 55 n. 150; Krämer, J. et al. Data Act: Towards a balanced EU data regulation, CERRE report, March 2023, p. 69.

7. Obligations of Public Sector Bodies Receiving Data (Art. 19)

Art. 19(1) obliges the public sector body receiving data pursuant to Chapter V to:

- not use the data in a manner incompatible with the purpose for which they were requested (lit. a);
- have implemented technical and organisational measures that preserve the confidentiality and integrity of the requested data and the security of the data transfers, in particular personal data, and safeguard the rights and freedoms of data subjects (lit. b);
- erase the data as soon as they are no longer necessary for the stated purpose and inform the data holder and individuals or organisations that received the data pursuant to Article 21(1) without undue delay that the data have been erased, unless archiving of the data is required in accordance with Union or national law on public access to documents in the context of transparency obligations (lit. c).

The obligation of Art. 19(1)(a) is connected with and secured by the obligation in Art. 19(1(c) to erase the data as soon as they are no longer necessary for the stated purpose. Correspondingly to the obligation to inform the data holder that the data have been destroyed, the data holder should also have the right to inquire whether the data is still stored.[624] Nevertheless, rec. 73 allows the use of the data for other purposes if the data holder that made the data available has expressly agreed for the data to be used for other purposes.

According to Art. 19(2) the public sector body or a third party receiving data should not use the data they receive to develop a product or service that competes with the product or service from which the data originated nor share the data with another third party for that purpose. This provisions mirrors the obligation of the data holder in Art. 4(10).

Additionally, rec. 74 obliges the public sector body receiving data when reusing it to “respect both existing applicable legislation and contractual obligations to which the data holder is subject”. This implies that contractual obligations of the data holder therefore might prevent data use on

624 Max Planck Institute for Innovation and Competition, Position Statement, 2022, p. 57 n. 157.

the basis of Chapter V.[625] Such a consequence should have been regulated directly in the provisions and not merely in a recital.[626] If contractual obligations always trump the obligation to make data available, it could pose an incentive for data holders and third parties to circumvent the obligation under Art. 14.[627] A provision similiar to Art. 7(2), declaring derogation clauses non-binding would have been better suited to foster B2G data sharing.[628] The recital also goes further than and even seems to contradict Art. 17(1)(j) which only requires the public sector body to "make its best efforts to avoid compliance with the data request resulting in the data holders's liability for infringement of Union or national law".

According to Art. 19(3) and rec. 74 the disclosure of trade secrets of the data holder to public sector bodies should only be required where it is strictly necessary to fulfil the purpose for which the data has been requested and confidentiality of such disclosure should be ensured to the data holder. The appropriate measures include the use of model contractual terms, technical standards and the application of codes of conduct. It has been suggested that technical and organisational measures could follow the approach of Art. 25 GDPR.[629]

According to Art. 19(4) a public sector body should be responsible for the security of the data it receives.

8. Compensation in Cases of Exceptional Need (Art. 20)

Whether the data holder may claim compensation depends on the kind of exceptional need which motivates the request.[630] Where the data is made

625 Max Planck Institute for Innovation and Competition, Position Statement, 2022, p. 59 n. 162.

626 Max Planck Institute for Innovation and Competition, Position Statement, 2022, p. 59 n. 162.

627 Max Planck Institute for Innovation and Competition, Position Statement, 2022, p. 59 n. 162.

628 Cf. Max Planck Institute for Innovation and Competition, Position Statement, 2022, p. 59 n. 162; Krämer, J. et al. Data Act: Towards a balanced EU data regulation, CERRE report, March 2023, p. 73.

629 Schröder, M., *MMR-Beil.* 2024, 104 (108); Specht-Riemenschneider *MMR-Beil.* 2022, 809 (825).

630 Various actors proposed that an adequate compensation mechanism should be implemented for all scenarios of an exceptional need that require the making available of data, see Leistner, M. / Antoine, L., IPR and the use of open data and data sharing

available to respond to a public emergency pursuant to Art. 15(a), according to Art. 20(1), the data holder should provide the data free of charge, as the safeguarding of a significant good is at stake in such cases, rec. 75. Rec. 75 gives further reason in this regard: "Public emergencies are rare events and not all such emergencies require the use of data held by enterprises. [...] The business activities of the data holders are therefore not likely to be negatively affected as a consequence of the public sector bodies having recourse to [the Data Act]." However, it is also argued that precisely the exceptional character of data requests in cases of public emergencies are the reason why data holders should be compensated.[631]

In other cases of exceptional need pursuant to Art. 15(b), the data holder should be entitled to fair remuneration as these cases might be more frequent, rec. 75. According to Art. 20(4), however, data holders cannot request compensation in cases of Art. 15(b), if the specific task is the production of official statistics and where the purchase of data is not allowed by national law. The member states should notify the commission about such laws (Art. 20(4) sent. 2).

Rec. 75 clarifies that the compensation should not be understood as constituting payment for the data itself and as being compulsory. According to Art. 20(2) such compensation shall cover the technical and organisational costs incurred to comply with the request including, where necessary, the costs of anonymisation, pseudonymisation, aggregation and of technical adaptation, plus a reasonable margin. The data holder should provide information on the basis for the calculation of the costs and the reasonable margin upon request of the public sector body. The public sector body can request that the data holder provides information on the basis for the calculation of the costs and the reasonable margin. It is neither clearly defined nor further elaborated in the recitals what a "reasonable margin" is and how it should be calculated, thus leading to legal uncertainty.

As the obligation to provide data might constitute a considerable burden on microenterprises and small enterprises (rec. 75), Art. 20(2) applies to small and micro enterprises in all scenarios, even in cases of public emergencies, Art. 20(1), (3).

---

initiatives by public and private actors, 2022, p. 111; Perarnaud, C. / Fanni, R., The EU Data Act – Towards a new European data revolution?, 2022, p. 4.

631 Höne, M. / Knapp, J., *ZGI* 2023, 168 (171).

In case the public sector body disagrees with the requested level of compensation, it may submit a complaint to the competent authority of the member state where the data holder is established, Art. 20(5).

9. *Contribution of Research Organisations or Statistical Bodies (Art. 21)*

Art. 21(1) entitles the public sector body to share data received under Chapter V with individuals or organisations in view of carrying out scientific research or analytics compatible with the purpose for which the data was requested (lit. a). It may also share the data with national statistical institutes and Eurostat for the compilation of official statistics (lit. b), if compatible with the purpose for which the data was requested. Regarding the meaning of "compatible with the purpose" of the request, it remains open how strict it should be interpreted especially concerning its link to the specific emergency.[632]

In such cases, the public sector body should notify the data holder from whom the data was received without undue delay, Art. 21(5). The notification should state the identity and contact details of the organisation or the individual receiving the data, the purpose of the transmission or making available of the data, the period for which the data will be used and the technical and organisational protection measures taken, including where personal data or trade secrets are involved. Where the data holder disagrees with the transmission or making available of data, it may lodge a complaint with the competent authority referred to in Art. 37 of the member state where the data holder is established.

The individuals or organisations receiving the data pursuant to Art. 21(1) should act either on a not-for-profit basis or in the context of a public-interest mission recognised in Union or member state law, not including organisations on which commercial undertakings have a significant influence which is likely to result in preferential access to the results of the research, Art. 21(2) and rec. 76. This resembles Art. 18(c) DGA which requires data altruism organisations to operate on a not-for-profit basis. The individuals or organisations receiving the data must also comply with the provisions of Art. 17(3) and Art. 19.

---

632 Max Planck Institute for Innovation and Competition, Position Statement, 2022, p. 57 n. 156; Schröder, M., *MMR-Beil.* 2024, 104 (107).

According to Art. 21(4) and notwithstanding Art. 19(1)(c) individuals and organisations within the scope of Art. 21(1) may keep the data received for up to 6 months following the erasure of the data by the public sector bodies.

The data sharing for research purposes allows for data sharing with individuals and organisations working on a non-profit basis. This ignores that also profit based research is valuable and often essential in cases of public emergencies, as proven during the pandemic.[633] The provisions on data sharing for scientific purposes are therefore not fully sufficient to enable effective research.[634]

However, according to rec. 63 research-performing organisations and research-funding organisations organised as public sector bodies or as bodies governed by public law already have access rights under Art. 14 and 15. Consequently, for research organisations governed by public law Art. 14 and 15 might even be more relevant than Art. 21. Generally, it is nevertheless an advantage that Art. 21-actors might not have to file a request by themselves, but receive data 'through' another public sector body.

10. Mutual Assistance and Cross-Border Cooperation (Art. 22)

Art. 22(1) obliges the public sector bodies and Union institutions, agencies, and bodies to cooperate and assist one another in order to implement Chapter V in a consistent manner. The following paragraphs (Art. 22(2) to (4)) clarify the preconditions of this assistance. Especially, the exchanged data may not be used in a manner incompatible with the purpose for which they were requested, Art. 22(2).

Art. 22(3) and (4) regulate the procedure in cases, in which the requesting eligible body and the data holder are not in the same member state or the request comes from a Union body. Union bodies as well as public sector bodies intending to request data from a data holder established in another member state should first notify the competent authority of that member state as referred to in Art. 37 (Art. 22(3)).

The competent authority should evaluate the request. The competent authority should examine the request in light of the requirements under Art. 17 and take one of the actions laid down in Art. 22(4)(a)-(b). It should either

633 Specht-Riemenschneider, L., *MMR-Beil. 2022*, 809 (826).
634 Specht-Riemenschneider, L., *MMR-Beil. 2022*, 809 (826).

- transmit the request to the data holder and advise the requesting public sector body, the Commission, the European Central Bank or Union body of the need, if any, to cooperate with public sector bodies of the Member State in which the data holder is established, with the aim of reducing the administrative burden on the data holder in complying with the request (lit. a); or
- alternatively, reject the request on duly substantiated grounds in accordance with Chapter V (lit. b).

The requesting public sector body should take into account the advice of and the grounds provided by the relevant competent authority before taking any further action such as resubmitting the request (Art. 22(4)). The competent authority should act without undue delay, Art. 22(4).

This structure parallels the approach followed by the GDPR. Therefore, the challenges and difficulties of establishing the cooperation structure according to Art. 60-62 GDPR might also be paralleled in the cooperation mechanism of the Data Act.[635]

In cases of a challenge according to Art. 18(5) it is unclear in which member state they should be brought before a competent authority and which possibility to challenge or complain the requesting body has in cases where either the data holder declines the request or the competent authority rejects it.[636]

11. Interplay with Art. 6 GDPR

While the request should as far as it is possible be limited to non-personal data, Art. 17(2)(e), and only include personal data where strictly necessary (rec. 72), cases of exceptional need might often necessitate a request concerning also personal data. Personal data, however, only falls in the scope of the request in cases of Art. 15(1)(a)

635 Leistner, M. / Antoine, L., IPR and the use of open data and data sharing initiatives by public and private actors, 2022, p. 111.
636 Schröder, M., *MMR-Beil.* 2024, 104 (107).

Relationship between Art. 15 and Art. 6 GDPR

As far as personal data is concerned, the making available of data according to Art. 14 and 15 would require a legal basis according to Art. 6 GDPR – as the Data Act is without prejudice to the GDPR (Art. 1(5)). However, Art. 1(5) leaves room for interpretation whether a potential legal basis according Art. 6 GDPR can be established by the Data Act. Some commentators interpret Art. 1(5) in such a way as precluding that the provisions of Chapter V constitute a legal basis according to Art. 6(1)(e), (3) GDPR.[637] Nevertheless, as Art. 6(1)(c), (e) GDPR already provides the possibility of a legal basis outside the GDPR, this would not create a conflict between the GDPR and the Data Act, as it actually complies with the provisions of the GDPR. Rec. 69 also provides that in "accordance with Article 6(1) and 6(3) of Regulation (EU) 2016/679 ... when providing for the legal basis for the making available of data by data holders, in cases of exceptional needs", clarifying that Chapter V should be understood as a legal basis in Union law for the processing of personal data according to Art. 6(1)(e), (c) and Art. 6(3) GDPR. Concurringly, *Leistner* and *Antoine* also argue that the GDPR itself provides the respective legal basis in Art. 6(1)(d) and (e) as situations of exceptional need as defined in Art. 15 will often also justify a need for personal data.[638] However, the threshold of Art. 6(1)(d) is high and cannot be assumed for any case of exceptional need but would have to be proven for each request.

Art. 6(1)(e) GDPR could justify that the public sector body receives and uses personal data, but needs a legal basis outside of the GDPR, Art. 6(3) GDPR. This legal basis could be the provisions of Chapter V, if they meet the requirements of Art. 6(3) GDPR. As a legal basis according to Art. 6(1)(e) GDPR it must either state the purpose of the data processing or the purpose should be necessary for the performance of a task carried out in the public interest, Art. 6(3) GDPR. Art. 14, 15(1)(a) state the aim of the data processing as combatting a public emergency. Art. 6(3) GDPR also requires that the legal basis meets an objective of public interest and be proportionate to the legitimate aim pursued. Art.15(1)(a) meets an objective of public interest. The processing of personal data is proportionate to the aim of

637 Specht-Riemenschneider, L., *ZEuP* 2023, 638 (669).

638 Leistner, M. / Antoine, L., IPR and the use of open data and data sharing initiatives by public and private actors, 2022, p. 111.

combatting public emergencies, Art. 15(1)(a), especially since it should be anonymised or pseudonymised were possible, Art. 18(4).

The data holder who makes personal data available based on a request under Art. 14 could be justified according to Art. 6(1)(c) GDPR, as it is necessary for compliance with a legal obligation.[639] According to Art. 6(1)(c), (3) GDPR it would need to determine the aim of the data processing it requires, Art. 6(3) GDPR, as Art. 14, 15(1)(a) do. However, it could also be argued that a separate justification for the data holder making the data available is not needed, as it could be seen as a specification under Art. 6(3) from whom the public sector body can request the data.

Under Art. 15(c) in the draft Data Act, data processing would have been allowed for various undetermined purposes. The significance of these tasks varied and not each task in the public interest would have justified the processing of any kind of personal data and also the extent of protection needed for different kinds of personal data.[640] Thus, it is understandable, that the corresponding Art.15(1)(b) of the final Data Act only applies to non-personal data. However, it also includes cases of preventing a public emergency, which could justify the making available of personal data and are similar to cases of combatting public emergencies and thus should have been included in Art. 15(1)(a).[641]

In the following articles, especially in Art. 18-21, the Data Act contains specific provisions to adapt the application of rules of the GDPR, as allowed in Art. 6(3) GDPR.

Relationship between Art. 18(5) and Art. 6 GDPR

It is also debated whether Art. 18(5) stipulates a legal ground for data processing according to Art. 6(1)(c) GDPR, as anonymisation and pseud-

---

639 See also Ducuing, C. / Margoni, T. / Schirru, L. (ed.), *CiTiP Working Paper* 2022, pp. 57 et seq.

640 Cf. Wienroeder, M, 2022, Part II (Art. 14-22), in: Hennemann, M. / Karsten, B. / Wienroeder, M. / Lienemann, G. / Ebner, G. (ed.), The Data Act Proposal – Literature Review and Critical Analysis, University of Passau Institute for Law of the Digital Society Research Paper Series No. 23-02, p. 25.

641 Cf. Wienroeder, M, 2022, Part II (Art. 14-22), in: Hennemann, M. / Karsten, B. / Wienroeder, M. / Lienemann, G. / Ebner, G. (ed.), The Data Act Proposal – Literature Review and Critical Analysis, University of Passau Institute for Law of the Digital Society Research Paper Series No. 23-02, p. 25.

onymisation constitute data processing under Art. 4(2) GDPR.[642] In the context of chapter V, Art. 18(5) has to be seen as a specific provision within the legal basis according to Art. 6(1)(c), (e), (3) GDPR adapting the application of rules of the GDPR on "processing operations and processing procedures" (see above). Thus, no further legal ground for the anonymisation and pseudonymisation of the requested data is needed.

Relationship between Art. 21 and Art. 6 GDPR

Regarding Art. 21 it is questionable whether it needs its own justification under Art. 6(1) or also falls under the specification according to Art. 6(3) GDPR, more specifically as a specification on "the entities to, and the purposes for which, the personal data may be disclosed". As the aim of data sharing for research purposes under Art. 21 is not only the disclosure of data but also further data processing by the research organisation, it is questionable whether this should be encompassed as a specification according to Art. 6(3) GDPR. Still, the purpose of data disclosure to other entities will usually be data processing in some form. So, Art. 6(3) could also be interpreted as allowing for provisions on data sharing such as Art. 21.

12. Legal Remedies and Liability

Chapter V provides the possibility to lodge a complaint with the competent authority designated pursuant to Art. 37 in the cases of disputes whether the conditions laid down in Art. 17 are met or over the decline of the request (Art. 18(5)), when the data holders rights under Chapter V have been infringed by the transmission or making available of data according to Art. 17(5), in cases of disputes over the amount of compensation (Art. 20(5)), or in cases of making data available to research organisations and statistical bodies according to Art. 21(5). Those provisions lack clarification with regard to the respective procedure, their legal nature, and their legal effects. Especially, the framework for interim proceedings and the legal protection in cross-border cases could have been further clarified.[643]

---

642 Max Planck Institute for Innovation and Competition, Position Statement, 2022, p. 58 n. 160.

643 Schröder, M., *MMR-Beil.* 2024, 104 (108).

Additionally, Art. 19(4) provides that the requesting bodies should be responsible for the security of the data they receive, without providing legal consequences when the responsibility is violated. It does not seem to entail an independent legal claim for the data holder.[644] However, a violation could be claimed through a complaint according to Art. 17(5).

644 Schröder, M., *MMR-Beil.* 2024, 104 (108).

IX. Switching and Interoperability between Data Processing Services (Art. 23-31, Art. 33-35)

Chapter VI ('Switching Between Data Processing Services', Art. 23-31) imposes "surprisingly radical"[645] regulatory requirements of a contractual, (pre-)commercial, technical and organisational nature on providers of cloud, edge and other data processing services, to enable switching between such services. Having apparently been negotiated last[646], the provisions of Chapter VI have emerged from the institutional trilogue (in a characteristic display of legislative "hypertrophy"[647]) as substantially lengthened, with four new articles altogether.

Chapter VIII ('Interoperability', Art. 33-36) provides for essential requirements regarding interoperability for participants in data spaces and data processing service providers as well as for essential requirements concerning smart contracts. Further technological convergence is envisioned through the development of open interoperability specifications and harmonised standards for the interoperability of data processing services.[648] The rules contained in Chapter VIII have likewise been lengthened significantly as a result of the institutional trilogue.

With the exception of smart contracts addressed in Art. 36 (a "foreign subject"[649] primarily discussed in this work as an avenue for executing data sharing agreements on FRAND terms), both chapters are inextricably linked with one another. Domain name systems (DNS) offer a fitting illustration: within the realm of a data processing service, IP addresses of proximate servers are assigned to users accessing a website. This represents a standard capability of the cloud service model known as infrastructure-

---

645 Bomhard, D. / Merkle, M., *RDi* 2022, 168 (175).

646 After the trilogue meeting on 27 June 2023, an unofficial transcript of the inter-institutional agreement was leaked from which Chapter VI was still missing.

647 Veil, W., Auch der Data Act folgt dem Hypertrophie-Prinzip (Twitter, 20 July 2023) https://twitter.com/winfriedveil/status/1682070656580476928?t=digziO8W0DX0UgOJUH-6RA&s=19 accessed 18 September 2023 (observing that the final text of the Data Act has grown by almost 20,000 words compared to the original Commission proposal).

648 Commission, COM(2022) 68 final Explanatory Memorandum, p. 16.

649 Siglmüller, J., *MMR-Beil.* 2024, 112 (115).

as-a-service (IaaS).[650] For domain names to be organised as they were before the switching process, the DNS service used at the destination needs to map the new server infrastructure correctly and consistently. While this might constitute a relatively simple task, it is hard to accomplish unless the file storing the DNS configuration is exportable.[651] Switching operations beyond such basic syntactic and semantic data portability[652] are even less conceivable without technical standardisation in the way of interoperability – which is the subject-matter regulated by Art. 33 and Art. 35.

The Commission's Rationale for Taking Regulatory Action

In its Impact Assessment Report, the Commission observed the trend of integrated cloud ecosystems combining a variety of services from which customers are in effect prevented to extricate themselves due to contractual, economic, and technical *switching costs*.[653]

The behavioural economic mechanics at play here merit further consideration. Typically, the value of a given cloud service is contingent upon the scale of its customer base. As a corollary, *network effects* – both direct and indirect – are bound to arise along with a significant agglomeration of customers. Particularly in software-as-a-service (SaaS) and platform-as-a-service (PaaS)[654] environments, customers will opt for a widely used platform that allows them to seamlessly exchange documents and applications with business partners.[655] Third-party developers will be drawn to the

650 Autorité de la concurrence, Avis 23-A-08 portant sur le fonctionnement concurrentiel de l'informatique en nuage (cloud), 2023, para. 28.

651 E.g., see the workflow for Google Cloud, Migrate to Cloud DNS https://cloud.google.com/dns/docs/migrating?hl=en accessed 24 September 2023.

652 Cf. Art. 33(2)(b) and the associated definition given by ISO/IEC 19941:2017(en), para. 3.2.3 and 3.2.4.

653 Commission, Impact Assessment Report Accompanying the document Proposal for a [...] Data Act, SWD(2022) 34 final, pp. 19 et seq.; Danyeli, G. ‚Die große Freiheit über die Wolke? Die Regelungen des Data Act zum Wechsel von Cloud-Anbietern und zur Interoperabilität, in Heinze, C. (ed.), Daten, Plattformen und KI als Dreiklang unserer Zeit, DSRI, 2022, p. 428 (rightly adding legal switching costs incurred from conducting data protection compliant transfers of digital assets).

654 Mentioned in rec. 81, among other cloud service models like IaaS; cf. the trichotomy, by now classical, put forth by Mell, P. / Grance, T., The NIST Definition of Cloud Computing (NIST Special Publication 800-145), 2011, p. 2.

655 Schnurr, D., Switching and Interoperability Between Data Processing Services in the Proposed Data Act, CERRE Report, 2022, p. 8.

marketplaces with the most customers. Similarly, their employees are likely familiar with (or even certified professionally for[656]) the particularities of the underlying IT system at the expense of lesser-known cloud service providers.[657] These network effects are further amplified by the fact that the cloud ecosystems with the greatest uptake are vertically integrated across several markets: they are able to source data from a given service to offer another one in a more targeted way[658] and to bundle together complementary products.[659]

As illustrated by the figures for 2022 in the public IaaS market[660], the resulting *lock-in effects* materialise in a concentration of market shares (81.1%) between five conglomerates based in the United States and in China (i.e., the so-called "hyperscalers" Amazon, Microsoft, and Google plus Alibaba and Huawei[661]), presently foiling what the Commission imagines as "the next-generation of fully interoperable, energy efficient and competitive European cloud-to-edge based services"[662]. Due to unabated growth in what customers expend on enterprise cloud solutions offered by these hyperscalers (an amount which has more than tripled from 2017 to 2023[663]), lock-in scenarios will certainly remain a valid concern in the years to come. The requirements under Chapter VI are therefore regarded as a necessary and potent policy option to lower market entry barriers for

656 Autorité de la concurrence, Avis 23-A-08, 2023, para. 267.

657 Autoriteit Consument & Markt (ACM), Market Study Cloud Services, ACM/INT/440323, 2022, p. 48; cf. Gans, J. / Herve, M. / Masri, M. (2023) 19:3 *European Competition Journal* 522 (562) (describing this as sunk costs for staff training).

658 ACM, Market Study Cloud Services, 2022, p. 50 (pointing to Google feeding search results into their cloud-based offerings).

659 ACM, Market Study Cloud Services, 2022, p. 62 (invoking the example of Microsoft 365).

660 Gartner, Gartner Says Worldwide IaaS Public Cloud Services Revenue Grew 30% in 2022, Exceeding $100 Billion for the First Time, 18 July 2023 https://www.gartner.com/en/newsroom/press-releases/2023-07-18-gartner-says-worldwide-iaas-public-cloud-services-revenue-grew-30-percent-in-2022-exceeding-100-billion-for-the-first-time accessed 16 September 2023; for a review of similar numbers in 2021, cf. Danyeli, G., Die große Freiheit über die Wolke? Die Regelungen des Data Act zum Wechsel von Cloud-Anbietern und zur Interoperabilität, in Heinze, C. (ed.), Daten, Plattformen und KI als Dreiklang unserer Zeit, DSRI, 2022, p. 429.

661 Note that in the EU, the fourth and fifth spots are instead occupied, respectively, by IBM and Oracle (cf. ACM, Market Study Cloud Services, 2022, pp. 34 et seq).

662 Council, SWD(2022) 34 final, p. 51.

663 Gans, J. / Herve, M. / Masri, M. (2023) 19:3 *European Competition Journal* 522 (524 et seq. and 538).

(European) data processing services (rec. 78) and to ultimately achieve an innovative "multi-vendor cloud environment" (rec. 100).

Self-regulatory approaches, most notably the SWIPO Codes of Conduct[664] developed in accordance with Art. 6 Regulation (EU) 2018/1807, have so far been unused save for a few providers (cf. rec. 79).[665] Curiously, despite the marginal success of this self-regulatory regime in addressing vendor lock-in (cf. rec. 78 and rec. 90), Art. 6 Regulation (EU) 2018/1807 is not repealed, but according to Art. 1(7) will remain applicable as a voluntary complement to the mandatory provisions of Chapter VI.

On the subject of *technical barriers* to switching, the Commission concurs with findings made by the OECD that a lack of common standards constitutes one of the most pressing barriers to data sharing and re-use.[666] Studies by market authorities have shown this lack to be especially prevalent in the PaaS and IaaS sub-sectors, owing to proprietary databases and unreleased application programming interfaces (APIs).[667] In reaction to the *status quo*, rec. 100 notes that where market dynamics towards harmonised technical specifications are absent, European standardisation bodies on the basis of Regulation (EU) 1025/2012 should intervene at the behest of the Commission.[668] Rec. 103 puts this into concrete terms for semantic interoperability.

1. Surveying the Range of Data Processing Services (Art. 2(8), Art. 31)

A first major point of analysis relates to who is bound by the various obligations stated in Art. 23-31. In spite of more popular labels such as "cloud computing services"[669] contemplated throughout the legislative de-

664 Now rolled into one by SWIPO, Converged Code of Conduct for Data Portability and Cloud Service Switching, 2023.

665 Commission, SWD(2022) 34 final, p. 20 (noting by way of contrast that industry leader AWS alone offers in excess of 200 data processing services); cf. https://swipo.eu/current-swipo-code-adherences accessed 23 September 2023.

666 Council, SWD(2022) 34 final, p. 22.

667 ACM, Market Study Cloud Services, 2022, p. 56; Autorité de la concurrence, Avis 23-A-08, 2023, para. 526 et seqq.

668 Note however that common specifications (based on market-driven open interoperability specifications) offer an alternative route that sticks to self-regulatory developments (cf. Art. 35(5)).

669 Advocated pre-trilogue by the European Parliament (IMCO PE736.701, pp. 23 et seq.).

liberations, the Data Act employs the umbrella term "data processing service". The two-fold reasoning behind this broad terminological choice was to factor in edge computing (i.e., utilising computational resources close to the customer instead of remote data centres[670]) and to capture the all-encompassing reach of cloud-based infrastructure across the digital economy. Crucially, the use of the term "data processing service" extends beyond the switching requirements of Chapter VI to the interoperability standards under Art. 35 (read in conjunction with Art. 30(3)) and to the restrictions on transfers of non-personal data under Art. 32. Conversely, "data processing services" are yet to appear in other pieces of EU data legislation. For instance, Art. 2(13) DMA still employs the conventional framing as "cloud computing services"[671], whereas rec. 28 DGA finds that cloud storage and data intermediation services will generally not intersect.[672]

The Definition Supplied in Art. 2(8)

According to Art. 2(8), 'data processing service' means a digital service enabling ubiquitous, and on-demand network access to a shared pool of configurable, scalable and elastic computing resources of a centralised, distributed or highly distributed nature, provided to a customer, that can be rapidly provisioned and released with minimal management effort or service provider interaction. Rec. 80 spells out in detail what is meant by the IT jargon making up various elements of this definition (ubiquitous, shared pool, scalable, elastic, (highly) distributed).

Proceeding in order of mention, what makes a data processing service 'ubiquitous' is the mechanisms via which resources are accessed in a given network promoting the use of thin clients (e.g., web browsers) and thick clients (i.e., equipment with significant processing capacity such as hard

670 Hon, W.K. et al., Cloud Technology and Services, in Millard, C. (ed.), *Cloud Computing Law* 2nd edn, OUP 2021, p. 17; Godlovitch, I. / Kroon, P., Interoperability, switchability and portability: Implications for the cloud, WIK-Consult Report, 2022, p. 14.

671 Further on their role as core platform services, cf. Geradin, D. / Bania, K. / Katsifis, D. / Circiumaru, A., The regulation of cloud computing: Getting it right (SSRN pre-print) pp. 6 et seq.

672 Specht-Riemenschneider, L., in id. / Hennemann, M. (ed.), Data Governance Act: DGA, Nomos 2023, Art. 2 para. 70.

drives[673]) alike. As rec. 80 elucidates, the pool of computing resources supplied is 'shared' in the sense that they are provided to multiple users, whereas the processing is carried out separately for each user (multi-client platforms[674]). Because outwards scalability and elasticity of computing resources according to fluctuating demand are phenotypical properties of cloud computing overall[675], a plethora of service models will fall firmly within the definition under Art. 2(8). Rec. 81 explicitly affirms this not only for IaaS, PaaS, and SaaS offerings, but is mindful of the existence of more granular or hybrid service models besides and beyond these three categories (sometimes represented in the label XaaS[676]). Rec. 80 and rec. 83 corroborate the rather wide-ranging impetus by recognising virtual IT infrastructure, most notably virtual machines, as a relevant type of computing resource. The stipulation in the concluding sentences of rec. 80 that resources can be allocated either in a distributed or highly distributed manner again embodies the juxtaposition of cloud and edge computing. On the flip side, not every XaaS provider will necessarily qualify as a data processing service because the server infrastructure they supply to the customer could be non-scalable by design.[677]

Online content services (Art. 2(5) Portability Regulation (EU) 2017/1128) such as linear (i.e. scheduled) broadcasting or non-linear (i.e. on-demand) music and video streaming services[678] had – quite controversially[679] – been dispensed from complying with all Chapter VI switching requirements un-

673 Oxford English Dictionary, s.v. "fat client (*n.*)," December 2023, https://doi.org/10.1093/OED/1155432750.

674 Bomhard, D., Auswirkungen des Data Act auf die Geschäftsmodelle von Cloud-Anbietern, *MMR* 2024, 109 (110).

675 Mell, P. / Grance, T., The NIST Definition of Cloud Computing. 2011, p. 2.

676 Boehm, F., Herausforderungen von Cloud-Computing-Verträgen: Vertragstypologische Einordnung, Haftung und Eigentum an Daten, *ZEuP* 2016, 358 (363) (mentioning sub-categories like data-as-a-service and communication-as-a-service); Max Planck Institute for Innovation and Competition, Position Statement, 2022, p. 62 para. 169.

677 Siglmüller, J., *MMR-Beil.* 2024, 112 (114) (raising the consequential question whether scalability should be construed in technical terms or per the stipulations in the service agreement).

678 Engels, S. / Nordemann, J.B., The Portability Regulation (Regulation (EU) 2017/1128) – A Commentary on the Scope and Application, 9 (2018) *JIPITEC* 179 para 22.

679 Max Planck Institute for Innovation and Competition, Position Statement, 2022, p. 62 para. 170; Geiregat, S., The Data Act: Start of a New Era for Data Ownership? (SSRN pre-print), 2022, pp. 30 et seq. at para. 31.

der pre-trilogue versions of the Data Act.[680] The final wording of Art. 2(8), which has dropped this passage, does not change the exclusion of online content services in effect. Namely, rec. 16 firmly states that "textual, audio, or audiovisual [...] content itself, which is often covered by intellectual property rights, inter alia for use by an online service, should not be covered by [the Data Act]".

In Particular: Cloud Switching Invoked by Consumers

By implication, defining data processing services extensively attributes significance to cloud switching in business-to-consumer (b2c) settings, especially compared with earlier drafts of the Act.[681] As Art. 2(30) lays out in the definition of "customer", the contracting party opposite a provider of data processing services can be a natural *or* a legal person. Consumers – a term defined in Art. 2(23) and sparsely used throughout Chapter II – do not unequivocally shine through in the notion of natural persons as customers. The same (tacit inclusion) is true of data subjects as per Art. 4(1) GDPR, which, again, are only related to their potential role as users under Chapter II (Art. 1(5)). To accommodate either concept, "customer" should be understood neither as presupposing legal or natural persons acting in a professional capacity nor as requiring a (monetary) payment to the provider.[682] On the latter point, Art. 23(c) (complemented by rec. 78) explicitly holds that entities supplying free-tier offerings count in among the targeted source providers.

Not having been fully anticipated by the legislator, the profound ramifications of the contractual clauses required by Art. 25(2) on existing rights granted to consumers and data subjects are in need of closer analysis. How these clauses interact with the right to erasure under Art. 17 GDPR, to have one's personal data ported under Art. 20 GDPR, and to retrieve digital content other than personal data in accordance with Art. 16(4) Digital Content

680 E.g., Commission, COM(2022) 68 final, p. 39.

681 Cf. Danyeli, G., Die große Freiheit über die Wolke? Die Regelungen des Data Act zum Wechsel von Cloud-Anbietern und zur Interoperabilität, in Heinze, C. (ed.), Daten, Plattformen und KI als Dreiklang unserer Zeit, DSRI, 2022, p. 430.

682 Geiregat, S., The Data Act: Start of a New Era for Data Ownership? (SSRN preprint), 2022, p. 29 para. 29; for instance, the provision of personal data pursuant to Art. 3(1) of the Digital Content Directive would suffice as the customer's contractual performance.

Directive (EU) 2019/770 (DCD) shall be explored below at the appropriate junctures.[683]

The Role of Data Processing Services in Operationalising Access and Sharing Rights

Chapter II, the access and portability regime for IoT-related data, should be an immediate consideration in the context of switching from one data processing service to another. Datasets stemming from the use of IoT devices will often be fed into a cloud-mediated system on which they are stored remotely.[684] What is more, providers of IoT services are increasingly relying on edge computing, processing data more locally to achieve quicker response times from sensors and mitigate privacy concerns.[685] "[L]imited possibilities regarding the portability of data generated by products connected to the internet " (rec. 20) are therefore bound to persist unless these data sets are easily unlocked from the existing and migrated to a new cloud environment by way of switching.[686]

Exemptions for Custom-Built Services and Beta Versions (Art. 31)

The switching requirements apply irrespective of the size and financial power of a data processing service. A proposal inspired by the rule devised for data holders in Art. 7(1), moving to exempt micro and small enterprises, did not gain sufficient traction in the legislative process.[687] Rather than bringing into play fixed quantitative criteria, the statutory exemptions for data processing services have shifted towards a more flexible situational assessment pursuant to Art. 31 ('Specific regime for certain data processing services'). Underpinning said article is the regulatory impetus to ease the

---

683 On Art. 17 GDPR and Art. 16(4) DCD, cf. sub 5; Art. 20 GDPR is discussed sub 9.

684 Cf. vbw, Data Act – Anpassungsbedarf aus Sicht der Bayerischen Wirtschaft, 2022, p. 16 (noting more generally that data holders and recipients will frequently rely on cloud solutions).

685 Hon, W.K. et al., Cloud Technology and Services in: Millard, C. (ed.), *Cloud Computing Law,* 2nd edn, OUP 2021, p. 17.

686 Max Planck Institute for Innovation and Competition, Position Statement, 2022, p. 60 para. 164.

687 Leistner, M. / Antoine, L., IPR and the use of open data and data sharing initiatives by public and private actors, 2022, pp. 112 et seq.

compliance burden on data processing services if they are not (yet) generally available on the market.

Art. 31(2) fully exempts those data processing services that have been made available temporarily in a non-production version for testing and evaluating purposes. Early access and beta testing programmes, whether private or public (i.e. restricted to the customer base at the time of release or open to new customers), should benefit from this exemption. As testing in late-stage development can typically last up to six months[688] depending on the number of beta testers and the complexity of the software architecture involved, the phrase "for a limited period of time" in Art. 31(2) should be interpreted liberally (in monthly intervals). This view is encouraged by the equivalent privilege for connected products undergoing testing pursuant to Art. 5(2), which altogether lacks a timeframe. Whether a non-production version for testing and evaluation purposes has been supplied by the provider of data processing services is therefore likely to emerge as the decisive question in interpreting Art. 31(2). Trial versions of a fully developed service do not qualify for a couple of reasons, chiefly among which is the fact that they are intended to promote the version with the full range of functionality and thus do not have testing and evaluation as their assigned purpose.[689]

Art. 31(1) addresses a different situation where (i) the majority of the service's main features has been custom-built to accommodate the specific needs of an individual customer *or* where (ii) all components have been developed for the purposes of an individual customer. In both cases, the data processing service must fall short of being offered at broad commercial scale via the provider's service catalogue, which roughly equates to the service being placed on the market (see Art. 2(22) and Art. 5(2) for connected products). Services falling within these parameters will not be required to deliver functional equivalence with the destination service (Art. 23(d), Art. 30(1)), can continue to charge for switching contrary to Art. 29, and do not have to ensure compatibility with harmonised standards and common specifications for the interoperability of data processing services (Art. 30(3), Art. 35). Because compliance with some of the more

688 For want of empirical data on this (at least concerning the public cloud sector), see the figure given by Google, What are software testing phases and GA? https://support.google.com/a/answer/11202276?hl=en accessed 22 September 2023.

689 Note as well that the text adopted by the European Parliament (P9_TA(2023)0069, p. 94) still featured data processing services "that operate on a trial basis".

invasive switching-related obligations is hence lifted by Art. 31(1), this exemption should be highly relevant in practice.[690] Still, providers must have in place a contractual environment that is conducive to switching (Art. 25) and which, on the technical side, is enabled by mandatory open interfaces (Art. 30(2) as well as by data exports upon request by the customer (Art. 30(5)). No further categorisation is made amongst custom-built or tailored services, meaning that providers of IaaS offerings could invoke a literal reading of Art. 30(2) ("data processing services other than those referred to in paragraph 1") to dismiss the associated duties. Paradoxically, their exemption from the far-reaching obligation to achieve functional equivalence would then leave almost no technical duties to implement switching, effectively upending Art. 30 and its division between IaaS providers on the one hand and (functionally more elaborate) SaaS / PaaS businesses on the other hand.[691] As this is hardly what the legislator will have intended by introducing Art. 31(1)[692], one should set the provision right through purposive construction, emphasising that *all* providers are subject to *all residual* technical obligations (i.e. apart from those governed by Art. 30(1) and Art. 30(3)).

Looking at the first scenario, the classification of a service as partially exempt hinges on what makes it "custom-built" and what its "main features" are under the law. As to the former, the notion of a custom-built service lends itself to particular legal uncertainty because such a binary criterion is ill-equipped to decide the nature of a cloud-based solution developed in multiple stages and processes.[693] A useful distinction could be drawn between custom-built and standardised software which was created for a reasonably broad range of customers and for a host of like use cases, with identical copies being marketed as such.[694] Regarding the latter, the main features of a data processing service will vary substantially case-by-case and (subjectively) from customer to customer. At any rate, said main features are to be appreciated in isolation and not with a view to functional equivalence and what destination services offer; they can therefore neither

690 Bomhard, D., *MMR-Beil.* 2024, 109 (110).

691 For the role of IaaS under Art. 30(1), see the concluding sentence of rec. 86 .

692 Cf. the last sentence of rec. 98 (acknowledging that once marketed at broad commercial scale, providers will eventually become subject to Chapter VI in its entirety).

693 Ennis, S. / Evans, B., Cloud Portability and Interoperability under the EU Data Act: Dynamism versus Equivalence (SSRN pre-print), 2023, p. 16.

694 Rebin, I., in Spickhoff, A (ed.), BeckOGK Produkthaftungsgesetz (C.H. Beck 2022) § 2 para. 55.

correspond to the "shared features" pursuant to Art. 2(37) nor (arguably) to which "same service type" (Art. 2(9)) binds together a group of data processing services. Since the *majority* of main features is at issue, an objective assessment could involve which features characteristically denote the service model (for SaaS, integrated applications[695] such as proprietary analytics tools, messaging clients and office suites come to mind).

The second scenario of Art. 31(1) appears remarkably similar to, if perhaps more narrow in scope ("*all* components") than the first scenario. With rec. 98 containing no guidance on the matter, one can do little more than surmise what sets one apart from the other. A viable explanation hones in on the phrase "developed for the purposes of the individual customer", which could signify that the data processing service has been created for them from scratch (as opposed to "custom-built", suggesting non-standard modifications to existing software components).

2. The Terminology of Customer Activation: Switching, On-Premises Transfers and Multi-Homing (Art. 25(3), Art. 34(1))

Despite what its uniform heading ("Switching between data processing services") might suggest, Chapter VI is not rooted in a single action of switching away from the customer's original provider (known as the *source provider*).[696] Customers are instead free to choose between four basic options, boiling down to which contractual relationship they intend to maintain with the source provider and if they want to instruct a new service provider (the so-called *destination provider*) with managing their data and digital assets:

(1) switching to the destination provider (Art. 23(c), Art. 25(2)(a), Art. 25(3)(a))
(2) transfer to on-premises infrastructure (Art. 23(c), Art. 25(2)(a), Art. 25(3)(b))
(3) erasure of the customer's exportable data and digital assets (Art. 25(2)(c)(ii), Art. 25(2)(h), Art. 25(3)(c))
(4) in-parallel use of data processing services (Art. 34(1))

---

695 Autorité de la concurrence, Avis 23-A-08, 2023, para. 24.

696 Bomhard, D., *MMR-Beil.* 2024, 109 (110) rightly points out that regrettably, neither the source nor the destination provider are defined within the Act.

Although Art. 25(3) seems to indicate that customers may exercise the first two options independently from one another ("one or more of the following actions", viz. switching and transfers to on-premises infrastructure *cumulatively*), this must be understood as being directed towards what the customer can request under Art. 25(3)(c). Namely, the erasure of applicable data sets is inherent to both switching and on-premises exports pursuant to Art. 25(2)(h).[697] A juxtaposition with the language used in Art. 25(2)(a) ("to switch to a data processing service [...] *or* to port [...] to an on-premise ICT infrastructure")[698] as well as in rec. 82 (" switch to a different service provided by a different provider of data processing services *or* move to an on-premises ICT infrastructure") reveals that providers are not actually encumbered with a dual obligation. As for the in-parallel use of multiple data processing services, the one-directional actions of switching and on-premises exports are logically incompatible with multi-homing.

Turning first to *switching* as the phenotypical scenario of exiting one data processing service to use another in its place, the statutory definition in Art. 2(34) reads as follows:

> "'switching' means the process involving a source provider of data processing services, a customer of a data processing service and, where relevant, a destination provider of data processing services, whereby the customer of a data processing service changes from using one data processing service to using another data processing service of the same service type, or other service, offered by a different provider of data processing services, or to an on-premises ICT infrastructure, including through extracting, transforming and uploading the data".

Rec. 85 explains these last-mentioned steps in the switching process (extraction, transformation, and uploading). Additionally, a clarification is made whereby switching does not need to involve a wholesale migration from one large-scale cloud environment, but can also consist in unbundling a particular service from the contract (say, moving from one natural language processing tool to the next[699]). The label "switching" does not come without a considerable degree of incoherent terminology. *Sensu stricto*, it denotes the process of migrating data sets to infrastructure controlled by the destin-

697 Erasure is already possible after the passage of the notice period, cf. Art. 25(2)(c)(ii).
698 On a previous draft, cf. Geiregat, S., The Data Act: Start of a New Era for Data Ownership? (SSRN pre-print), 2022, p. 34 para. 34.
699 See the list compiled by Autorité de la concurrence, Avis 23-A-08, 2023, para. 32.

ation provider (e.g., according to Art. 25(3)(a)). More broadly speaking, "switching" is in use as the umbrella term for the three relevant actions sketched above (e.g., in Art. 2(34)). Problematically, the term is also affixed (in Art. 25(3)(b) and rec. 93) to operations destined for an on-premises infrastructure, thereby conflating both customer actions unnecessarily.

It is more accurate to frame *on-premises exports* not as a subset of (essentially cross-platform) switching, but as a distinct possibility of repatriating cloud-based resources. By choosing the expression on-premises ICT infrastructure, the Data Act ostensibly subscribes to the idea of making available exportable data and digital assets via on-premises (*in situ*) portals operated by the source provider. This has been favoured by some economists, particularly for business customers, to overcome information asymmetries to their detriment since multi-dimensional information is rather presented in its full context instead of being packaged and exported *ex situ*.[700] Crucially, on-premises ICT infrastructure is given precisely the opposite meaning under the terms of Art. 2(33), defining it as "ICT infrastructure[701] and computing resources leased, rented or owned by the customer, located in its own data centre and operated by the customer or by a third-party". On-premises transfers are hence construed not as *in-situ* access rights, but as a legal interest to receive[702] data sets akin to Art. 20(1) GDPR (or, perhaps, Art. 16(4) of Directive (EU) 2019/770). Because on-premises infrastructure is housed in the customer's data centre, lock-in effects are perceived as minor in comparison to remote data processing, which is why the actions laid out in Art. 25(2) do not cover on-premises infrastructure as the source of a switching operation.[703]

Finally, pursuant to Art. 23(1), the Data Act's regulatory regime for cloud switching now recognises the in-parallel (i.e., simultaneous) use of several data processing services, a usage pattern otherwise known as *multi-homing*. Non-business customers will often choose to engage with more than one platform (e.g., for cloud storage) in order to have multiple access and

700 Martens, B. / Parker, G. / Petropoulos, G. / van Alstyne, M., Towards Efficient Information Sharing in Network Markets, TILEC Discussion Paper DP 2021-014), 2 November 2021, p. 21.

701 "ICT infrastructure" does not appear to be a legal term of art, especially given that Regulation (EU) 2022/2554 (the Digital Operational Resilience Act) leaves the concept undefined, too.

702 Geiregat, S., The Data Act: Start of a New Era for Data Ownership? (SSRN preprint), 2022, p. 34 para. 34.

703 Criticised by Lagoni, J., *CR* 2024, 91 (95).

backup methods with respect to the relevant data stock.[704] In business contexts, more than 80%[705] of customers have been found to deploy a so-called multi-cloud strategy (mentioned as such in rec. 99), spreading their digital assets between differently operated, complementary cloud services. However, a multi-cloud strategy is by no means tantamount to multi-homing in the sense that two services of the *same* service type are in use for the *same* sets of data.[706] Since well-known technical barriers to switching take hold and hamper multi-homing, Art. 34(1), oddly positioned in Chapter VIII, seeks to provide redress to customers. Apart from functional equivalence and – evidently – the clauses relating to the termination of service and the erasure of data at the source, providers are obliged to enable multi-homing both from a contractual and a technical angle.

3. Guiding Principles and Legal Status of the Switching-related Rights and Duties

For all its detailed provisions, Chapter VI is built on two remarkably short rules guiding the switching process end-to-end and determining the duty-based contractual, commercial, and technical framework which is meant to incentivise switching operations by customers. As expressions of the settled principles of proportionality (Art. 24) and of good faith (Art. 27), these related rules mark the general boundaries of providers' obligations and of the corresponding legal entitlements that customers hold.

In light of these principles, the present section also explores the (semi-contractual) legal nature of the rights and obligations created by Art. 23 et seq., paying particular attention to the construct of portability rights.

Scope of the Technical Obligations (Art. 24)

Art. 24 provides that the responsibilities of providers of data processing services laid down in Art. 23, 25, 29, 30 and 34 shall apply only to the ser-

704 Goode, S., Understanding Single Homing and Multihoming User Switching Propensity in Cloud File Hosting Service Relationships (2020) *e-Service Journal* 34 (42).

705 See the surveys cited by Gans, J. / Herve, M. / Masri, M. (2023) 19:3 *European Competition Journal* 522 (542 et seq.).

706 Autorité de la concurrence, Avis 23-A-08, 2023, para. 76.

vices, contracts or commercial practices provided by the source provider. This is a direct consequence of Chapter VI targeting the source provider exclusively[707] (and not the destination provider, the exception being Art. 27). In essence, the underpinning idea is one of establishing a proportional sphere of responsibility so as not to overburden the source provider: it would be unreasonable (and likely detrimental to innovation and consumer choice[708]) to have the source provider recreate the contractual, commercial, and technical environment to the extent that all service features and contractual clauses of the destination provider can be linked to counterparts at the source.

Even more so, replicating (unknown or unique) functionalities of the destination service would be quasi-impossible without the source provider having some measure of access to the infrastructure of the destination provider[709], thus potentially compromising trade secrets. It is imperative to highlight that this concern was first raised with the objective of stifling the obligation of *functional equivalence* (Art. 2(37), 23(d), 30(1)).[710] While unsuccessful, the criticism impacted the position of the European Parliament[711] and of the Council[712], which ultimately prevailed in the form of rec. 86:

> "Providers of data processing services can only be expected to facilitate functional equivalence for the features that both the source and destination data processing services offer independently."

Further to that end, Art. 30(6) makes it plain that (source) providers are not required to develop new technologies or services in response to a request to switch or transfer made under Art. 25(2)(a), let alone proactively.

707 Cf. Bomhard, D., *MMR-Beil.* 2024, 109 (110); Geradin, D. / Bania, K. / Katsifis, D. / Circiumaru, A., The regulation of cloud computing: Getting it right (SSRN pre-print) p. 15 point out that other switching regimes under EU law such as Art. 106 of the Electronic Communications Code distributes the burden of compliance between the source and destination providers.

708 Ennis, S. / Evans, B., Cloud Portability and Interoperability under the EU Data Act: Dynamism versus Equivalence (SSRN pre-print), 2023, p. 9 (fearing an incentive for firms to "dumb down" complex products).

709 Similarly, Schnurr, D., Switching and Interoperability between Data Processing Services in the Proposed Data Act, CERRE Report, 2022, p. 17.

710 IMCO PE736.701, p. 3.

711 ITRE PE732.704, p. 44 ("shared core functionalities").

712 Council Presidency 2022/0047(COD) – 13342/22, p. 29 ("functionalities that both the originating and destination services offer").

The law therefore acknowledges the – far from unlikely – scenario that the destination provider offers functionalities which are absent from the service at the source (take certain applications and channels for team collaboration within an elaborate SaaS environment).

Against this backdrop, Art. 24 has generalised the rule that source providers are only liable to what pertains to their own service offering with the customer, and thus their sphere of influence.

Cooperation in Good Faith (Art. 27)

Art. 27 requires the parties (and in particular, the destination provider) to cooperate in good faith to make the switching process effective, enable the timely transfer of data, and maintain the continuity of the data processing service. Rec. 97 adds that data should be transferred securely in a commonly used, machine-readable format, and by means of open interfaces. For it not to pre-empt the more detailed modalities of data transfers under Art. 30, this latter regulatory commitment should be read to address destination providers transmitting necessary data to destination providers prior to switching.

The provision marks a logical continuation of Art. 24, reaching into the sphere of influence managed by the destination provider, and stands alone in targeting them. It remains to be seen in (judicial) practice, however, when a refusal to cooperate will be considered in bad faith and what consequences such a refusal would elicit. While Art. 27 means more than a mere encouragement to good-will cooperation, it hardly serves as a legal basis to compel destination providers to execute a technical action or specific business commitments.[713] By contrast, financial penalties pursuant to member state legislation made under Art. 40 or compensatory damages seem a more plausible prospect.[714]

On the opposite side of the switching process, source providers may likewise not obstruct its efficacy, for instance by mandating a single form or gateway for the customer to communicate their switching request.[715]

713 Bomhard, D., *MMR-Beil.* 2024, 109 (111 et seq.).
714 Bomhard, D., *MMR-Beil.* 2024, 109 (112).
715 Piltz, C. / Zwerschke, J., *CR* 2024, 153 (157).

Chapter VI: Basis for a Dedicated 'Cloud Portability Right'?

The duty to remove obstacles to the "porting" of exportable data and other digital assets to a destination service or to on-premises infrastructure (Art. 23(c)) stands out as a firmly data-centric obligation. Were it not formulated *ex negativo*, this obligation could translate to a distinct right that customers may invoke against providers in broadly the same way as the right granted in Art. 5(1). Still, the nature of the underlying legal interest has stirred up some debate – a discussion which should be kept separate from the question if a new portability right in the cloud sector is necessary as well as conducive to the current framework under European Union law.

Geiregat extrapolates from Art. 23(c), jointly read with Art. 25(2)(a) and Art. 30, the creation of a statutory, i.e. "self-standing, immediately enforceable subjective right"[716]. The MPIIC proceeds on the assumption of a contractual right that entails both switching and portability obligations.[717] Relatedly, the Weizenbaum Institute derives from Art. 25(2)(a) a right to switch between providers, along with the conditions for exercising that right.[718] The members of CiTiP take a similar view, interpreting Art. 25(2)(a) in the sense of a "positive obligation to deliver on switching", which the co-legislators failed to frame as an explicit right to switch.[719]

While open to a wide margin of interpretation, caution is merited on what the obligations presented in Art. 23(c) and carved out in greater detail by Art. 25(2)(a) and Art. 30 truly amount to. Ultimately, the hypothesis of a self-standing "cloud portability right"[720] does not hold up to scrutiny. Art. 25(1) does not emulate the language of Art. 5(1), which is generally understood as a dedicated right to port IoT-related data bearing some

716 Geiregat, S., The Data Act: Start of a New Era for Data Ownership? (SSRN pre-print), 2022, p. 40 at para. 43; cf. also p. 29 at para. 28 (with regard to the original Commission Proposal); in apparent agreement: Ennis, S. / Evans, B., Cloud Portability and Interoperability under the EU Data Act: Dynamism versus Equivalence (SSRN pre-print), 2023, p. 11 (noting an "extreme rebalancing of rights in cloud-based assets").

717 Max Planck Institute for Innovation and Competition, Position Statement, 2022, p. 61 n. 167.

718 Weizenbaum Institute for the Networked Society, Position Paper regarding Data Act, 2022, p. 24.

719 Ducuing, C. / Margoni, T. / Schirru, L. (ed.), *CiTiP Working Paper* 2022, p. 60.

720 Geiregat, S., The Data Act: Start of a New Era for Data Ownership? (SSRN pre-print), 2022, p. 29 at para. 28 and *passim*.

resemblance to Art. 20(2) GDPR.[721] Instead, it prescribes a contractual framework for the "rights (...) in relation to switching". To fully grasp the ramifications of this subtle yet crucial difference in semantics (plural instead of singular), Art. 25(1) has to be related back to the overarching mandate under Art. 23(c) to remove all obstacles to porting – commercially, contractually, technically or otherwise. Accordingly, the source provider mainly has a *negative obligation* to refrain from obstructing the switching process, on top of which they are bound by a *positive obligation* to assist in the course of switching under Art. 25(2)(a)(i).

The first-mentioned obligation, surfacing in Art. 23(c), lays the ground for uninhibited porting to take place and, from the perspective of the customer, could be regarded as part of a "right to switchability".[722] Critically, this was also how the Commission's Impact Assessment Report designated a policy option which prevailed over keeping the self-regulatory framework of Regulation (EU) 2018/1807.[723] Switchability, a concept underpinning Art. 23 on the whole, describes the ease – both in time and fees spent – by which customers can terminate a contract and rely on a workable technical framework in order to migrate their data and digital assets to a destination service.[724]

The subsequent obligation, i.e., to assist with the switching process (what brings to mind a *Mitwirkungspflicht* under German legal terminology), should technically be regarded as a right to receive migration support[725] or, economically, as mandatory 'exit management'. Art. 25(2)(b) now consolidates this viewpoint by requiring the source provider to support the customer's exit strategy.

A duty to complete the switching process, which had formed part of the initial proposal[726], is presently not owed by the source provider unless, as

721 Commission, Impact Assessment Report Accompanying the document Proposal for a [...] Data Act, SWD(2022) 34 final, p. 67; cf. Max Planck Institute for Innovation and Competition, Position Statement, 2022, p. 27 n. 69 and *passim*; Ducuing, C. / Margoni, T. / Schirru, L. (ed.), *CiTiP Working Paper* 2022, p. 28.

722 Commission, COM(2022) 68 final Explanatory Memorandum, p. 11.

723 Commission, Impact Assessment Report Accompanying the document Proposal for a [...] Data Act, SWD(2022) 34 final, p. 37.

724 Cf. Godlovitch, I. / Kroon, P., Interoperability, switchability and portability, WIK-Consult Report, 2022, p. 29.

725 For the situation under prior law, cf. Schuster, F. / Hunzinger, S., *CR* 2015, 277 (278 et seq.).

726 Commission, COM(2022) 68 final, Art. 24(1)(a)(1) ("assist and, where technically feasible, complete the switching process").

rec. 85 puts it, "specific professional transition service has been obtained". Migration assistance to the customer and good faith-collaboration with the destination provider (Art. 27) aside, holding the source provider to the successful completion of the switching process has therefore become a matter for private ordering. The exception in this regard, reaching into the sphere of influence managed by the destination provider, is the duty under Art. 23(d) and Art. 30(1) (read with a view to the *caveat* under Art. 24) to facilitate that the highest possible degree of functional equivalence is achieved at the destination. On principle, however, the source provider is not liable to see the customer through the latter stages of the switching process. As rec. 85 elucidates, said responsibility is jointly borne by the destination provider and by the customer themselves:

> "Providers of data processing services and customers have different levels of responsibilities, depending on the steps of the process referred to. For instance, the source provider of data processing services is responsible for extracting the data to a machine-readable format, but *it is the customer and the destination provider who will upload the data to the new environment*, unless specific professional transition service has been obtained." (emphasis added)

Consistent with the plural form used in Art. 25(1) ("rights"), Chapter VI then does not give rise to a directly enforceable cloud portability right, but to a bundle of three interconnected entitlements by virtue of the contract between the customer and the source provider:

(1) the right to demand a position at the source free from (pre-)commercial, technical, contractual, and organisational obstacles to 'switchability' (Art. 23)
(2) the right to have the source provider assist with the switching process, including through appropriate information and security measures (Art. 25(2)(a)(i), (iii), and (iv)), and to insist on good faith-collaboration with the parties involved (Art. 27)
(3) for data processing services of the IaaS variety[727], the right to obtain functional equivalence at the destination through the active contribution of the source provider (Art. 23(d), Art. 30(1))

727 See the final part of rec. 86.

Contrasted with the statutory right to (exportable) data portability found in Art. 30(5)[728], what these rights have in common is their origin within the contract. The concern that the source provider may conceivably take advantage of their bargaining position and alter its contents in a manner contrary to Art. 25(2) should therefore not be neglected.[729] For this provision especially, relying solely on public enforcement by the competent authority under Art. 37(1) falls short in remediating the switching-related obstacles faced by customers.[730] Calls for effective private enforcement in the court system are well-founded so that the conformity of a given contract with the requirements of Art. 25 can be adequately reviewed.[731]

4. *Removing Obstacles to 'Switchability' (Art. 23)*

Art. 23 merges the specific means and ends of regulation to ensure that customers can switch to one or more destination services (or conduct on-premises transfers). As to the enabling means of switching, providers of data processing services are obliged to positively implement the measures fleshed out in the subsequent articles. Art. 23 itself unites beneficial outcomes or ends of a customer-friendly switching process under the overarching ideal of *switchability* (on this term, see the preceding section). Namely, to accomplish switchability, providers shall not impose (or, if they have done so in the past, remove) the following obstacles to effective switching.[732] The provision thereby aligns with Art. 6(6) DMA, with the latter obliging gatekeepers to refrain from restricting users' ability to switch to another platform or remove obstacles to that effect.[733]

728 Cf. below at 9.

729 Geiregat, S., The Data Act: Start of a New Era for Data Ownership? (SSRN pre-print), 2022, p. 40 at para. 42.

730 Max Planck Institute for Innovation and Competition, Position Statement, 2022, p. 67 n. 182.

731 Max Planck Institute for Innovation and Competition, Position Statement, 2022, pp. 67 et seq. n. 183 et seq.; *contra* Geiregat, S. The Data Act: Start of a New Era for Data Ownership? (SSRN pre-print), 2022, p. 40 at para. 43 (criticising this approach as a "detour around national private-law remedies").

732 The wording at the start of the second sentence of Art. 23 ("In particular") does not seem to imply that the measures would have to go beyond what is prescribed in Art. 25 et seq.

733 Louven, S., 'DMA Art. 6', in BeckOK Informations- und Medienrecht (42nd edn, C.H. Beck 2023) para 89.

Firstly, customers should not be deprived of their ability to terminate the original service agreement with the source provider after the statutory notice period has elapsed and the switching process has been completed (Art. 23(a), Art. 25). Secondly, the freedom of contract, that is to conclude a new service agreement with the destination provider covering the same service type (Art. 23(b)) may not be curtailed. Both provisions have to be regarded as safeguards of the customer's private autonomy and as prohibitions on imposing dark patterns, e.g., in the way of hidden terms and conditions.[734] Thirdly, Art. 23(c) stipulates that existing barriers for customers to port their exportable data and digital assets must be removed, including where the customer has benefitted from a free-tier (i.e., non-paid) offering by the source provider. This component of the right to switchability is available to customers irrespective of whether they have elected (phenotypical) switching, multi-homing, or on-premises transfers.

Crucially, digital assets (the most important subset of which are applications) and exportable data are mutually exclusive concepts. Under the Commission's proposal, data and applications both formed part of the umbrella term digital assets[735], which drew criticism for disregarding the diverging needs for data portability or application portability across the spectrum of IaaS, SaaS, and PaaS business models.[736]

By "digital assets" (Art. 2(32)), elements in digital format are meant, including applications, for which the customer has the right of use, independently from the contractual relationship of the data processing service it [the customer] intends to switch from.[737] Rec. 83 brings some clarity which elements besides applications qualify as digital assets: meta-data related to the configuration of settings, security, and access and control rights management, and other elements such as virtual machines and containers fall under the notion of digital assets. Some confusion remains over the meaning of 'applications.' The term could be misconstrued to cover the whole service offered to the customer by a source provider.[738] To avoid ambiguity, 'applications' are best interpreted in terms of IT architecture, for instance as computer programs that the customer could use on the

734 Martini, M. / Kramme, I. / Kamke, A., *MMR* 2023, 399 (402).
735 Commission, COM(2022) 68 final, rec. 72 ("all its digital assets, including data").
736 Ennis, S. / Evans, B., Cloud Portability and Interoperability under the EU Data Act: Dynamism versus Equivalence (SSRN pre-print), 2023, p. 9.
737 Taken from Council Presidency 2022/0047(COD) – 14019/22, p. 37.
738 Bitkom, 'Bitkom Position Paper EU Data Act Proposal', 19 April 2022, 2022, p. 10.

source provider's cloud infrastructure.[739] In any case, the peculiar choice of 'digital assets' – a term that has hitherto largely been endemic to debates on so-called 'digital inheritance'[740] – demonstrates that the rules for switching embrace data portability and application portability alike.[741]

According to Art. 2(38), "exportable data" mean input and output data, including metadata, directly or indirectly generated, or cogenerated, by the customer's use of the data processing service, excluding any data processing service provider's or third party's assets or data protected by intellectual property rights or constituting a trade secret. Rec. 82 goes on to exclude data related to the integrity and security of the service from being exportable. Art. 2(38) is prefaced by the limitation "for the purpose of [Art.] 23 to 31 and [Art.] 35", probably to avoid applying the definition to data sets not concerning data processing services.[742] The omission of Art. 34 is easily adjusted for because that provision, in turn, references Art. 23(c) (amongst other parts of Chapter VI).

The inclusion of co-generated data as exportable has been welcomed in order to prevent lock-in effects.[743] Co-generated data sets can conceivably involve the source or destination providers as well as third parties like other customers; else, the parallelism of granting both groups the same exception for IP rights and trade secrets is hard to explain. *Schnurr* emphasises that the burden of proof rests with the source provider.[744] In any case, it would contravene the spirit of Art. 23 if the source provider could invoke IP rights or trade secrets as an all-out obstruction of migrating to the destination service – namely where the excluded data sets are not clearly specified.[745]

Fourthly, Art. 23(d) highlights functional equivalence in the use of destination services covering the same service type as the final objective of the switching process. Heralded by some as "practically central" *en route*

739 Geiregat, S., The Data Act: Start of a New Era for Data Ownership? (SSRN preprint), 2022, p. 32 at para. 33.

740 Geiregat, S. The Data Act: Start of a New Era for Data Ownership? (SSRN preprint), 2022, p. 33 at para. 33 with further references.

741 Which is made plain in Art. 35(2).

742 Cf. Art. 1(2)(e): "any data and services processed by providers of data processing services".

743 Geiregat, S. The Data Act: Start of a New Era for Data Ownership? (SSRN preprint), 2022, p. 32 at para. 32; precisely to that effect, cf. ALI-ELI Principles for a Data Economy, Pr. 19(2)(e).

744 Schnurr, D., Switching and Interoperability between Data Processing Services in the Proposed Data Act, CERRE Report, 2022, p. 15.

745 See below on Art. 25(2)(e)-(f).

to interoperable ecosystems and IT infrastructures between the source and destination providers[746], functional equivalence is *not* a binding condition that source providers have to actively ensure. This is made clear not least by the passage "in accordance with [Art.] 24", meaning that source providers will ultimately not be liable for the performance of a competitor service outside their sphere of influence. Furthermore, Art. 23(d) does not anticipate or reference Art. 30(1), which establishes further duties concerning functional equivalence.[747] Rec. 86 corroborates said important division:

> "This Regulation does not constitute an obligation to facilitate functional equivalence for providers of data processing services other than those offering services of the IaaS delivery model."

Other data processing services – mainly those of the SaaS and PaaS variety – will only have to comply with Art. 23(d) and may simply not impose obstacles to achieving functional equivalence (as opposed to actively facilitating it pursuant to Art. 30(1)).[748] As drawing the line between IaaS and PaaS has become "an increasingly challenging and artificial pursuit"[749] in practice, one should expect source providers to assert that the majority of their data processing services fall within the PaaS bracket.

Lastly, Art. 23(e) addresses obstacles to unbundling data processing services referred to in Art. 30(1) from other data processing services provided by the source provider. The action of unbundling is intended to separate out IaaS services from the source provider's offering on the whole, thereby overcoming the aforementioned issues with classifying the service model. A comparison with a similar provision in Art. 12(a) DGA suggests that unbundling entails a structural separation, and would not prohibit a continued economic unity between all service models (including IaaS).[750] Alas, structural separation could only succeed where – as Art. 23(e) puts it – this is "technically feasible" in the first place. Rec. 93 frames the viability of un-

746 Leistner, M. / Antoine, L., IPR and the use of open data and data sharing initiatives by public and private actors, 2022, pp. 113 et seq.; further, see below on Art. 30(1).

747 Functional equivalence is therefore discussed in greater detail sub 8.

748 Oblivious to this distinction: Bomhard, D., *MMR-Beil.* 2024, 109 (110 et seq.).

749 Ennis, S. / Evans, B., Cloud Portability and Interoperability under the EU Data Act: Dynamism versus Equivalence (SSRN pre-print), 2023, p. 6; cf. Autorité de la concurrence, Avis 23-A-08, 2023, para. 26.

750 v. Ditfurth, L. / Lienemann, G., The Data Governance Act: – Promoting or Restricting Data Intermediaries? (2022) 23 *Competition and Regulation in Network Industries* 270 (284).

bundling differently as "the absence of major and demonstrated technical obstacles" that prevent it. Interconnected and integrated cloud ecosystems with IaaS elements will typically not be built on a modular architecture, which could in itself amount to a major technical obstacle.[751]

5. Contractual Enablers of Switching (Art. 25)

Whereas Art. 23 requires *ex negativo* that providers of data processing services do away with certain obstacles to 'switchability', Art. 25(2) stipulates the minimum content (rights and corresponding obligations) arising from the contractual agreement between the customer and source provider when it comes to switching to the destination service or moving to on-premises infrastructure. Art. 25(3)-(5) refine these obligations with special regard to the notice and transition periods triggered upon switching.

Art. 25(2) lists a wealth of clauses which to include in the contract between customer and source provider on a mandatory basis. The clauses drastically improve upon the bargaining position of customers of cloud and edge computing services and should have lasting impact on designing terms and conditions for service agreements in the cloud sector.[752] Rec. 96 goes further and encourages relying on (non-binding) standard contractual clauses and other tools for compliance – once adopted before the compliance date of 12 September 2025 (cf. Art. 41) – to foster both legal certainty and trust in data processing services.

Levelling the playing field, smaller source providers will often honour the customer's rights under one service agreement while holding co-extensive rights under a different service agreement with another (upstream) data processing service. Rec. 91 acknowledges this likely dual role:

> "Where providers of data processing services are in turn customers of data processing services provided by a third party provider, they will benefit from more effective switching themselves, while simultaneously invariably bound by this Regulation's obligations regarding their own service offerings."

---

751 Ennis, S. / Evans, B., Cloud Portability and Interoperability under the EU Data Act: Dynamism versus Equivalence (SSRN pre-print), 2023, p. 14.

752 Bomhard, D., *MMR-Beil.* 2024, 109 (111).

Form of the Service Agreement (Art. 25(1))

Per its opening paragraph, Art. 25 requires that a written contract is to be concluded with the customer in a way that allows them to store and reproduce the contract. Any agreement in electronic form with the customer should be sufficient to meet this requirement[753], provided that the agreement has been made available for download before they sign it. A useful point of comparison can be drawn from Art. 28(9) GDPR, according to which an agreement in electronic form qualifies as a contract concluded "in writing".[754]

30-day Transition Period and Other Time Frames

Taken as an ensemble, the clauses required by Art. 25(2)(a), Art. 25(2)(d), and Art. 25(2)(g) determine the general timeline for the switching process. Accordingly, the procedure consists of four major steps.

At the outset, the customer submits a *request* indicating their broad intention to switch, that is without necessarily specifying if they prefer cross-platform switching, erasure of their data and digital assets at the source, multi-homing, or on-premises transfers. The wording of Art. 25(3) ("may notify the provider of data processing services of its decision to perform one or more of the following actions upon termination of the maximum notice period") appears to grant the customer discretion over disclosing their choice, but in doing so remains strikingly vague. The final sentence of rec. 85 errs the other way, stating that customers "should inform" the source provider about their decision. Art. 25(3) therefore lends itself to (at least two) diametrically opposed readings: according to the first, the customer may *only* notify the source provider of their decision upon termination of the maximum notice period (Art. 25(2)(d)), which is indeed reflected in

753 Leistner, M. / Antoine, L., IPR and the use of open data and data sharing initiatives by public and private actors, 2022, p. 114 (referencing Art. 1:301(6) of the Principles of European Contract Law); similarly, see Geiregat, S., The Data Act: Start of a New Era for Data Ownership? (SSRN pre-print), 2022, pp. 39 et seq. at para. 41 (advocating for the phrase "durable medium"); moreover, cf. Piltz, C. / Zwerschke, J., *CR* 2024, 153 (156) (pointing to Sec. 126b German Civil Code).

754 Seegel, A., Cloud-Switching nach Data Act: Der Vorhang fällt, die Fragen offen!, CR-online.de Blog, 15 November 2023.

the syntax of the German-language version.[755] A second – more plausible – reading hones in on the source provider and suggests that they have to start the lengthy process of executing the requested customer action upon termination of the maximum notice period, *until* which point the customer may change their mind.[756]

The initial request is followed by the so-called *notice period,* which has to be specified in the contract. Under Art. 25(2)(d), the period shall not exceed two months, i.e., the customer at most has to give two months' notice. The maximum notice period has been criticised for clashing with widely accepted commercial practices, namely with a fixed minimum duration which is distinctive for some contractual arrangements.[757] It is unclear if the maximum notice period is set in stone or whether it can be extended or otherwise modified by way of private ordering. Because the idea of an alternative (agreed upon) notice period fell through in the trilogue negotiations, one could argue that the two-months limit cannot be prolonged.[758] The answer lies somewhat hidden in rec. 89, holding that "[n]othing in this Regulation prevents [...] parties from agreeing on contracts for data processing services of a fixed duration, including proportionate early termination penalties to cover the early termination of such contracts". Hence, the notice period can be lengthened as a matter of private ordering.

Subject to possible extensions as per Art. 25(4)-(5), the ensuing *maximum mandatory transitional period* under Art. 25(2)(a) lasts 30 calendar days during which the service contract remains in operation. Providers can seek to extend the period prescribed to up to 7 months on the grounds of technical unfeasibility for a switching process to conclude within that time frame (Art. 25(3)). Broadly reminiscent of Art. 12(2) GDPR, due justification for the delay of the switching process must be given within 14 working days of making the switching request. Rec. 87 clarifies that the onus for circumstances constituting technical unfeasibility is fully on the

755 Unlike the English text, the sub-clause "wonach der Kunde den Anbieter von Datenverarbeitungsdiensten *nach Ablauf der maximalen Kündigungsfrist* gemäß Absatz 2 Buchstabe d über seine Entscheidung unterrichten kann" (emphasis added) removes any ambiguity, but is most likely the result of an error in translation.

756 This reading can draw upon Art. 25(2)(c)(ii), in which the end of the notice period coincides with the customer's declaration to erase exportable data and digital assets.

757 Schnurr, D., Switching and Interoperability between Data Processing Services in the Proposed Data Act, CERRE Report, 2022, p. 14.

758 Cf. Ennis, S. / Evans, B., Cloud Portability and Interoperability under the EU Data Act: Dynamism versus Equivalence (SSRN pre-print), 2023, p. 14.

source provider.[759] Capping the transition period at 7 months has drawn criticism for not being workable in more complex cases, e.g. when moving fully integrated enterprise IoT platforms.[760] Finally, a clause to extend the transition period for the purposes of the customer must also be included in the contract according to Art. 25(5) – an option which the customer may invoke prior to or during the transitional period in order to ensure the continuity of service (rec. 87).

After the transition period has elapsed, Art. 25(2)(g) mandates that a further 30 days (or more) be given to customers as the minimum *period for data retrieval.* During this time, the continued security of the relevant data must be ensured pursuant to Art. 25(2)(a)(iv), thus marking the end of the source provider's obligations in assisting with the switching process.

Exit Management through Comprehensive Information (Art. 25(2)(a)-(b))

Time frames aside, Art. 25(2)(a) goes on to establish detailed rules for source providers to offer various aspects of migration support to the customer; at the same time, Art. 25(2)(a)(ii) clarifies that they have to maintain business continuity under the contract. Essentially, source providers have to carry out a form of "exit management"[761] for their customers. Art. 25(2)(b) explicitly requires providers to support the customer's exit strategy relevant to the contracted services, including by providing all relevant information. Rec. 92 and rec. 95 flesh out the contents of the resulting to duty to inform: *inter alia,* customers have to be let in on the scope of the exportable data and digital assets, the intended procedures, tools and available machine-readable data formats involved, known technical restrictions, and the estimated time to complete the switching process. Further information is to be given on known risks to continuity in the provisions of the original service (Art. 25(2)(a)(iii)).

Importantly, Art.25(2)(a)(i) implies the possibility for customers to enlist the services of third parties in the switching process, to whom the source provider needs to furnish the above information as well. Apart from the fact

759 As proposed by Schnurr, D., Switching and Interoperability between Data Processing Services in the Proposed Data Act, CERRE Report, 2022, p. 15.
760 ITRE PE732.704, p. 55.
761 Bomhard, D. / Merkle, M., *RDi* 2021, 168 (175).

that the customer may compensate these third parties, no further mention is made of their involvement.[762]

Effects on Termination of the Contract (Art. 25(2)(c))

Art. 25(2)(c)(i) deems the contract between the customer and the source provider terminated upon the successful completion of the switching process. Art. 25(2)(c)(ii) antedates the point of termination in case the customer merely wishes to have their exportable data and digital assets erased (i.e., without any switching intentions). The contract must contain a corresponding clause, along with a duty to notify the customer that termination has occurred. The notion of a "successfully completed switching process", is not detailed in either Art. 23(a) or Art. 25(2)(c)(i). This lack of conceptual clarity begs the question how "successful completion" is measured.[763] Rec. 92 underscores the successful, effective and secure nature of the switching process, which could point to an objective standard in the sense that the relevant exportable data and digital assets have been migrated to the destination service (as opposed to a perhaps more subjective effectiveness from the customer's point of view). Given the duty of notification, it appears that the source provider – and not the customer – should decide upon successful completion based on objective criteria.

The interplay of this termination *ipso iure* per Art. 25(2)(c) with statutory rights to terminate[764] the contract is entirely left unaddressed and is obfuscated by the wording of Art. 23(a): if the contract automatically ends by successfully completing the switching process, why do source providers have to remove obstacles against (ineffectual) termination thereafter?[765] A haphazard explanation would account for the edge case that customer and source provider have exceptionally agreed to revive the contract, perhaps

762 Cf. rec. 89, third sentence; *vice versa*, the first sentence of rec. 89 concerns the provider outsourcing parts of the switching operation to third parties.

763 Seegel, A., Cloud-Switching nach Data Act: Der Vorhang fällt, die Fragen offen!, CR-online.de Blog, 15 November 2023.

764 In Germany, under the prevailing – if over-simplifying – classification of SaaS arrangements as leases and PaaS / IaaS arrangements as service contracts (*Dienstverträge*), rights of termination are available under Sec. 543 and Sec. 626 German Civil Code, respectively (cf. Strittmatter, M., § 22 Cloud Computing in Auer-Reinsdorff, A. / Conrad, I. (ed.), Handbuch IT- und Datenschutzrecht, 3rd edn, C.H. Beck 2019, para. 31).

765 Seegel, A., Cloud-Switching nach Data Act: Der Vorhang fällt, die Fragen offen!, CR-online.de Blog, 15 November 2023.

because certain data sets were accidentally omitted during the retrieval period.

Art. 25(2)(c) creates further uncertainties regarding the effects of termination on the remuneration owed by the customer. Because termination is tied to the switching process, it is conceivable that the source provider could no longer demand compensation for its services once the transition period has started. Conversely, rec. 89 states that standard service fees do not constitute switching charges under Art. 2(36), pointing to a continuity of remuneration throughout the switching process.[766] Even so, the prospect of a long-term contract being terminated *ipso iure* is bound to impact the revenue recognition of cloud and edge computing businesses.[767]

Exportable Data and Digital Assets (Art. 25(2)(e)-(f))

The categories of data and digital assets which are subject to cross-platform switching or on-premises exports must be specified in a dedicated contractual clause (Art. 25(2)(e)). At a minimum, all exportable data pursuant to Art. 2(38) must be reflected in these data categories.[768] Read in conjunction with rec. 82, those categories must include the customer's input and output data, along with pertinent meta-data, that have been (co-)generated by the customer's use of the data processing service. Furthermore, the exclusion of particular data sets protected by intellectual property would have to be listed. As to the exclusion of trade secrets represented within the exportable data, Art. 25(2)(f) contains a distinct rule. Accordingly, the contract must identify which data categories are exempt from porting or on-premises transfers since they are specific to the internal functioning of the source provider's data processing service and their disclosure would pose the risk of a breach of trade secrets. Art. 25(2)(f) goes on to state that this exemption may not delay or impede the switching process.[769] Source providers may therefore not invoke the extension of the transition period under Art. 25(4) solely because trade secrets are affected; in other words, the effort needed to separate out the data sets concerned does not in itself constitute technical unfeasibility.

766 Extensively, Bomhard, D., *MMR-Beil.* 2024, 109 (111).
767 Id. and Bomhard, D./ Merkle, M. *RDi* 2022, 168 (175).
768 See above on Art. 23(c).
769 Taken from Council Presidency 2022/0047(COD) – 14019/22, p. 56.

Erasure of Data Held by the Source Provider after the Retrieval Period (Art. 25(2)(h))

Finally, the contract must guarantee full erasure of all exportable data and digital assets generated directly by the customer, or relating to the customer directly, after the expiry of the retrieval period (Art. 25(2(g)). Erasure can exceptionally occur *after* the window for data retrieval has drawn to a close if the customer and source provider have agreed to do so (e.g., after reviewing a complex and lengthy switching process). As Art. 25(2)(c)(ii) makes plain, erasure does not have to be linked to a switching request, but may be requested in isolation.

As a result, the scope of the data that are subject to erasure does not mirror the definition of exportable data and digital assets given in Art. 2(32) and Art. 2(38) respectively, instead limiting it to data generated directly by the customer or relating to them directly. Despite apparent intersections with the concept of personal data (Art. 4(1) GDPR: any information *relating* to an identified or identifiable natural person), Art. 25(2)(h) fails to take note of the fact that this contractual agreement on erasure will apply next to the data subject right under Art. 17 GDPR in applicable b2c cases.[770] However, such a complementary relationship can be deduced from rec. 94, stipulating that existing rights relating to the termination of contracts under the GDPR should not be affected. The data subject's right to erasure is hereby addressed given that the absence of a contract will remove the (future) basis for legitimate processing (Art. 17(1)(d), jointly read with Art. 6(1)(b) GDPR).[771]

Interplay with the Digital Content Directive

The contractual arrangements to be taken in accordance with Art. 25(2) are "[w]ithout prejudice to Directive (EU) 2019/770" (i.e. the DCD). Rec. 94 modifies this apodictic statement by maintaining that the Directive's rights relating to the termination of contracts "should not be affected". Another

770 For Chapter II rights, rec. 39 makes this clarification in unmistakable terms; generally, see Art. 1(5).

771 Paal, B.P., DS-GVO Art. 17 Recht auf Löschung ("Recht auf Vergessenwerden"), in id. / Pauly, D.A. (ed.), Datenschutz-Grundverordnung. Bundesdatenschutzgesetz, 3rd edn, C.H. Beck 2021, para. 26.

inclusive conflict rule is found in Art. 1(9), which encompasses the DCD[772] along with other pieces of legislation promoting consumer protection: the Data Act "complements and is without prejudice" to these laws. Crucially, data processing services have to be regarded as digital services within the meaning of Art. 2(2)(b) of the Directive.[773] A conflict therefore arises with the Data Act, at least on the subject of termination-related rights.

The uncertainties of both instruments being applicable to the same set of circumstances have spurred different proposals on how to achieve a workable complementary relationship between the Data Act and the DCD. In the view endorsed by the MPIIC, both laws should not apply in parallel. Because Art. 25 offers a greater level of interoperability and technological governance, it should exclusively apply to digital content, including in b2c relations, thereby pre-empting the directive as the less "ambitious" porting regime.[774] The members of CiTiP concur in the result that Art. 24 constitutes a *lex specialis* to the Directive, finding that Art. 11 et seq. DCD are not suitable for the intricacies of switching operations.[775] Conversely, *Geiregat* argues for dual application in the b2c sphere, with greater consumer protection in effect.[776] This stance deserves support, not least because violations of Art. 25(2) could thus be framed as lack of conformity with the subjective requirements of the contract (Art. 7 DCD).[777]

For example, the customer can elect to retrieve digital content other than personal data (Art. 16(4) DCD) from the source provider's infrastructure rather than conducting a (not dissimilar) on-premises transfer or initiating the cross-platform switching process. Again, as with the interplay between on-premises exports and switching *sensu stricto,* this should not duplicate the burden on the source provider. In the style of a *ius eligendi*[778], the in-parallel application of the Directive and the Data Act therefore stops where the customer has exercised one right over the other.

772 Schmidt-Kessel, M., *MMR-Beil.* 2024, 122 (125).
773 Rec. 19 of Directive (EU) 2019/770 (explicitly mentioning SaaS); cf. Schmidt-Kessel, M., *MMR* 2024, 122 (126).
774 Max Planck Institute for Innovation and Competition, Position Statement, 2022, p. 65 n. 177.
775 Ducuing, C. / Margoni, T. / Schirru, L. (ed.), *CiTiP Working Paper* 2022, 62.
776 Geiregat, S. The Data Act: Start of a New Era for Data Ownership? (SSRN preprint), 2022, pp. 37 et seq. at para. 39.
777 Schmidt-Kessel, M., *MMR-Beil.* 2024, 122 (127).
778 Cf. Sec. 265 German Civil Code.

Private Enforcement?

Unlike the unfair terms regime established by Art. 13, the consequences of failing to include the contractual minimum as prescribed by Art. 25(2) are not mentioned by the legislator.[779] While the service agreement between customer and service provider would remain in operation, violations could lead to financial penalties (Art. 40) or could justify awarding compensatory damages to the customer.[780] With respect to private enforcement, one must differentiate between provisions that are directly enforceable (e.g., Art. 25(2)(d)) and those which require a close review of the stipulations made in the individual contract (e.g., the list under Art. 25(2)(e)-(f)).[781]

6. *Transparency Obligations next to the Contract (Art. 26 and 28)*

Notwithstanding Art. 23, one of the key (if somewhat implicit) conditions for an environment of switchability between data processing services is providing all relevant information to the customer in a clear manner. Various facets of this all-round duty to inform the customer manifest themselves throughout the switching process, namely with regard to exit management (Art. 25(2)(a)(iii), Art. 25(2)(b)), switching charges (Art. 29(4)-(6)), and multi-homing (Art. 31(3)).

Art. 26 expands upon the duty to inform in a discrete provision. It should mainly be understood as an annex to parts of Art. 25 in the sense that the relevant information cannot (or need not) be included in the original contract with the customer.

As for Art. 26(b), this auxiliary role *besides the contract* is accurate: accordingly, source providers have to refer the customer (via hyperlink, etc.) to a self-hosted up-to-date online register (e.g., a restricted website) with details of all data structures[782] and data formats as well as the relevant standards and open interoperability specifications in which the covered

779 *Contra* Piltz, C. / Zwerschke, J., *CR* 2024, 153 (156) (holding that the contractual clauses between source providers and (business) customers will be subject to unfair terms control under Art. 13).

780 Bomhard, D., *MMR-Beil.* 2024, 109 (111).

781 Max Planck Institute for Innovation and Competition, Position Statement, 2022, p. 118 n. 330.

782 Cf. rec. 24 and Art. 33(1)(b); on this and related terminology, see below in the section on Art. 33.

data sets under Art. 25(2)(e) are available.[783] Art. 30(4) adds an obligation to update the register to reflect timely compliance with the standards that are currently in force.[784]

As for Art. 26(a), its content presents a significant overlap with the aforementioned Art. 25(2)(b), essentially re-stating what is listed in rec. 95. Because Art. 25(2)(b) requires that "all relevant information" should be provided, with rec. 95 elaborating on said information in the context of supporting the customer's exit strategy (i.e., precisely the subject matter of Art. 25(2)(b)), the repetition in Art. 26(a) has merely declaratory value.

In light of cloud computing resources being spread between data centres across the globe, most notably in the United States[785], the provision of data processing services carries a momentous international dimension. Art. 28 takes into consideration the prospect of international access and transfer of non-personal data[786] from an information and transparency point of view. Customers are to be informed via the source provider's websites, the URLs of which have to be listed in the service agreement pursuant to Art. 28(2).

First, according to Art. 28(1)(a), customers must be given notice which jurisdiction the physical ICT infrastructure (e.g., servers[787]) deployed for data processing of their individual services is subject to. In line with similar language introduced to the Data Governance Act, "jurisdiction" should be construed broadly enough to cover both EU member states and third countries[788], whilst accounting for jurisdictions in federal legal systems (e.g., in the United States).[789]

Second, Art. 28(1)(b) obliges source providers to make available a general description of the technical, organisational, and contractual measures ad-

783 Council Presidency 2022/0047(COD) – 14019/22, p. 57.

784 See below on Art. 30(3).

785 Taylor, P., Number of data centers worldwide 2023, by country (Statista, 17 September 2023) https://www.statista.com/statistics/1228433/data-centers-worldwide-by-country/.

786 With regard to personal data, Art. 13(1)(f) GDPR – potentially coupled with Art. 49(1) sent. 4 GDPR -- applies as the relevant notice obligation; cf. Paal, B.P. / Hennemann, M., in Paal, B.P. / Pauly, D.A. (ed.), Datenschutz-Grundverordnung. Bundesdatenschutzgesetz, 3rd edn, C.H. Beck 2021, Art. 13 DSGVO para. 19.

787 Cf. rec. 80.

788 Cf. Specht-Riemenschneider, L., in id. / Hennemann, M. (ed.), Data Governance Act, Nomos 2023, Art. 7 mn. 37 (deeming the wording of Art. 7(3)(d) DGA inconclusive on the matter of which jurisdictions are encompassed).

789 Hennemann, M. in Specht-Riemenschneider, L. / id. (ed.), Data Governance Act, Nomos 2023, Art. 21 mn. 83.

opted by them in order to prevent unlawful international governmental access to or governmental transfer of non-personal data held in the European Union. The provision has to be juxtaposed with Art. 32(1), which orders providers to adopt said measures, and could trigger a similar practice to exporting controllers under Art. 44 et seq. GDPR conducting transfer impact assessments.[790] Crucially, the information given only has to relate to the data held by the source provider[791] – and not to those (already) held by the customer or by the destination provider.

7. Commercial Enablers of Switching – Reduced Switching Charges (Art. 29)

On top of data-induced vendor lock-in, customers with large quantities of data have so far been discouraged to switch to a new data processing service because source providers often charge significantly for the retrieval of data (so-called data transfer-out fees[792]) and for their onwards transfer (so-called transport fees[793]). Art. 29 aims to gradually put an end to these commercial obstacles. Relating back to Art. 23(b), the withdrawal of switching charges thereby fosters the ability for customers to conclude new contracts with destination providers.[794]

Key Concepts

According to Art. 2(36), switching charges are "charges, other than standard service fees or early termination penalties, imposed by a provider of data processing services on a customer for the actions mandated by this Regulation for switching to the system of a different provider or to on-premises ICT infrastructure, including data egress charges." Data egress charges, in turn, signify "data transfer fees charged to customers for extracting their data through the network from the ICT infrastructure of a provider of data processing services to the system of a different provider or to on-premises ICT infrastructure" (Art. 2(35)). The term therefore collectively addresses the aforementioned data transfer-out and transport fees.

790 With further references: Piltz, C. / Zwerschke, J., *CR* 2024, 153 (157).
791 Bomhard, D., *MMR-Beil.* 2024, 109 (111); cf. Art. 1(2)(f).
792 Gans, J. / Herve, M. / Masri, M. (2023) 19:3 *European Competition Journal* 522 (530).
793 Commission, Switching of Cloud Services Providers, 2018), pp. 42 et seqq.
794 Bomhard, D., *MMR-Beil.* 2024, 109 (110).

Rec. 89 reiterates that proportionate early termination fees can be agreed (in line with so-called "commitment models"[795]) and that standard service fees can be chargeduntil the contract with the source provider becomes inoperable. Crucially, additional services beyond the switching-related obligations of the source provider can still be performed at cost if the customer has agreed tothe price in advance (consider the specific professional transition service mentioned in rec. 85). In light of the wide range of such professional (transition) services as well as the standard service offering, it has been argued that the quantitative impact of removing switching charges remains limited.[796]

On the other hand, if the provider outsources certain tasks within the switching process to a third-party entity, rec. 89 demands that outsourcing remains cost-neutral to the customer. Finally – in the case of multi-homing – the source provider can only demand data egress charges to the extent that they have incurred such costs (Art. 34(2)).

The Timeline for Withdrawing Switching Charges (Art. 29(1)-(3))

For a period of three years starting on 11 January 2024 (cf. Art. 50), source providers may impose reduced charges compared to the amount they have previously billed their customers for switching to a new service (Art. 29(2)). As evidenced by Art. 29(3), these reduced charges shall only cover the costs for providers directly linked to the switching process, hence eliminating commercial incentives to make a profit at the expense of their customers.

Once the transitional three years have passed (i.e., from 12 January 2027 onwards), switching charges shall be abolished altogether under Art. 29(1). During the legislative process, it was suggested (in vain) to further accelerate the total withdrawal of switching charges for consumers, eliminating them by the date on which the Data Act enters into force.[797]

Going in the opposite direction, some commentators have fiercely criticised the regime established in Art. 29(1)-(3). *Gans* and co-authors fear that the removal of data transfer-out costs in particular will materially shift the price structure to the effect that customers not intending to switch, trans-

795 Lagoni, J., *CR* 2024, 91 (94).
796 Id., at 93.
797 IMCO PE736.701, p. 41.

fer on-premises or multi-home will cross-subsidize customers that do.[798] *Leistner* and *Antoine* point out the financial burden linked to complex switching operations, calling into question the layered 'sunset period' for switching charges.[799] According to *Schnurr*, the burden would especially put a strain on smaller providers of cloud services as they would typically struggle to compensate for the lost switching charges through other revenue streams.[800] Following this line of reasoning, asymmetries in the financial capabilities of differently sized enterprises could have been remedied by allowing microenterprises and small enterprises (especially given their favourable treatment elsewhere in the Act[801]) to continue to claim reduced switching charges even after the sunset period under Art. 29(2) has elapsed.

Monitoring Mechanism (Art. 29(7))

In order to reach the targets set by Art. 29(1)-(3), the Commission may adopt delegated (i.e. tertiary) legislation to monitor the progress of diminishing switching charges during the 3-years transition period (Art. 29(7)). In other words, the Commission is empowered to verify if the respective deadlines under Art. 29(1) and Art. 29(2) have been met. Conversely, it does not follow that the Commission can object to any increase of switching charges within the cost-covering threshold of Art. 29(3) – as may be the case when accounting for inflation.

A delegated act adopted on the basis of Art. 29(7) must comply with the procedural requirements of Art. 45 and take into account the advice of the EDIB pursuant to Art. 42(c)(iii).

Pre-Contractual Notice Obligations (Art. 29(4)-(6))

Art. 29(4) imposes a pre-contractual obligation on providers of data processing services to supply customers with clear information on standard

---

798 Gans, J. / Herve, M. / Masri, M. (2023) 19:3 *European Competition Journal* 522 (528); with similar concerns on price setting: Bomhard, D., *MMR-Beil.* 2024, 109 (111).

799 Leistner, M. / Antoine, L., IPR and the use of open data and data sharing initiatives by public and private actors, 2022, p. 115.

800 Schnurr, D., Switching and Interoperability between Data Processing Services in the Proposed Data Act, CERRE Report, 2022, p. 15.

801 Cf. Art. 7(1), Art. 15(2) and Art. 20.

service fees, early termination penalties, and reduced switching charges. Art. 25(2)(i) repeats this obligation as far as switching charges are concerned. Possibly because of their volatility, applicable switching charges have to be (re-)stated in a dedicated contractual clause.

Art. 29(5) obliges the provider to flag data processing services within their service offering that involve highly complex or costly switching or even make switching impossible without significant interference in the data, digital assets or service architecture.

In a similar vein to Art. 28, providers shall make the just-mentioned pieces of information available via a dedicated section of their website or in any other easily accessible way (Art. 29(6)).

8. Functional Equivalence across IaaS Environments (Art. 30(1))

Art. 30 strikes a key distinction within the vast range of data processing services. Some providers will supply scalable and elastic computing resources limited to infrastructural elements such as servers, networks and the virtual resources necessary for operating the infrastructure. On top of that, they do *not* provide access to the operating services, software and applications that are stored, otherwise processed, or deployed on those infrastructural elements. These providers are subject to an enhanced switching-related obligation. Not only do they have to refrain from imposing obstacles to achieving functional equivalence (Art. 23(d)), but the providers of these services are bound by a much higher standard under Art. 30(1):

> "Providers [...] shall, in accordance with Article 27, take all reasonable measures in their power to facilitate that the customer, after switching to a service covering the same service type, achieves functional equivalence in the use of the destination data processing service."

In its final sentence, rec. 86 sheds light on the addressees of this obligation, revealing (*e contrario*) that Art. 30(1) targets providers offering services of the IaaS delivery model. As previously sketched, the resulting distinction between IaaS and PaaS (and, to a lesser degree, SaaS) is often hardly achievable.[802] For example, Identity and Access Management services (IAM) speak to this point because they are found across the PaaS / IaaS spec-

802 Ennis, S. / Evans, B., Cloud Portability and Interoperability under the EU Data Act: Dynamism versus Equivalence (SSRN pre-print), 2023, p. 6 with further references.

trum.[803] Even if the lines were less blurred, Art. 30(1) can still be criticised for missing a clear justification to hold the providers of IaaS offerings to a tougher standard.[804] In search of a rationale, the observation that a given service within heterogeneous ecosystems of the PaaS or SaaS varieties will lack a clear equivalent or correspond to multiple counterpart services at the destination more often is not fully convincing (or indeed, alien to IaaS).[805]

Functional Equivalence – A Feasible Concept?

According to Art. 2(37) "functional equivalence" means "re-establishing on the basis of the customer's exportable data and digital assets, a minimum level of functionality in the environment of a new data processing service of the same service type after the switching process, where the destination data processing service delivers a materially comparable outcome in response to the same input for shared features supplied to the customer under the contract." The "same service type", in turn, signifies a set of data processing services that share the same primary objective, data processing service model and main functionalities (Art. 2(9)).

Rec. 81 clarifies that the conventional data processing models (IaaS, SaaS, PaaS, and so forth) are not necessarily coextensive with the operational characteristics defining a service type. As to these operational characteristics, the legislation remains silent: what constitutes the primary objective and main functionalities of a given service and, conversely, which functionalities are merely of ancillary or secondary importance to this primary objective? Whilst attempts to pinpoint the main functionalities of multipurpose business cloud platforms (e.g., AWS, Microsoft Azure, Salesforce or SAP S/4HANA) would have proven as futile[806], examples based on less complex service types such as cloud storage could have shed some light on what the same service type – and thus, functional equivalence – actually entails. Rec. 81 partly remedies this vagueness by opening up the notion "same service type" and accepting that data processing services "of the same service type may have different [...] characteristics such as performance, security, resilience, and quality of service".

---

803 Autorité de la concurrence, Avis 23-A-08, 2023, para. 32.

804 Ennis, S. / Evans, B., Cloud Portability and Interoperability under the EU Data Act: Dynamism versus Equivalence (SSRN pre-print), 2023, p. 11.

805 Gans, J. / Herve, M. / Masri, M. (2023) 19:3 *European Competition Journal* 522 (559).

806 Cf. Siglmüller, J., *MMR-Beil.* 2024, 112 (115).

The definition of "functional equivalence" in Art. 2(37) is itself not immune to regulatory friction for it does not consider the interplay with a similar term defined in Art. 2(12) DCD:

> "'functionality' means the ability of the digital content or digital service to perform its functions having regard to its purpose;"

One is naturally drawn to compare both definitions and wonder if the yardstick of functionality has a bearing on "functional equivalence" within the meaning of the Data Act.[807] If answered in the affirmative, specific contractual assurances on what the source provider may perform in terms of output could come into play.[808] While the Act cannot be construed to conclusively lean one way or the other on this question, it should be noted that the *removal* of contractual obstacles to the detriment of switching – as the overarching theme to ensuring functional equivalence under Art. 23(d) – would hardly require *preserving* each contractual arrangement on the main functionalities at the source.

The Best Effort to Achieving Functional Equivalence (Art. 30(1), Art. 30(6))

Source providers have to take all reasonable measures *within their power* to facilitate that the customer achieves functional equivalence post-switching. By making reference to Art. 27, the provision demonstrates that functional equivalence hinges upon the source provider's in cooperating with the destination provider *bona fide*. The emphasis on cooperation also marks a minor contrast to Art. 23(d) citing Art. 24, whereby efforts regarding functional equivalence are directly limited to the source provider's sphere of influence. Nonetheless, the principle of proportionality enshrined in Art. 24 holds sway over the cases governed by Art. 30(1) as well. For one thing, functional equivalence does not amount to duplication of service at the destination. For another, source providers are not required to develop new technologies and services in the name of functional equivalence according to Art. 30(6).[809] Rec. 92 confirms these observations:

> "A source provider of data processing services does not have access to or insights into the environment of the destination provider of data

807 Ducuing, C. / Margoni, T. / Schirru, L. (ed.), *CiTiP Working Paper* 2022, 63.
808 Ducuing, C. / Margoni, T. / Schirru, L. (ed.), *CiTiP Working Paper* 2022, 63.
809 Cf. Bomhard, D., *MMR-Beil.* 2024, 109 (110).

> processing services. Functional equivalence should not be understood to oblige the source provider of data processing services to rebuild the service in question within the infrastructure of the destination provider of data processing services."[810]

The remaining part of Art. 30(6) states that source providers do not have to disclose or transfer (unlicensed) IP-protected digital assets or those containing trade secrets. This assertion is likely redundant since the customer could no longer claim the right of use for the respective digital assets in these cases anyway (cf. Art. 2(32)).

9. *Interoperability Requirements Aimed at Data Processing Services other than IaaS (Art. 30(2)-(5), Art. 35)*

Continuing the division along the lines of IaaS delivery models on the one hand, and PaaS / SaaS delivery models on the other, Art. 30(2)-Art. 30(5) turn to the latter. Coupled with Art. 35, intricate rules for the standardisation of data processing services are introduced, most of which revolve around the pivotal notion of interoperability.

Cloud Interoperability in a Nutshell (Art. 2(40), Art. 35(2))

As a concept, "interoperability" carries connotations of openness and interconnectedness, which is why it is generally thought to enhance innovation and consumer choice in data ecosystems.[811] In the realm of data processing services, linking them by way of interoperability could give rise to complex and diverse service ensembles.[812] Where the level of interoperability is high (bordering on over-standardisation), the concept can however exert precisely the opposite effects in negatively impacting security and reliability of service as well as innovation incentives on digital markets.[813] A balanced

810 Gans, J. / Herve, M. / Masri, M. (2023) 19:3 *European Competition Journal* 522 (558) attributes this recital to the European Parliament's mandate for negotiation.

811 Gasser, U., Interoperability in the Digital Ecosystem, 2015, pp. 9 et seq.

812 Schnurr, D., Switching and Interoperability between Data Processing Services in the Proposed Data Act, CERRE Report, 2022, p. 12.

813 Gasser, U., Interoperability in the Digital Ecosystem, 2015, at pp. 14 et seq.; Godlovitch, I. / Kroon, P., Interoperability, switchability and portability, WIK-Consult Report, 2022, p. 26.

calibration of interoperability requirements and definitions is therefore needed.

According to Art. 2(40), interoperability means the ability of two or more data spaces or communication networks, systems, connected products, applications, data processing services or components to exchange and use data in order to perform their functions. This definition, which borrows from long-standing jargon in computer science[814] essentially applies to digital infrastructure *in toto*, addressing their ability to exchange data on multiple levels of abstraction. An interesting parallel can be drawn to Art. 2(29) DMA, which goes further by blending in certain aspects of functional equivalence ("[...]so that all elements of hardware or software work with other hardware and software and with users in all the ways in which they are intended to function"). Conversely, *Siglmüller* approximates interoperability under Art. 2(40) to "compatibility" as understood by Art. 2(10) DCD, describing the ability of digital content to function with hardware or software typically used for digital content of the same type, without the need for conversion.[815]

For the purposes of data processing services, the above definition is incomplete without looking at the specifics of cloud interoperability. Art. 35(2)(a) reproduces, to the letter, the five layers advanced by the International Standards Organization (ISO) as standards for cloud interoperability.[816] The first three layers relate to the ability of systems to communicate through common infrastructures (transport interoperability), data formats (syntactic interoperability), and data models (semantic interoperability). At the fourth layer, "behavioural interoperability" seems to describe a lesser form of functional equivalence by focusing on the result of the data exchange, which has to match the expected outcome (cf. Art. 35(1)(c)). Finally, the policy layer of interoperability essentially reflects compliance with legal and organisational frameworks.

Art. 35(2) goes on to codify the remaining components of the aforementioned ISO standard. Whereas (b) enumerates syntactic, semantic, and policy data portability, (c) turns to application portability with distinct

814 Cf. ISO-Norm ISO/IEC 19941:2017, Information technology — Cloud computing — Interoperability and portability (mentioned twice in rec. 90 and rec. 100); IEEE Standard Glossary of Software Engineering Terminology, 1990, p. 42.

815 Siglmüller, J., *MMR-Beil.* 2024, 112 (115).

816 ISO-Norm ISO/IEC 19941:2017, Information technology — Cloud computing — Interoperability and portability, pp. 36 et seq.

facets such as metadata portability. It remains unclear if this dual terminology mirrors the migration of exportable data and digital assets, of which applications form part pursuant to Art. 2(32). *Schnurr* points out the dependency of workable application portability and switching-related "service portability" on existing vertical interoperability between the service and the underlying platform infrastructure.[817]

Open Interfaces (Art. 30(2))

Data processing services not designated as IaaS (including edge computing services) need not cater for functional equivalence, but have to set up open interfaces, at no additional cost to customers or concerned destination providers (Art. 30(2)). Along with other avenues for access and communication such as websites or intranet portals, Application Programming Interfaces (APIs, the importance of which is singled out in Art. 33(1)(c)) qualify as open interfaces.[818] In recognition of APIs fundamentally contributing to (various levels of) cloud interoperability when made available, the second sentence of Art. 30(2) stipulates that the obligation to share APIs or open up other interfaces is designed and shall include sufficient information "for the purposes of data portability *and interoperability*".[819]

Under the approach put into effect by Art. 30(2), interfaces only have to be made available between the parties, i.e. not publicly.[820] More importantly, the defence not to disclose digital assets that are protected as intellec-

817 Schnurr, D., Switching and Interoperability between Data Processing Services in the Proposed Data Act, CERRE Report, 2022, p. 12; for a different understanding of vertical interoperability (namely between upstream and downstream services), cf. Godlovitch, I. / Kroon, P., Interoperability, switchability and portability, WIK-Consult Report, 2022, p. 27.

818 Cf., e.g., Commission, Explanatory Notes on VAT e-commerce rules, September 2020, pp. 8 et seq.

819 First suggested by ACM, Proposal to enhance the draft Data Act: Based on a national market study into Cloud services, 2022 https://www.acm.nl/system/files/documents/proposal-to-enhance-the-draft-data-act.pdf;cf. Schnurr, D., Switching and Interoperability between Data Processing Services in the Proposed Data Act, CERRE Report, 2022, pp. 18 et seq.;Ennis, S. / Evans, B., Cloud Portability and Interoperability under the EU Data Act: Dynamism versus Equivalence (SSRN pre-print), 2023, p. 8.

820 By contrast, cf. the initial wording given by COM(2022) 68 final, p. 54 ("providers of data processing services shall make open interfaces publicly available and free of charge.").

tual property or as trade secrets as granted by Art. 30(6) will come into play. It therefore becomes a highly relevant question to which extent providers can claim copyright protection over or trade secrets represented in APIs. As to the former, while a majority of commentators dismisses the idea, the Court of Justice is yet to rule squarely on whether software copyright covers APIs.[821] As to the latter, APIs lend themselves to being protected as trade secrets (Art. 2(18)) owing to the underlying, potentially marketable source code.[822]

Even if invoked successfully, one could argue that the defence arising from Art. 30(6) cannot deprive the customer of the necessary technical means for switching. In other words, the general prohibition on imposing obstacles of a technical nature stated (Art. 23) implies that at least one viable open interface should be at hand.[823]

Standardisation En Route to Fully Fledged Interoperability (Art. 30(3), Art. 35)

Besides making available open interfaces, non-IaaS data processing services have to adhere to further regulatory standards. Art. 30(3) - extrapolated in Art. 35 - mandates that providers have to ensure compatibility with common specifications based on open interoperability specifications *or* with harmonised standards for interoperability. The relevant services have to be brought into compliance with these standards at least 12 months after the Commission has published references in a designated Union standards repository for the interoperability of data processing services (Art. 35(8)).

In stark contrast with Art. 33(5) and Art. 36(6), harmonised standards made by European standardisation organisations under Regulation (EU) No. 1012/2012 do not take precedence over common specifications adopted by the Commission.[824] Instead, the Commission enjoys discretion

---

821 Aplin, T. / Radauer, A. / Bader, M.A. / Searle, N., The Role of EU Trade Secrets Law in the Data Economy: An Empirical Analysis, *IIC* 2023, 826 (850); concurringly, Leistner, M. / Antoine, L., IPR and the use of open data and data sharing initiatives by public and private actors, 2022, p. 46 (on interface specifications).

822 From a transnational perspective cf. Irion, K., 'Algorithms Off-limits', *FaccT '22,* 1561 (1566).

823 Cf. Max Planck Institute for Innovation and Competition, Position Statement, 2022, p. 66 n. 180.

824 Rec. 100 even points the other way: " [...] where market-driven processes have not demonstrated a capacity to establish common specifications or standards that facil-

over whether to initiate the drafting process for harmonised standards (Art. 35(4): "may request") and / or seize its own regulatory authority through common specifications (Art. 35(5): "may [...] adopt"). This has rightly been identified as an oversight on the part of the legislator for it may lead to conflicting interoperability requirements.[825] The undesirable prospect of two standardisation instruments covering the same subject-matter could be resolved, however, by understanding the Commission's discretion as a binary choice between harmonised standards and common specifications in practice. Said interpretation aligns with the limits on the Commission's regulatory power regarding common specifications, given that the views of member state authorities and other relevant expert groups and bodies need to be taken into account pursuant to Art. 35(6). In another deviation from the otherwise parallel regimes for data spaces (Art. 33(7)) and smart contracts (Art. 36(8)), the EDIB is not expressly mentioned here.

Crucially, common specifications adopted by the Commission are not a stand-alone regulatory instrument according to Art. 30(3), but find their basis in so-called *open interoperability specifications.* Art. 2(41) defines open interoperability specifications as technical specifications in the field of information and communication technologies which are performance oriented towards achieving interoperability between data processing services. Art. 35(3) adds that these specifications need to have been developed through an open-decision making process, thereby avoiding the prevalence of dominant firms' proprietary standards.[826] Also, they need to have gained market acceptance, among other procedural and substantive requirements laid down in Annex II of Regulation (EU) No. 1025/2012. Rec. 100 further sheds light on the self-regulatory origin of open interoperability specifications, noting that the Commission should rely "on parties in the market to develop relevant open interoperability specifications to keep up with the fast pace of technological development in this industry."

Irrespective of which standardisation instrument is chosen, the aforementioned layers of cloud interoperability as per Art. 35(2) ought to be adequately addressed. Other than interoperability, Art. 35(1) demands that the broader objectives in regulating data processing services (portability of

itate effective cloud interoperability at the PaaS and SaaS levels, the Commission should be able, on the basis of this Regulation and in accordance with Regulation (EU) No 1025/2012, to request European standardisation bodies to develop such standards [...]".

825 Siglmüller, J., *MMR-Beil.* 2024, 112 (116).

826 Cf. Paal, B. / Fenik, M., *ZfDR* 2023, 249 (260).

digital assets, functional equivalence, security and integrity of service) must be taken into account as well. Lastly, Art. 35(1)(e) pays heed to technological neutrality and fast-paced evolution and innovation (cf. rec. 100).

Art. 30(5) – An Oblique Right to (Exportable) Data Portability

Should no relevant standards under Art. 30(3), read jointly with Art. 35(8), exist as of yet, Art. 30(5) contains a fall-back provision whereby all exportable data shall be exported in a structured, commonly used, and machine-readable format at the customer's request. This provision, which does not have an exact counterpart in Art. 4 et seq., responds to a problem frequently voiced during the consultation period, namely lacklustre standardisation in data formats.[827]

As with the access right under Art. 4(1), the mandate to use a "structured, commonly used, and machine-readable format" emulates the wording of Art. 20(1) GDPR.[828]

Unlike the switching-related rights bundled together in the contract with the source provider, Art. 30(5) codifies a discrete *statutory right to data portability* held by the customer. However, its inapplicability to IaaS offerings, exacerbated by the residual role as a fall-back provision for Art. 30(3), arguably limit the practical reach of the right considerably.[829] If deemed applicable, Art. 30(5) could transcend Art. 20(1) GDPR. While both provisions exclude inferred and derived data[830] and safeguard IP rights and trade secrets in similar ways[831], the notion of exportable data is broader in extending to non-personal data as well (cf. Art. 28(1)(b)).

827 Podzsun, R., Der EU Data Act und der Zugang zu Sekundärmärkten am Beispiel des Handwerks, 2022, p. 45.

828 On these format requirements, cf. sub V.2., above.

829 Cf. Schnurr, D., Switching and Interoperability between Data Processing Services in the Proposed Data Act, CERRE Report, 2022, p. 23 (advocating for Art. 30(5) to be elevated to the default requirement for all exportable data).

830 Cf. rec. 15 on the one hand ("[...]information inferred or derived from such data, which is the outcome of additional investments into assigning values or insights from the data, in particular by means of proprietary, complex algorithms, including those that are a part of proprietary software, should not be considered to fall within the scope of this Regulation [...]"; on the other hand, cf. Article 29 Working Party, 'Guidelines on the right to data portability' WP 242 rev.01, 5 April 2017, p. 10.

831 On the one hand, see Art. 2(38); on the other hand, cf. the settled interpretation of Art. 20(4) GDPR, e.g., by Brandt, E. / Grewe, M., 'Datenportabilität 2.0', *MMR* 2023, 928 (930).

Consequently, the question arises to which extent Art. 30(5) can operate next to (or is superseded by) the GDPR right to personal data portability where customers are data subjects, too. In order to give a sound answer, one must turn to Art. 1(5) which calibrates the interface of the Act's provisions with data protection law. In principle, both regulatory regimes are positioned in a complementary relationship, which the second sentence of Art. 1(5) explicitly affirms for the interplay of Art. 15, 20 GDPR with Chapter II's access and sharing rights. Where a conflict with data protection law presents itself, however, the rights enshrined in the GDPR are set to prevail.[832] A *conflict* in the established (technical) sense of the word goes beyond a simple disparity, and cannot be reconciled through a normative device that allows for the two colliding rules to co-exist.[833] For exportable data that prove to be personal data, given the switching-related notification and transition periods, the time frame under Art. 30(5) to respond to a porting request would typically exceed one month as per Art. 12(3) GDPR. To avoid having to separate personal and non-personal exportable data, that is to achieve a coherent data export despite the (perhaps unforeseen) conflict, the one-month period under Art. 12(3) GDPR could be integrated into Art. 30(5). At any rate, having the customer decide between a GDPR or a Data Act "route" to exporting their data hardly serves a practical demand.[834]

10. Interoperability Requirements within Data Spaces (Art. 33)

Data spaces are part and parcel of the European Data Strategy, with the "establishment of EU-wide common, interoperable data spaces in strategic sectors"[835] being regarded as a key priority for boosting data sharing in the public and private sectors. To date, although 14 of the so-called Common

832 Conducting a holistic analysis of Art. 1(5), Schmidt-Kessel, M., *MMR-Beil.* 2024, 122 (126) argues that the precedence of data protection law already follows from the "without prejudice" clause in the first sentence, thus regarding the conflict rule in the third sentence as "obsolete at best".

833 Specht-Riemenschneider, L., *ZEuP* 2023, 638 (647) (quoting authority, specifically Joined Cases C-54/17 and C-55/17 *Autorità Garante della Concorrenza e del Mercato v. Wind Tre SpA & Vodafone Italia SpA* at para. 60).

834 Steinrötter, B., *GRUR* 2023, 216 (223) (with respect to Art. 4 and Art. 5).

835 Commission, COM(2022) 66 final, p. 16.

European Data Spaces have been announced[836], none has been fully implemented. Presently, the Regulation on the European Health Data Space, a political agreement on which has been reached on 22 March 2024[837], appears to be the singular regulatory instrument underway. In part, this is due to the Commission choosing not to rely on "overly detailed, heavy-handed ex ante regulation"[838] in favour of agile tools such as regulatory sandboxes.

Crucially, Art. 33 is not necessarily concerned with sector-specific considerations, but sets out a high-level, i.e. sector-agnostic interoperability framework for all kinds of data spaces.[839]

Defining Data Spaces

In Art. 33(1) and rec. 103, the legislator restates the definition given in Art. 30(h) DGA, which frames Common European Data Spaces as "purpose- or sector-specific or cross-sectoral interoperable frameworks of common standards and practices to share or jointly process data for, *inter alia*, the development of new products and services, scientific research or civil society initiatives" (emphasis added). The umbrella term "data spaces", however, continues to lack a legislative definition. Turning to the main policy documents on the matter, one can deduce at least that data spaces make up larger data ecosystems (and eventually, a single market for data[840]) as characteristically open infrastructures allowing for the pooling, access, and sharing of data sources.[841] Moreover, data sharing where one parti-

836 Common European Data Spaces are envisioned to serve the needs of the following sectors and policy areas: high-level environmental initiatives ("European Green Deal"), industrial manufacturing, healthcare, energy, mobility, financial services, research, agriculture, employable skills, media, cultural heritage, and the public administration; for an in-depth synopsis, cf. Commission, SWD(2022) 45 final, pp. 12 et seq.

837 Cf. the original proposal of the Commission, COM(2022) 197 final.

838 Commission, COM(2022) 66 final, p. 12; further on the Commission's agile governance approach, cf. Ducuing, C. / Margoni, T. / Schirru, L. (ed.), *CiTiP Working Paper* 2022, pp. 97 et seq.

839 As is noted by Ducuing, C. / Margoni, T. / Schirru, L. (ed.), *CiTiP Working Paper* 2022, p. 16.

840 Schmidt-Kessel, M., *MMR-Beil.* 2024, 75 (76) (referring to Commission, COM(2022) 66 final, p. 6).

841 Bitkom, Data Spaces and Data Ecosystems - First Explainer and Current Status, 2022, p. 5 (citing Council, SWD(2022) 45 final, p. 2 and documentation on the GAIA-X project).

cipant in the infrastructure offers data or data services falls within the ambit of data spaces and, consequently, triggers the applicability of Art. 33.[842] Rec. 103 supports this finding in defining "participants" (formerly: operators[843]) in data spaces as entities facilitating or engaging in data sharing within common European data spaces, including data holders. Data spaces can accordingly be understood as forums for exchanging product and related services data as well.[844]

Art. 33 as an Overarching Rule Governing Data Processing Services?

Ushering in the standardisation regime of Chapter VIII, it has been posited that Art. 33 represents a *lex generalis* which governs data processing services as well. Consequently, Art. 35 would merely modify and build on the general interoperability requirements of Art. 33 by way of a *lex specialis.*[845] This supposition is mainly substantiated through the use of the label "data services" in Art. 33(1), which allegedly ties in with the narrower concept of data processing services.[846]

"Data services", however, does not unequivocally constitute the hypernym for data processing services. For one thing, rec. 113 plainly mentions both concepts without hinting at any terminological hierarchy between them.[847] Secondly, the term "data services" has hitherto solely been brought up in a policy context, with no clear technical (let alone statutory) meaning attributed to it.[848] Even if "data services" could be identified as a term of art with data processing services as its sub-set, Art. 33(1) and the rules of Chapter VI display too many incongruities to support a hierarchical (rather than separate) design of Art. 33 and Art. 35. To give an example, it is hard to square with a hierarchical understanding why the transparency obligation pursuant to Art. 26(b) stops at data structures and data formats when Art. 33(1)(b) further requires that vocabularies, classification

842 Extensively, Siglmüller, J., *MMR-Beil.* 2024, 112 (113).
843 Council Presidency 2022/0047(COD) – 14019/22, p. 38.
844 Take the mention of connected products in Art. 33(1)(c).
845 Siglmüller, J., *MMR-Beil.* 2024, 112 (113).
846 Id. at 113.
847 As is conceded by Siglmüller, J., *MMR-Beil.* 2024, 112 (112).
848 E.g. Commission, COM(2022) 66 final, p. 27 ("Roll out re-usable data-services on a large scale to assist in collecting, sharing, processing and analysing large volumes of data") or Gaia-X, Gaia-X Federation Services (GXFS)', 1 December 2021, p. 3 ("This is how new data services providing value to all participants will be created").

schemes, taxonomies, and code lists shall be described in a publicly available and consistent manner. Additionally, the vision of automatic access and transmission of data within data spaces, possibly continuously and in real-time, provide a clear indication that Art. 33(1)(c) is not intended to subvert the time frames for complex switching operations set out in Art. 25. Instead, connected products and data sharing agreements are mentioned, which fits more adequately into the data access and sharing ecosystem for IoT products and services that is germane to Chapters II and III of the Act.

Essential Requirements for Data Spaces (Art. 33(1)-(2))

Per its opening paragraph, Art. 33 enumerates, on a high level of abstraction, four categories of essential requirements to facilitate the interoperability of data, data sharing mechanisms, and services. The following paragraphs supply a variety of regulatory instruments (delegated acts, harmonised standards, common specifications, and guidelines) to flesh out the finer points of these essential requirements for a specific sector or for data spaces in general. These avenues for direct regulatory intervention have been interpreted as a consequential reaction to the limited success of the market-driven approach under Art. 20 GDPR to develop interoperable formats.[849]

According to Art. 33(1)(a), key properties of a given data set relating to its usability (content, use restrictions, licences, data collection methodology, data quality and uncertainty, i.e. likelihood of veracity[850]) shall be sufficiently described so that recipients can find, access, and use the data set. Where applicable, this information shall be given in a machine-readable[851] format. Art. 33(1)(b) mandates that formal aspects of the data set, most notably its format and structure as elaborated through relevant vocabularies, classification schemes and data taxonomies, shall be described in a publicly available and consistent manner. *Siglmüller* identifies (somewhat illogical) differences between the two norms as far as the modalities of disclosure are concerned. It would seem that the description per Art. 33(1)(b) need

849 Callewaert, C., Data Act und Datenportabilität - Lesson Learned?, in Heinze, C. (ed.), Daten, Plattformen und KI als Dreiklang unserer Zeit, DSRI, 2022, pp. 422 et seq.; cf. rec. 68 GDPR.

850 Butterfield, A. / Ngondi, G.E. / Kerr, A. (ed.), A Dictionary of Computer Science, s.v. "uncertainty", 7th edn, OUP 2016.

851 On the notion of machine readability, cf. sub V.2.

not be in a machine-readable format, and *vice versa,* the information under Art. 33(1)(a) could also be made available under the terms of a data licensing agreement.[852] Likewise, it does not stand to reason why Art. 33(1)(b) refrains from stating the usability of the data set for recipients as the intended regulatory goal, which – as in Art. 33(1)(a) – would imply a sufficient quantity of the information as well as the absence of data dumps.[853]

Art. 33(1)(c) highlights APIs as an imperative tool to access and transmit data automatically and, where technically feasible, do so continuously, in bulk download, or in real-time in a machine-readable format. Not least by referencing connected products at the end, the provision is clearly geared towards realising the user's right to access and share readily available data pursuant to Art. 4(1) and Art. 5(1), respectively. Again (as in the case of Art. 30(2)), the potential of awarding intellectual property rights over APIs needs to be accounted for.[854] This should however not thwart the mere description (i.e., documentation[855]) as required by Art. 33(1)(c).

Going beyond documentation, Art. 33(1)(d) stands out as the only genuine interoperability mandate for participants in data spaces.[856] Accordingly, participants have to provide the means to enable the interoperability of tools for automating the execution of data sharing agreements. Special emphasis is put on smart contracts, thus pointing to the requirements of Art. 36.[857]

Art. 33(2) acknowledges that the essential requirements under Art. 33(1) are, by their very nature, non-descript and in a state of constant flux due to technological and market developments. To remedy the inherent vagueness, the Commission is given the power to adopt delegated acts. These delegated acts must comply with the procedural requirements of Art. 45 and take into account the advice of the EDIB pursuant to Art. 42(c)(iii).

---

852 Siglmüller, J., *MMR-Beil.* 2024, 112 (113 et seq.).

853 A similar issue concerning the same piece of statutory language arises in the context of Art. 3(2)(a) and rec. 24 (cf. sub IV.3.).

854 Max Planck Institute for Innovation and Competition, Position Statement, 2022, p. 82 n. 223.

855 Siglmüller, J., *MMR-Beil.* 2024, 112 (114).

856 Id. at 114.

857 Cf. sub VI. 7.

Harmonised Standards (Art. 33(3)-(4))

Adhering to Art. 33(4), the Commission shall request one or more of the three European standardisation organisations (CEN, Cenelec, and ETSI[858]) to draft harmonised standards on the matter of essential requirements for data spaces.

Art. 33(3) institutes a (non-rebuttable) presumption of conformity with the essential requirements prescribed by Art. 33(1) if a participant offering data or data services in the data space can show compliance with the relevant parts of the harmonised standards.

Common Specifications (Art. 33(5)-(10))

Where the Commission's request under Art. 33(4) has not been accepted by the European standardisation organisation in question, or where the harmonised standards are not delivered within the applicable deadline or within the parameters of the request, the Commission may intervene in the absence of harmonised standards published in the Official Journal and adopt common specifications (Art. 33(5)). Rec. 103 makes it clear that these common specifications rank lower than harmonised standards: they represent "an *exceptional fall-back solution* to facilitate compliance with the essential requirements of this Regulation, or when the standardisation process is blocked, or when there are delays in the establishment of appropriate harmonised standards" (emphasis added).[859]

The subsidiary power of the Commission is affirmed through the duties to notify a committee established under Art. 22 of Regulation (EU) No. 1025/2012 (Art. 33(6)) and to consider the advice of expert groups as well as consult with relevant stakeholders (Art. 33(7)). The obligations to review and, if necessary, amend common specifications upon the intervention of member states (Art. 33(10)) and to repeal common specifications where harmonised standards have been published (Art. 33(9)) further attest to this.

In parallel with Art. 33(3), Art. 33(8) raises a presumption of conformity if a participant offering data or data services in the data space can show compliance with the relevant parts of the common specifications.

858 Annex I of Regulation (EU) No. 1025/2012.
859 Cf. sub VI. 7. (regarding the parallel regime for smart contracts in Art. 36).

Guidelines (Art. 33(11))

Art. 33 concludes by affording the Commission the opportunity to adopt guidelines regarding the aforementioned (sectorial) common European data spaces. Importantly, Art. 30(h) DGA comes into play, according to which the guidelines are proposed to the Commission by the EDIB, specifically its third sub-group pursuant to Art. 29(2)(c) DGA.[860]

While the EDIB is accounted for here, the same cannot be said of the equally relevant Data Spaces Support Centre.[861]

860 Cf. Hennemann, M., in Specht-Riemenschneider, L. / id. (ed.), Data Governance Act: DGA, Nomos 2023, Art. 30 para. 28.

861 Max Planck Institute for Innovation and Competition, Position Statement, 2022, p. 84 n. 232; cf. Council, SWD(2022) 45 final, p. 8.

X. International Governmental Access and Transfer (Art. 32)

Chapter VII ('Unlawful International Governmental Access and Transfer of Non-Personal Data', Art. 32) aims to prevent unlawful governmental access to non-personal data held in the Union by data processing services offered on the Union market through technical, legal, and organisational safeguards.[862] Rec. 101 argues respectively that "third countries may adopt laws, regulations and other legal acts that aim to directly transfer or provide governmental access to non-personal data located outside their borders, including in the Union."

The provision of Art. 32 recalls similar provisions first in the GDPR (Art. 44-50) for personal data and then in the DGA (Art. 31); the latter being concerned with non-personal data as well as with data sharing services, public sector bodies, natural or legal persons with the right to re-use data and recognised data altruism organisations. Generally, the structure and provisions of Art. 32 mirror the approach of Art. 31 DGA, with few differences.

The terms "access" and "transfer" are not defined in the Data Act. As Art. 32 uses the same wording as Art. 31 DGA and mirrors its provisions, it seems plausible to also apply the definition in Art. 2(13) DGA for "access" as meaning "data use, in accordance with specific technical, legal or organisational requirements, without necessarily implying the transmission or downloading of data". While neither the Data Act nor the DGA define "transfer", it still seems plausible to understand it similarly. For Art. 31 DGA it is argued to understand "transfer" in contrast to the definition of "access" as only meaning the active disclosure of data to third-countries.[863]

Art. 32 only addresses data held by data processing services according to Art. 2(12).[864] Thus, other activities of a company that is not only active as a

862 Commission, COM(2022) 68 final Explanatory Memorandum, p. 16.

863 Hennemann, M., in: Specht-Riemenschneider, L./Hennemann, M., Data Governance Act, 2023, Art. 31 DGA, mn. 32; Schreiber, K. / Pommerening, P. / Schoel, P., Das neue Recht der Daten-Governance, § 5 mn 6 et seq.

864 The broad term "providers of data processing services" also includes cloud storage providers, thus leading to an efficient protection of data which is not stored in in-house infrastructure, see Leistner, M. / Antoine, L., IPR and the use of open data and data sharing initiatives by public and private actors, 2022, p. 115.

data processing service are not covered by Art. 32.[865] They might, however, fall under the scope of the GDPR or the DGA (Art. 31).

According to Art. 32 and as a general rule, the transfer of non-personal data is generally allowed and partially regulated by Art. 32 (while the transfer of personal data is according to Art. 44-50 GDPR generally forbidden and only in specific cases allowed).[866] In practice, however, it might become difficult to determine whether Art. 44-50 GDPR or Art. 32 apply, as firstly personal and non-personal data may be mixed in datasets and secondly it is increasingly hard to distinguish personal and non-personal data.[867]

Generally, the approach of Art. 32 is not free of doubt. There is the risk that it hinders the objectives of Art. 23-31 to enable switching between data processing services, which means a transfer of data, by obliging the providers of data processing services to prevent international governmental access and transfer. It is therefore questioned whether Art. 32 is in line with the principal objective of the Data Act to enhance data sharing.[868] Some commentators have advocated that Art. 32 is not necessary and justified as – with regard to non-personal data – its prime objective is not the protection of fundamental rights and freedoms of the data subject.[869] However, non-personal data can have implications for the public interest, for example related to trade secrets, intellectual property, and public security that can justify the restriction of international data transfer.

1. Preventing International and Third-Country Governmental Access and Transfer of Non-Personal Data (Art. 32(1))

Where a governmental access or transfer would create a conflict with Union law or the national law of the relevant member state, Art. 32(1) obliges the providers of data processing services to take all adequate technical, legal, and organisational measures, including contracts, in order to prevent

865 Max Planck Institute for Innovation and Competition, Position Statement, 2022, p. 69 n. 189.

866 Hennemann, M., in: Specht Riemenschneider, L./Hennemann, M., Data Governance Act, 2023, Art. 31 DGA, mn. 1.

867 Ducuing, C. / Margoni, T. / Schirru, L. (ed.), *CiTiP Working Paper* 2022, 69.

868 Max Planck Institute for Innovation and Competition, Position Statement, 2022, p. 69 n. 189.

869 Max Planck Institute for Innovation and Competition, Position Statement, 2022, p. 69 n. 190.

international and third-country governmental access and transfer of such non-personal data held in the Union.

The MPIIC argued concerning the provision of the draft Data Act, that it could lead to data processing service providers completely refraining from transferring data to countries outside of the EU.[870] According to its interpretation of the provision of the draft Data Act it could have required the monitoring of the content of all data, although a provider of data processing services is not a content provider.[871] Insofar, the wording of the final provision indicates more clearly that only governmental access and transfer and not any international transfer creating a conflict with union law should be prevented. Still as no specific event as for example a judgement is required (as in paragraph (2) and (3)),[872] the requirement to take all reasonable measures to prevent any governmental access or transfer creating a conflict with union law is a considerable burden on providers of data processing services.

The assessment of this provision depends in particular on the understanding of "create a conflict with union law". The MPIIC interprets it as even requiring less than an actual violation of the law by the data access or transfer.[873] Also, a different interpretation of Art. 32(1) seems possible. One might argue that that the transfer shall only be restricted in specific cases where legislation specifically prohibits governmental access or transfer.[874] In light of the final wording of the provision this interpretation seems more plausible. Potentially along these lines, rec. 101 specifies such potential conflicts with Union or member state law as conflicts with obligation to protect such data, in particular as regards the protection of fundamental rights of the individual, such as the right to security and the right to an effective remedy, or the fundamental interests of a member state related to national security or defence, as well as the protection of commercially

870 Max Planck Institute for Innovation and Competition, Position Statement, 2022 p. 73 n. 197.

871 Max Planck Institute for Innovation and Competition, Position Statement, 2022 p. 73 n. 200.

872 Max Planck Institute for Innovation and Competition, Position Statement, 2022 p. 73 n. 198 et seq.

873 Max Planck Institute for Innovation and Competition, Position Statement, 2022 p. 75 n. 206.

874 See also in the context of the parallel rule of Art. 31 DGA Hennemann, M., in: Specht-Riemenschneider, L./Hennemann, M., Data Governance Act, 2023, Art. 31 DGA, mn. 24.

sensitive data, including the protection of trade secrets, and the protection of intellectual property rights, and including its contractual undertakings regarding confidentiality in accordance with such law. The obligation to prevent governmental access to and transfer of non-personal data should thus not be understood as an independent liability provision for the data processing services.[875]

The draft Data Act followed the wording of the DGA and required providers of data processing services to take all "reasonable [...] measures", while the final wording differs from the DGA, requiring "adequate [...] measures". While both have a similar meaning, the deliberate deviation from the wording of Art. 31 DGA indicates that indeed a different standard is required. In rec. 102 "the encryption of data, the frequent submission to audits, the verified adherence to relevant security reassurance certification schemes, and the modification of corporate policies" are given as exemplary measures that should be taken by the providers of data processing services.

2. *Enforcement of Foreign Judgements and Decisions (Art. 32 paras. 2 and 3)*

Judgments of third-country courts or tribunals or decisions of third-country administrative authorities, including law enforcement authorities requiring such transfer or giving access to non-personal data should only be recognised or enforceable when based on an international agreement, such as a mutual legal assistance treaty[876], in force between the requesting third country and the Union or a member state, Art. 32(2) and rec. 101. If such an agreement exists, it sets a clear legal standard.[877] Rec. 101 further explains that

> "in other cases, situations may arise where a request to transfer or provide access to non-personal data arising from a third country law conflicts with an obligation to protect such data under Union law or under the national law of the relevant Member State, in particular regarding

875 See in the context of the parallel rule of Art. 31 DGA Hennemann, M., in: Specht-Riemenschneider, L. / Hennemann, M., Data Governance Act, 2023, Art. 31 DGA, mn. 40.

876 For example the Agreement on mutual legal assistance between the European Union and the United States of America (2003) or the Agreement between the European Union and Japan on mutual legal assistance in criminal matters (2010).

877 Max Planck Institute for Innovation and Competition, Position Statement, 2022 p. 70 n. 193.

the protection of fundamental rights of the individual, such as the right to security and the right to an effective remedy, or the fundamental interests of a Member State related to national security or defence, as well as the protection of commercially sensitive data, including the protection of trade secrets, and the protection of intellectual property rights, including its contractual undertakings regarding confidentiality in accordance with such law."

In the absence of international agreements regulating such matters and if compliance with the decision would risk putting the addressee in conflict with Union law or the relevant national law, transfer or access should only be allowed according to Art. 32(3), if

(a) the third-country system requires the reasons and proportionality of such a decision or judgement to be set out and requires such a decision or judgement to be specific in character (...); and
(b) the reasoned objection of the addressee is subject to a review by a competent third-country court or tribunal; and
(c) the competent third-country court or tribunal issuing the decision or judgement or reviewing the decision of an administrative authority is empowered under the law of that third country to take duly into account the relevant legal interests of the provider of the data protected by Union law or by the national law of the relevant Member State.

Art. 32(3) regulates in particular scenarios in which the data processing service is in a conflict of contradictory duties according to different legal systems.[878] To determine, whether the conditions laid down in the first subparagraph are met, according to Art. 32(3)(2) the addressee of the decision can ask the opinion of the relevant national body or authority competent for international cooperation in legal matters, notably when it considers that the decision may relate to trade secrets and other commercially sensitive data as well as to content protected by intellectual property rights or the transfer may lead to re-identification. This mitigates the burden on the service provider.[879] If the addressee considers that the decision may impinge on national security or defence interests of the Union or its member states,

878 See in the context of the parallel rule of Art. 31 DGA Hennemann, M., in: Specht-Riemenschneider, L. / Hennemann, M., Data Governance Act, 2023, Art. 31 DGA, mn. 53.

879 Max Planck Institute for Innovation and Competition, Position Statement, 2022 p. 71 n. 194.

it shall ask the opinion of the national competent bodies or authorities with the relevant competence, in order to determine whether the data requested concerns national security or defence interests of the Union or its member states, Art. 32(3) subpara. 2 sent. 2. If the addressee has not received a reply within a month, or if the opinion of the competent authorities concludes that the conditions are not met, the addressee may deny the request for transfer or access on those grounds, Art. 32(3) subpara. 2 sent. 3. The wording of this subparagraph clarifies that the determination whether there is a conflict with EU or national law according to Art. 32(1) is not covered in its provisions,[880] although also in this scenario the possibility to ask the opinion of the national competent bodies would have helped foster legal certainty for data processing services.

The wording "may reject" implies that the issued opinions of the competent authorities are not binding, as the addressee of the decision is not obliged to deny the transfer of data. It is however questionable that the case of not receiving a reply should be treated the same as when the conditions of the first subparagraph are not met.

The EDIB shall advise the Commission on developing guidelines on the assessment of whether the conditions laid down in Art. 32(3) are met.[881]

Leistner and *Antoine* see the conditions for transferring or making data available laid down in Art. 32(3) as an adequate and structured framework for protecting non-personal data against inadequate international transfer or governmental access.[882] In contrast, the BDI criticises, that it implements a level of protection for non-personal data which is usually only known for the protection of personal data as protection of fundamental rights.[883]

3. Minimisation and Informational Duty (Art. 32 (4) and (5))

According to Art. 32(4), "if the conditions laid down in para. 2 and 3 are met, the provider of data processing services shall provide the minimum

880 This was less clear under the original proposal, cf. Max Planck Institute for Innovation and Competition, Position Statement, 2022 p. 71 n. 195.

881 Welcomed bv Leistner, M. / Antoine, L., IPR and the use of open data and data sharing initiatives by public and private actors, 2022, p. 116; BDI Stellungnahme zum Legislativvorschlag des EU-Data Act, 2022, p. 21.

882 Leistner, M. / Antoine, L., IPR and the use of open data and data sharing initiatives by public and private actors, 2022, p. 115.

883 BDI Stellungnahme zum Legislativvorschlag des EU-Data Act, 2022, p. 21.

amount of data permissible in response to a request". The "minimum amount of data" should be determined based on either the provider's reasonable interpretation of the request or that of the relevant competent body's or authority's, Art. 32(4). Referring to the "amount of data" is rather misguided, as often the informational content is more important than its amount.[884]

The rule of Art. 32(4) applies if the transfer of non-personal data is not in conflict with Union law or the national law of the relevant member state. If such a conflict exists the data should not be transferred.[885]

The provision refers to the reasonable interpretation of the respective request by the relevant national body or authority referred to in Art. 32(3) and (2). This approach does not really clarify this vague requirement, which was already criticised in the parallel Art. 31(4) DGA[886].

According to Art. 32(5) the provider of data processing services should inform the customer about the existence of a request of a third-country authority to access its data before complying with that request, except where the request serves law enforcement purposes and for as long as this is necessary to preserve the effectiveness of the law enforcement activity. Rec. 101 adds, that the provider of data processing services should,

> "wherever possible under the terms of the data access request of the third country's authority, be able to inform the customer whose data are being requested before granting access to those data in order to verify the presence of a potential conflict of such access with Union or national rules, such as those on the protection of commercially sensitive data, including the protection of trade secrets and intellectual property rights and the contractual undertakings regarding confidentiality."

---

884 Max Planck Institute for Innovation and Competition, Position Statement, 2022 p. 72 n. 196.

885 See in the context of the parallel rule of Art. 31 DGA Hennemann, M., in: Specht-Riemenschneider, L. / Hennemann, M., Data Governance Act, 2023, Art. 31 DGA, mn. 60.

886 Hennemann, M., in: Specht-Riemenschneider, L. / Hennemann, M., Data Governance Act, 2023, Art. 31 DGA, mn. 59.

XI. Implementation and Enforcement (Art. 37-42)

Chapter IX ('Implementation and Enforcement', Art. 37-42) lays down the implementation and enforcement framework with regard to competent authorities in each member state, including a complaints mechanism and cooperation with data protection authorities.[887] Thereby, Chapter IX focuses on public enforcement and fails to address private enforcement. However, the mentioning of collective actions in rec. 108 as well as direct references to contractual relationships throughout the Data Act (e.g., Art. 13(1)) imply private enforcement.[888]

1. Competent Authorities (Art. 37)

According to Art. 37(1) and rec. 107, member states should designate one or more competent authorities to ensure the application and enforcement of the Data Act. The member states can either establish new authorities or rely on existing ones. The competent authorities should cooperate with each other, Art. 37(2). If a member state designates more than one competent authority, it should also designate a data coordinator from among them to facilitate cooperation between the competent authorities and to assist the entities in the scope of the Data Act on all matters related to its enforcement and implementation, Art. 37(2).

Therefore, the Data Act opts for a decentralised (member state-driven) enforcement structure which corresponds to the policy of the DGA (but contrasts the policy of the DMA and partially also of the DSA).[889]

The competent authorities shall remain impartial and free from any external influence, whether direct or indirect, and shall neither seek nor take instructions from any other public authority or any private party, Art. 37(8). The member states should ensure that the competent authorities are provided with the necessary resources to this end, Art. 37(9). According

887 Commission COM(2022) 68 final Explanatory Memorandum, p. 16.

888 Furthermore, Art. 10(7) assumes that national courts take cases on FRAND litigation.

889 Krämer, J. et al. Data Act: Towards a balanced EU data regulation, CERRE report, March 2023, p. 32.

to Art. 37(4)(b), the competent authority responsible for the application and enforcement of Art. 23 to 31 and Art. 34 and 35 shall have experience in the field of data and electronic communications services.

Where either the protection of personal data or specific sectoral data access and use issues are concerned the respective competent authorities should also have the responsibility for the application of the Data Act in the respective fields, Art. 37(3) and Art. 37 (4)(a). When a member state designates more than one competent authority which monitor sectors in an overlapping manner, their competences have to be distributed carefully between them.[890]

Member states should clearly define the tasks and powers of the competent authorities which – according to Art. 37(5) – should include among others promoting data literacy and awareness of the rights and obligations under the Data Act (a) and monitoring technological and commercial developments of relevance for the making available and use of data (e). According to Art. 37(5)(b) they should especially handle complaints arising from alleged infringements of the Data Act. They should also investigate the subject matter of complaints as well as matters that concern the application of the Data Act, including on the basis of information received from another competent authority or other public authority (c). The legislator further elaborates on these powers of investigation and especially the cooperation of the competent authorities regarding investigations in rec. 107.

According to Art. 37(5)(d) the competent authorities should impose effective, proportionate and dissuasive financial penalties which may include periodic penalties or penalties with retroactive effect as well as initiating legal proceedings for the imposition of fines.[891] While Art. 40 is not solely focused on financial penalties, only this type of penalty is mentioned in Art. 37(5).[892] Competent authorities should cooperate with competent authorities of other member states and, where relevant, with the Commission or the EDIB (f); with the relevant competent authorities responsible for the implementation of other Union or national legal acts (g) and with the relevant competent authorities to ensure that Art. 23 to 31 and Art. 34 and 35 are enforced consistently with other Union law and self-regulation applicable to providers of data processing services (h). This cooperation

890 Leistner, M. / Antoine, L., IPR and the use of open data and data sharing initiatives by public and private actors, 2022, p. 117.

891 Cf. also below sub XI. 4.

892 Wiebe, A., *GRUR* 2023, 227 (237).

should be facilitated by the data coordinator if one is designated (Art. 37(5) subpara. 2).

According to Art. 37(6), the data coordinator if designated should:

"(a) act as the single point of contact for all issues related to the application of this Regulation;
(b) ensure the online public availability of requests to make data available made by public sector bodies in the case of exceptional need under Chapter V and promote voluntary data sharing agreements between public sector bodies and data holders;
(c) inform the Commission, on an annual basis, of the refusals notified under Article 4(2) and (8) and Article 5(11)".

The Commission should maintain a public register of the competent authorities based on the information the member states should communicate, Art. 37(7).

According to Art. 37(14) competent authorities have the power to request all the information that is necessary to verify compliance with the requirements of the Data Act from users, data holders and data recipients or their legal representatives. These requests have to be proportionate to the performance of the task and should be reasoned. Competent authorities can also submit a reasoned request for assistance or enforcement from a competent authority in another member state. Upon receiving such a request, the respective other authority should provide a response without undue delay, detailing the actions that have been taken or which are intended to be taken (Art. 37(15)).

Competent authorities should respect the principles of confidentiality and of professional and commercial secrecy and should protect personal data in accordance with Union and national law, Art. 37(16). Any information exchanged in the context of assistance requested and provided under Art. 31 should only be used in respect of the matter for which it was requested (Art. 37(16)).

Jurisdiction concerning Entities within the Scope of the Data Act

Art. 37(10) also regulates the jurisdiction of which member state an entity will be subject to. This is the member state in which it is established or in which it has its main establishment. As its main establishment will be considered where it has its head office or its registered office within which the principal financial functions and operational control of the entity are exercised.

Entities within the scope of the Data Act should also designate a legal representative in one of the member states (Art. 37(11)). The entity should mandate the legal representative to be addressed in addition to or instead of the entity itself regarding all issues related to the compliance with the Data Act (Art. 37(12)). The legal representative should cooperate with the competent authorities and comprehensively demonstrate to them upon request, the actions taken, and provisions put in place by the entity to ensure compliance (Art. 37(12)).

An entity is deemed to be under the jurisdiction of the member state in which the legal representative is located, Art. 37(13) sent. 1. The designation of a legal representative should be without prejudice to any legal actions which could be initiated against the entity, Art. 37(13) sent. 2. Until an entity has designated a legal representative it will be under the competence of all member states, so that any competent authority may exercise its competence if the same entity is not subject to enforcement proceedings under the Data Act for the same facts by another competent authority (Art. 37(13)).

2. Right to Lodge a Complaint with a Competent Authority (Art. 38)

In order to enforce their Data Act rights, natural and legal persons should be entitled to seek redress for the infringements of their rights under the regulation by lodging complaints with competent authorities (Art. 38(1) and rec. 108). These complaints can be lodged individually or collectively. The data coordinator should upon request provide all the necessary information to natural and legal persons for lodging their company to the appropriate competent authority, Art. 38(1) sent. 2.

According to Art. 38(2) the competent authority with which the complaint has been lodged shall inform the complainant of the progress of the proceedings and of the decision taken in accordance with national law (similarly to Art. 58(4) GDPR).[893]

Competent authorities should be obliged to cooperate to ensure the complaint is appropriately handled and resolved effectively and in a timely manner (Art. 38(3) and rec. 108). The cooperation should include exchanging all relevant information by electronic means without undue delay,

893 Remke, C., *MMR-Beil.* 2024, 117 (119).

however without any effect on the cooperation mechanisms provided for by Chapters VI and VII of Regulation (EU) 2016/679 and by Regulation (EU) 2017/2394, Art. 38(3).

The right to lodge a complaint under Art. 38 is without prejudice to any other administrative or judicial remedy (Art. 38(1)), thus not precluding private enforcement.[894] Despite the focus on contractual relations in the Data Act, it does not address comprehensively the role of private enforcement.[895] This lack of harmonisation of private enforcement may lead to disharmony concerning claims by users, but also unfair competition law-based actions and national legislation on private remedies concerning the rights under the Data Act.[896] Harmonisation could have also clarified the relationship between public enforcement and private remedies.[897]

3. *Right to an Effective Judicial Remedy (Art. 39)*

Art. 39(1), (2) regulates the right to an effective judicial remedy with regard to legally binding decisions taken (or failures to act) by competent authorities. Any affected natural and legal person has a respective right notwithstanding any administrative or other non-judicial remedies. The proceedings pursuant to Art. 39 should be brought before the courts or tribunals of the member state of the competent authority against which the judicial remedy is sought, Art. 39(3).

4. *Penalties (Art. 40)*

The member states should lay down rules on penalties applicable to infringements of the Data Act. Penalties shall be effective, proportionate and

894 Leistner, M. / Antoine, L., IPR and the use of open data and data sharing initiatives by public and private actors, 2022, p. 118; Steinrötter, B., *GRUR* 2023, 216 (225).

895 Leistner, M. / Antoine, L., IPR and the use of open data and data sharing initiatives by public and private actors, 2022, p. 118; Schwamberger, S., Der Datenzugang im Data Act: Fortschritt oder Rückschritt?, in: Bernzen, A. K. et al., Immaterialgüter und Medien im Binnenmarkt, Nomos 2022, p. 88 (110); Steinrötter, B., *GRUR* 2023, 216 (225).

896 Leistner, M. / Antoine, L., IPR and the use of open data and data sharing initiatives by public and private actors, 2022, p. 118.

897 Leistner, M. / Antoine, L., IPR and the use of open data and data sharing initiatives by public and private actors, 2022, p. 119.

dissuasive, and should take all measures necessary to ensure that they are implemented (Art. 40(1)). Rec. 109 gives as examples "financial penalties, warnings, reprimands or orders to bring business practices into compliance with the obligations imposed by" the Data Act.

Until the Data Act applies, the member states should notify the Commission of those rules and measures as well as of any subsequent amendment affecting them (Art. 40(2)). The Commission should maintain and regularly update an easily accessible public register of those measures.

Additionally, rec. 109 states that it is the task of the competent authorities to ensure that infringements of the obligations laid down in the Data Act are sanctioned by penalties. Art. 40(3) and rec. 109 add a list of non-exhaustive and indicative criteria for the imposition of penalties, such as for example the nature, gravity, scale and duration of the infringement (a) in view of the public interest at stake, the scope and kind of activities carried out, and the economic capacity of the infringing party; whether the infringing party systematically or recurrently fails to comply with its obligations under the Data Act and any action taken by the infringing party to mitigate or remedy the damage caused by the infringement (b).

As Art. 40 leaves it to the member states to lay down rules, different standards within the member states are possible.[898] Additionally, the data protection authorities remain competent to impose administrative fines for the infringement of the GDPR.[899] Altogether this may lead to overlapping and parallel enforcement and thus to inefficient results and legal uncertainty.[900] This is partly addressed by Art. 40(3), stating that the member states should take into account the recommendations of the EDIB.

Rec. 109 adds that – in order to avoid that the same infringement is penalised more than once – a member state that intends to exercise its competence in relation to an infringing party that is not established and has not designated a legal representative in the Union should – without undue delay – inform all data coordinators as well as the Commission.

898 Leistner, M. / Antoine, L., IPR and the use of open data and data sharing initiatives by public and private actors, 2022, p. 118.

899 Leistner, M. / Antoine, L., IPR and the use of open data and data sharing initiatives by public and private actors, 2022, p. 118.

900 Leistner, M. / Antoine, L., IPR and the use of open data and data sharing initiatives by public and private actors, 2022, p. 118.

Concerning the role of the EDIB[901] for imposing penalties, rec. 110 adds:

> "Among other functions, the competent authorities should make use of the EDIB as a platform to evaluate, coordinate and adopt recommendations on the setting of penalties for infringements of this Regulation. It should allow for competent authorities, with the assistance of the Commission, to coordinate the optimal approach to determining and imposing such penalties. That approach prevents fragmentation while allowing for Member State's flexibility, and should lead to effective recommendations that support the consistent application of this Regulation."

5. Model Contractual Terms (Art. 41)

In order to assist parties in drafting and negotiating contracts with fair, reasonable and non-discriminatory contractual rights and obligations, the Commission should develop and recommend non-binding model contractual terms on data access and use as well as non-binding standard contractual clauses for cloud computing contracts, Art. 41. The first should include "reasonable compensation and the protection of trade secrets".

According to rec. 111 model contract terms should also "where necessary take into account the conditions in specific sectors and the existing practices with voluntary data sharing mechanisms". This should be done before the 12.09.2025.[902] Rec. 111 further explains:

> "These model contractual terms should be primarily a practical tool to help in particular smaller enterprises to conclude a contract. When used widely and integrally, these model contractual terms should also have the beneficial effect of influencing the design of contracts about access to and use of data and therefore lead more broadly towards fairer contractual relations when accessing and sharing data."

The model contractual terms and the standard contractual clauses are an important instrument for making the Data Act work effectively in prac-

901 On the role of the EDIB in general cf. below XI. 6.

902 The Commission has set up an expert group to help draft the model contractual terms which plans to recommend them by autumn 2025: https://digital-strategy.ec.europa.eu/en/policies/data-act-explained.

tice.[903] Thus, *Leistner* and *Antoine* point to draft model contract terms for data sharing on a contractual basis, on the necessary protection of trade secrets, the fairness test for B2B data sharing contracts and the minimum content for cloud service contracts defined in Art. 24.[904]

With a similar aim of assisting parties in drafting and negotiating contracts with balanced contractual rights and obligations, the American Law Institute (ALI) and the European Law Institute (ELI) developed "Principles for a Data Economy", which do function as an example and / or blueprint for the model contractual terms and standard contractual clauses.[905] The same holds true for the default rules on data provision contracts currently developed by the UNCITRAL Working Group IV.[906]

6. *Role of the European Data Innovation Board (Art. 42)*

The EDIB that has been set up[907] under Art. 29 DGA[908] as a Commission expert group should also support the consistent application of the Data Act. It should thus advise and assist the Commission developing a consistent practice of competent authorities (Art. 42(a)). It should also facilitate cooperation between competent authorities through capacity-building and the exchange of information as well as comprehensive discussions between the competent authorities (Art. 42(b) and rec. 110). This shall "increase

903 Leistner, M. / Antoine, L., IPR and the use of open data and data sharing initiatives by public and private actors, 2022, p. 119.

904 Leistner, M. / Antoine, L., IPR and the use of open data and data sharing initiatives by public and private actors, 2022, p. 119.

905 See https://europeanlawinstitute.eu/projects-publications/completed-projects/data-economy/.

906 UNCITRAL, Report of the Working Group IV (Electronic Commerce) on the work of its sixty-fifth session (New York, 10–14 April 2023), A/CN.9/1132, pp. 3 et seq.; UNCITRAL, Working Group IV (Electronic Commerce), Sixty-fifth session, New York, 10–14 April 2023, Default rules for data provision contracts, A/CN.9/WG.IV/WP.180; UNCITRAL, Report of the Working Group IV (Electronic Commerce) on the work of its sixty-sixth session (Vienna, 16–20 October 2023), A/CN.9/1162, pp. 10 et seq.; UNCITRAL, Working Group IV (Electronic Commerce) Sixty sixth session, Vienna, 16–20 October 2023, Default rules for data provision contracts (first revision), A/CN.9/WG.IV/WP.183.

907 Further details: https://ec.europa.eu/transparency/expert-groups-register/screen/expert-groups/consult?lang=en&groupID=3903.

908 Commentary on Art. 29 DGA: Hennemann, M., in: Specht-Riemenschneider, L. / Hennemann, M., Data Governance Act, 2023, Art. 29 DGA.

effective access to justice as well as enforcement and judicial cooperation across the Union", rec. 101.

Especially, it shall advise and assist with regard to the request of the drafting of harmonised standards (Art. 33(4), Art. 35(4) and Art. 36(5)), the preparation of the drafts of the implementing acts (Art. 33(5), Art. 35(5), (8) and Art. 36(6)), the preparation of the delegated acts (Art.29(7) and Art. 33(2)) and the adoption of guidelines laying down interoperability specifications for the functioning of common European data spaces (Art. 33(11)).

Rec. 110 further explains, that the EDIB should "advise and assist the Commission in coordinating national practices and policies on the topics covered by the Data Act as well as in delivering on its objectives in relation to technical standardisation to enhance interoperability."

XII. Final Provisions (Art. 45-48)

Chapter XI ('Final Provisions') encompasses *inter alia* rules for the Commission to adopt delegated acts on monitoring switching charges and on further specifying standards for interoperability and smart contracts.[909]

1. Exercise of the Delegation (Art. 45)

Art. 45(1) confers the power on the Commission to adopt delegated acts in accordance with Art. 290 TFEU. Rec. 113 concisely sums up the areas specified in Art. 29(7) and Art. 33(2) to which this regulatory power applies. The Commission shall by these means

> "establish a monitoring mechanism on switching charges imposed by providers of data processing services on the market, and [...] further specify the essential requirements in respect of interoperability for participants in data spaces that offer data or data services to other participants."

The power to adopt delegated acts starts with the enactment of the Data Act (cf. Art. 45(2)).

When preparing a delegated act, experts designated by each member state as well as those from the European Parliament and of the Council are invited to relevant meetings of Commission expert groups, which is followed by a timely consultation of the member state-appointed experts on the draft of the delegated act in question (Art. 45(4); referring to the Interinstitutional Agreement on Better Law-Making of 13 April 2016, of which Sec. 28 and Sec. 3 of the Annex are pertinent). Upon adoption of the delegated act, the Commission is then to notify the European Parliament and the Council as per Art. 45(5) so that these institutions are in a position to object to the piece of legislation in question within three months (Art. 45(6) and Art. 290(2)(b) TFEU).

Ultimately, either the European Parliament or the Council can revoke the delegated power conferred upon the Commission, albeit with no retro-

909 Please see above sub II. 7.-9. for Art. 45, 49, and 50.

active effect on delegated acts which are already in force (Art. 45(3) and Art. 290(2)(a) TFEU).

2. Committee Procedure and Implementing Powers (Art. 46 and Rec. 114)

According to rec. 114 implementing powers should be conferred on the Commission to ensure uniform conditions for the implementation of the Data Act. Where it is permitted to do so in the absence of (adequate) harmonised standards, the Commission should adopt

> "common specifications to ensure the interoperability of data, of data sharing mechanisms and services, as well as of common European data spaces, common specifications on the interoperability of data processing services, and common specifications on the interoperability of smart contracts".

It should also publish "the references of harmonised standards and common specifications for the interoperability of data processing services in a central Union standards repository for the interoperability of data processing services".

Art. 46 states that the Commission should be assisted by a committee within the meaning of Regulation (EU) No 182/2011[910].

3. Amendments (Art. 47 and 48)

In order to make use of the consumer protection cooperation network mechanism and to enable representative actions, Art. 47 and Art. 48 amend the Annexes to the Regulation (EU) 2017/2394 and Directive (EU) 2020/1828, as explained in rec. 108.

910 Regulation (EU) No 182/2011 of the European Parliament and of the Council laying down the rules and general principles concerning mechanisms for control by member states of the Commission's exercise of implementing powers.

Data Act Bibliography

ACM, Market Study Cloud Services, 2022

Aplin, T. / Radauer, A. / Bader, M. A. / Searle, N., The Role of EU Trade Secrets Law in the Data Economy: An Empirical Analysis, IIC 2023, 826-858

Assion, S. / Willecke, L., Der EU Data Act, *MMR* 2023, 805-810

Auernhammer, H. (ed.) DSGVO, BDSG: Datenschutz-Grundverordnung, Bundesdatenschutzgesetz und Nebengesetze, Carl Heymanns Verlag 2024

BDI Stellungnahme zum Legislativvorschlag des EU-Data Act, 2022

Bernzen, A. K. / Grisse, K. / Kaesling, K., Immaterialgüter und Medien im Binnenmarkt – Europäisierung des Rechts und ihre Grenzen, Nomos 2022

Bitkom, 'Bitkom Position Paper EU Data Act Proposal' (19 April 2022)

Bitkom, Data Spaces and Data Ecosystems - First Explainer and Current Status (September 2022)

Boehm, F., Herausforderungen von Cloud-Computing-Verträgen: Vertragstypologische Einordnung, Haftung und Eigentum an Daten, *ZEuP* 2016, 358-387

Bomhard, D. / Merkle, M., Der Entwurf des Data Act – Neue Spielregeln für die Data Economy, *RDi* 2022, 168-176

Bomhard, D., Auswirkungen des Data Act auf die Geschäftsmodelle von Cloud-Anbietern, *MMR* 2024, 109-107

Bräutigam, P. / Schmidt-Wudy, F., Das geplante Auskunfts- und Herausgaberecht des Betroffenen nach Art. 15 der EU-Datenschutzgrundverordnung, Ein Diskussionsbeitrag zum anstehenden Trilog der EU- Gesetzgebungsorgane, *CR* 2015, 56-63

Butterfield, A. / Ngondi, G. E. / Kerr, A. (eds.), A Dictionary of Computer Science, (OUP 2016)

Callewaert, C., Data Act und Datenportabilität - Lesson Learned? in Heinze, C. (ed.), Daten, Plattformen und KI als Dreiklang unserer Zeit, DSRI, 2022

Casolari, F. / Taddeo, M. / Turillazzi, A. / Floridi, L., How to Improve Smart Contracts in the European Union Data Act, *DISO* 2, 9 (2023)

Danyeli, G., Die große Freiheit über die Wolke? Die Regelungen des Data Act zum Wechsel von Cloud-Anbietern und zur Interoperabilität, in: Heinze, C. (ed.), Daten, Plattformen und KI als Dreiklang unserer Zeit, DSRI, 2022

Derclaye, E. / Husovec, M., Why the sui generis database clause in the Data Act is counter-productive and how to improve it? (8 March 2022, available at https://papers.ssrn.com/sol3/papers.cfm?abstract_id=4052390)

von Ditfurth, L. / Lienemann, G., The Data Governance Act: – Promoting or Restricting Data Intermediaries? Competition and Regulation in Network Industries, 23 (4) 2022, 270-295

Ducuing, C. / Margoni, T. / Schirru, L. (ed.), White Paper on the Data Act Proposal, *CiTiP Working Paper* 2022

Ebner, G., Information Overload 2.0? – Die Informationspflichten gemäß Art. 3 Abs. 2 Data Act-Entwurf, *ZD* 2022, 364-369

Ebner, G., Weniger ist Mehr?, Nomos 2022

Ebner, G., LG Kiel: Scraping von Daten auf Facebook, *ZD* 2023, 282-287

Ebner, G., Die Novellierung der datenschutzrechtlichen Informationspflichten, Impulse für eine Optimierung der Art. 12 bis 14 DS-GVO, *ZfDR* 2023, 299-314

Eckardt, M. / Kerber, W., Property rights theory, bundles of rights on IoT data, and the EU Data Act (December 2023).

Efroni, Z. / Metzger, J. / Mischau, L. / Schirmbeck, M., Privacy Icons: A Risk-Based Approach to Visualisation of Data Processing, *EDPL* 2019, 352-366

Ehmann, E. / Selmayr, M. (eds.), Datenschutz-Grundverordnung - DS-GVO, 3rd ed., C.H. Beck 2024

Engels, S. / Nordemann, J. B., The Portability Regulation (Regulation (EU) 2017/1128) – A Commentary on the Scope and Application, *JIPITEC* 9 (2) 2018, 179-200

Ennis, S. / Evans, B., Cloud Portability and Interoperability under the EU Data Act: Dynamism versus Equivalence (SSRN pre-print)(13 April 2023, available at https://papers.ssrn.com/sol3/papers.cfm?abstract_id=4395183)

Finck, M. / Mueller, M-S., Access to Data for Environmental Purposes: Setting the Scene and Evaluating Recent Changes in EU Data Law, Journal of Environmental Law 35 (1) 2023, 109-131

Funk, A., Das Prinzip der Nutzerzentriertheit des Data Act – ein gravierender Strukturfehler — Untersuchung und Bewertung der zentralen Rolle des Nutzers in der Datenökonomie nach der Konzeption des Data Act, *CR* 2023, 421-427

Gans, J. / Herve, M. / Masri, M., Economic analysis of proposed regulations of cloud services in Europe, European Competition Journal, 19 (3) 2023, 522-568

Gasser, U., Interoperability in the Digital Ecosystem, Harvard University - Berkman Klein Center for Internet & Society 2015

Geiregat, S., 'The Data Act: Start of a New Era for Data Ownership?' (SSRN print) (27 Sep 2022, available at https://papers.ssrn.com/sol3/papers.cfm?abstract_id=4214704)

Geminn, C. / Francis, L. / Herder, K., Die Informationspräsentation im Datenschutzrecht – Auf der Suche nach Lösungen, *ZD-Aktuell* 2021, 05335

Geradin, D. / Bania, K. / Katsifis, D. / Circiumaru, A., The regulation of cloud computing: Getting it right (SSRN pre-print)(11 Dec 2022, available at https://papers.ssrn.com/sol3/papers.cfm?abstract_id=4285731)

Gerpott, T., Vorschlag für ein europäisches Datengesetz Überblick und Analyse der Vorgaben für vernetzte Produkte, *CR* 2022, 271-280

Godlovitch, I. / Kroon, P., Interoperability, switchability and portability: Implications for the cloud, WIK-Consult Report, 2022

Goode, S., Understanding Single Homing and Multihoming User Switching Propensity in Cloud File Hosting Service Relationships, E-Service Journal 11(2) 2020, 34-73

Grapentin, S., Datenzugangsansprüche und Geschäftsgeheimnisse der Hersteller im Lichte des Data Act, *RDi* 2023, 173-182

Hartmann, B. / McGuire, M. R. / Schulte-Nölke, H., Datenzugang bei smarten Produkten nach dem Entwurf für ein Datengesetz (Data Act): Rechtliche Rahmenbedingungen für die Vertragsgestaltung, *RDi* 2023, 49-59

Heinzke, P., Data Act: Auf dem Weg zur europäischen Datenwirtschaft, *BB* 2023, 201-209

Heinzke, P. / Herbers, B. / Kraus, M., Datenzugangsansprüche nach dem Data Act, BB 2024, 649-655

Hennemann, M., A Fair Share? – Data Contracts and Unfair Terms Control, in: Lohsse, S. / Schulze, R. / Staudenmayer, D., Private Law and the Data Act, Nomos 2024 (forthcoming)

Hennemann, M. (ed.), Global Data Strategies – A Handbook, C.H. Beck 2023

Hennemann, M., Datenportabilität, *PinG* 2017, 5-8

Hennemann, M. /Specht-Riemenschneider, L. (eds.), Data Governance Act: DGA, Nomos 2023

Hennemann, M. / Steinrötter, B., Data Act – Fundament des neuen EU-Datenwirtschaftsrechts?, *NJW* 2022, 1481-1485

Hennemann, M. / Steinrötter, B., Der Data Act, Neue Instrumente, alte Friktionen, strukturelle Weichenstellungen, *NJW* 2024, 1-8

Hilgendorf, E. / Vogel, P., Datenrecht im Umbruch. Aktuelle Herausforderungen von Datenschutz und Datenwirtschaft in Europa, *JZ* 2022, 380-388

Hon, W. K. et al., Cloud Technology and Services, in Millard, C. (ed.), Cloud Computing Law (OUP 2021)

Höne, M./Knapp, J., Von Daten- und Diskurssilos, ZGI 2023, 168-171

Irion, K., Algorithms Off-limits? If digital trade law restricts access to source code of software then accountability will suffer, (SSRN-print)(11 Jul 2022, available at https://papers.ssrn.com/sol3/papers.cfm?abstract_id=4147375)

Kerber, W., Governance of IoT Data: Why the EU Data Act Will not Fulfill Its Objectives, *GRUR-Int.* 2023, 120-135

Kerber, W., Towards a dynamic concept of competition that includes innovation, OECD, DAF/COMP/WD(2023)42

Kettner S. / Thorun, C. / Vetter, M., Wege zur besseren Informiertheit, ConPolicy 2018

Klink-Straub, J. / Straub, T., Data Act als Rahmen für die gemeinsame Datennutzung ZD-Aktuell 2022, 01076

Kollmar, F. / El-Auwad, M., Grenzen der Einwilligung bei hochkomplexen und technisierten Datenverarbeitungen, *K&R* 2021, 73-78

Krämer, J. et al. Data Act: Towards a balanced EU data regulation, CERRE, 2023

Krämer, J., Improving The Economic Effectiveness of the B2B and B2C Data Sharing Obligations in the Proposed Data Act, CERRE, 2022

Lagoni, J., Cloud Switching gemäß Data Act: Die Abschaffung von Switching Charges, *CR* 2024, 91-95

Leistner, M. / Antoine, L., IPR and the use of open data and data sharing initiatives by public and private actors, 2022

Lewinski, K. v. / Hähnle, J., Was informatisch richtig ist, kann auch juristisch recht sein, *DuD* 2021, 686-690Louven, S., DMA Art. 6, in BeckOK Informations- und Medienrecht (C.H. Beck 2023)

Louven, S., Vorschriften im Data Act zur Ausgestaltung und Kompensation von Datenbereitstellungspflichten, *MMR-Beil.* 2024, 82-86

Macher, E. / Ballestrem, J., Der neue EU Data Act: Zugang zu Daten – und Geschäftsgeheimnissen?, *GRUR-Prax* 2023, 661-664

Margoni, T. / Ducuing, C. / Schirru, L., Data property, data governance and Common European Data Spaces (SSRN print)(8 May 2023, available at https://papers.ssrn.com/sol3/papers.cfm?abstract_id=4428364)

Martens, B. / Parker, G. / Petropoulos, G. / van Alstyne, M., Towards Efficient Information Sharing in Network Markets, TILEC Discussion Paper DP 2021-014, 2021

Martini, M. / Kramme, I. / Kamke, A., KI-VO, DMA und DA als Missing Links im Kampf gegen dunkle Designmuster? *MMR* 2023, 399-403

Max Planck Institute for Innovation and Competition, Position Statement of 25 May 2022 on the Commission's Proposal of 23 February 2022 for a Regulation on Harmonised Rules on Fair Access to and Use of Data (Data Act), 2022

Mell, P. / Grance, T., The NIST Definition of Cloud Computing, *NIST Special Publication* 800-145, 2011

Mik, E., Smart Contracts and the Myth of Transparency, EuCML 2024, 1-3

MyData Global response of the Data Act, 2022

Niedermaier, T. / Picht, P., FRAND ADR under the Data Act and the SEP Regulation, (SSRN print)(18 May 2023, available at https://papers.ssrn.com/sol3/papers.cfm?abstract_id=4447930)

Nüske, N. / Olenberger, C. / Rau, D. / Schmied, F., Privacy Bots: Digitale Helfer für mehr Transparenz im Internet, *DuD* 2019, 28-32

Paal, B. / Pauly, D. A. (eds.), Datenschutz-Grundverordnung. Bundesdatenschutzgesetz, 3rd ed., C.H. Beck 2021

Paal, B. / Fenik, M., Access to Data in the Data Act Proposal, *ZfDR* 2023, 249-262

Pauly, D.A. / Wichert, F. / Baumann, J., Schutz von Geschäftsgeheimnissen nach dem Data Act, *MMR* 2024, 211-216

Perarnaud, C. / Fanni, R., The EU Data Act – Towards a new European data revolution?, 2022

Picht, P. G., Caught in the Acts – Framing Mandatory Data Access Transactions under the Data Act, further EU Digital Regulation Acts, and Competition Law, 2022

Piltz, C. / Zwerschke, J., Cloud Switching nach dem Data Act aus der Beratungsperspektive, *CR* 2024, 153-160

Podszun, R. / Pfeifer C., Datenzugang nach dem EU Data Act: Der Entwurf der Europäischen Kommission, *GRUR* 2022, 953-961

Podszun, R., Der EU Data Act und der Zugang zu Sekundärmärkten am Beispiel des Handwerks, Nomos 2022

Rebin, I., § 2, in Spickhoff, A (ed.), BeckOGK Produkthaftungsgesetz (C.H. Beck 2022)

Remke, C., Rechtsdurchsetzung unter dem Data Act, *MMR-Beil.* 2024, 117-121

Richter, F., Aus Sicht der Stiftung Datenschutz – Datenschutz – kein Wahlkampfschlager (?), *PinG* 2017, 122-123

Richter, S., Vereinbarkeit des Entwurfs zum Data Act und der DS-GVO - Der schmale Grat zwischen Schutz personenbezogener Daten und Datenkommerzialisierung, *MMR* 2023, 163-168

Roßnagel, A., Wie zukunftsfähig ist die Datenschutz-Grundverordnung?, *DuD* 2016, 561-565

Schaller, T. / Zurawski, P., Staatlicher Kompetenzaufwuchs im Data-Act-Entwurf, ZD-Aktuell 2022, 01169

Schmidt-Kessel, M., Heraus- und Weitergabe von IoT-Gerätedaten - Analyse des Vertragsnetzes unter dem Data Act, *MMR-Beil.* 2024, 75-82

Schnurr, D., Switching and Interoperability between Data Processing Services in the Proposed Data Act, CERRE Report, 2022

Schreiber, K., Revolutioniert der Data Act die Datenwirtschaft?, *MMR* 2023, 541-542

Schreiber, K./Pommerening, P./Schoel, P., Das neue Recht der Daten-Governance, Nomos 2022

Schröder, M., Bereitstellung von Daten wegen außergewöhnlicher Notwendigkeit, *MMR-Beil. 2024*, 104-109

Schuster, F. / Hunzinger, S., Vor- und nachvertragliche Pflichten beim IT-Vertrag – Teil II: Nachvertragliche Pflichten, *CR* 2015, 277-286

Schwamberger, S., Der Datenzugang im Data Act: Fortschritt oder Rückschritt?, in: Bernzen, A. et al., Immaterialgüter und Medien im Binnenmarkt, Nomos 2022

Schwamberger, S., Die Klauselkontrolle in Art. 13 Data Act, *MMR-Beil.* 2024, 96-101

Schwartmann R. / Jaspers, A. / Thüsing, G. / Kugelmann, D. (eds.), DS-GVO/BDSG, 2nd ed., C.F. Müller 2020

Schweitzer, H. / Metzger, A. / Blind, K. / Richter, H. / Niebel, C. / Gutmann, F., The legal framework for access to data in Germany and in the EU, BMWK, 2022

Schweitzer, H. / Metzger, A., Shaping Markets: A Critical Evaluation of the Draft Data Act, *ZEuP* 2023, 42-82

Schweitzer, H. / Metzger, A., Data Access under the Draft Data Act, Competition Law and the DMA: Opening the Data Treasures for Cowmpetition and Innovation?, *GRUR Int.* 2023, 337-356

Seegel, A., Cloud-Switching nach Data Act: Der Vorhang fällt, die Fragen offen!, CR-online.de Blog, 15 November 2023

Siglmüller, J., Standardisierungsbestrebungen für das Rückgrat der europäischen Digitalwirtschaft, *MMR-Beil.* 2024, 112-116

Simitis, S. / Hornung, G. / Spiecker gen. Döhmann, I. (eds.), Datenschutzrecht: DSG-VO mit BDSG, Nomos 2019

Specht-Riemenschneider, L., Datennutz und Datenschutz: Zum Verhältnis zwischen Datenwirtschaftsrecht und DSGVO, *ZEuP* 2023, 638-672

Specht-Riemenschneider, L., Der Entwurf des Data Act, *MMR* 2022, 809-826

Specht-Riemenschneider, L. / Blankertz, A. / Sierek, P. / Schneider, R. / Knapp, J. / Henne, T., Die Datentreuhand, Ein Beitrag zur Modellbildung und rechtlichen Strukturierung zwecks Identifizierung der Regulierungserfordernisse für Datentreuhandmodelle, *MMR-Beil.* 2021, 25-47

Staudenmeyer, D., Der Verordnungsvorschlag der Europäischen Kommission zum Datengesetz, *EuZW* 2022, 596-602

Steege, H., Technische Schutzmaßnahmen des Dateninhabers im Data Act, *MMR-Beil.* 2024, 91-95

Steinrötter, B., Verhältnis von Data Act und DS-GVO, Zugleich ein Beitrag zur Konkurrenzlehre im Rahmen der EU-Digitalgesetzgebung, *GRUR* 2023, 216-226

Strittmatter, M., § 22 Cloud Computing, in Auer-Reinsdorff, A. / Conrad, I. (eds.), Handbuch IT- und Datenschutzrecht, C.H. Beck 2019

vbw, Data Act – Anpassungsbedarf aus Sicht der Bayerischen Wirtschaft, 2022

Weiß, R., Streitbeilegung nach Art. 10 Data Act, *MMR-Beil.* 2024, 101-104

Weizenbaum Institute for the Networked Society, Position paper regarding Data Act, 2022

Wiebe, A., Der Data Act – Innovation oder Illusion, *GRUR* 2023, 1569-1578

Wiebe, A., Access rights at the Intersection with Database Rights and Trade Secret Protection, *GRUR* 2023, 227-238

Wienroeder, M., Sind der Data Act und die DSGVO miteinander kompatibel?, PinG 2024, 103-108

Zech, H., Information als Schutzgegenstand, Mohr Siebek 2012

Zech, H., Daten als Wirtschaftsgut – Überlegungen zu einem „Recht des Datenerzeugers", *CR* 2015, 137-146